I0796217

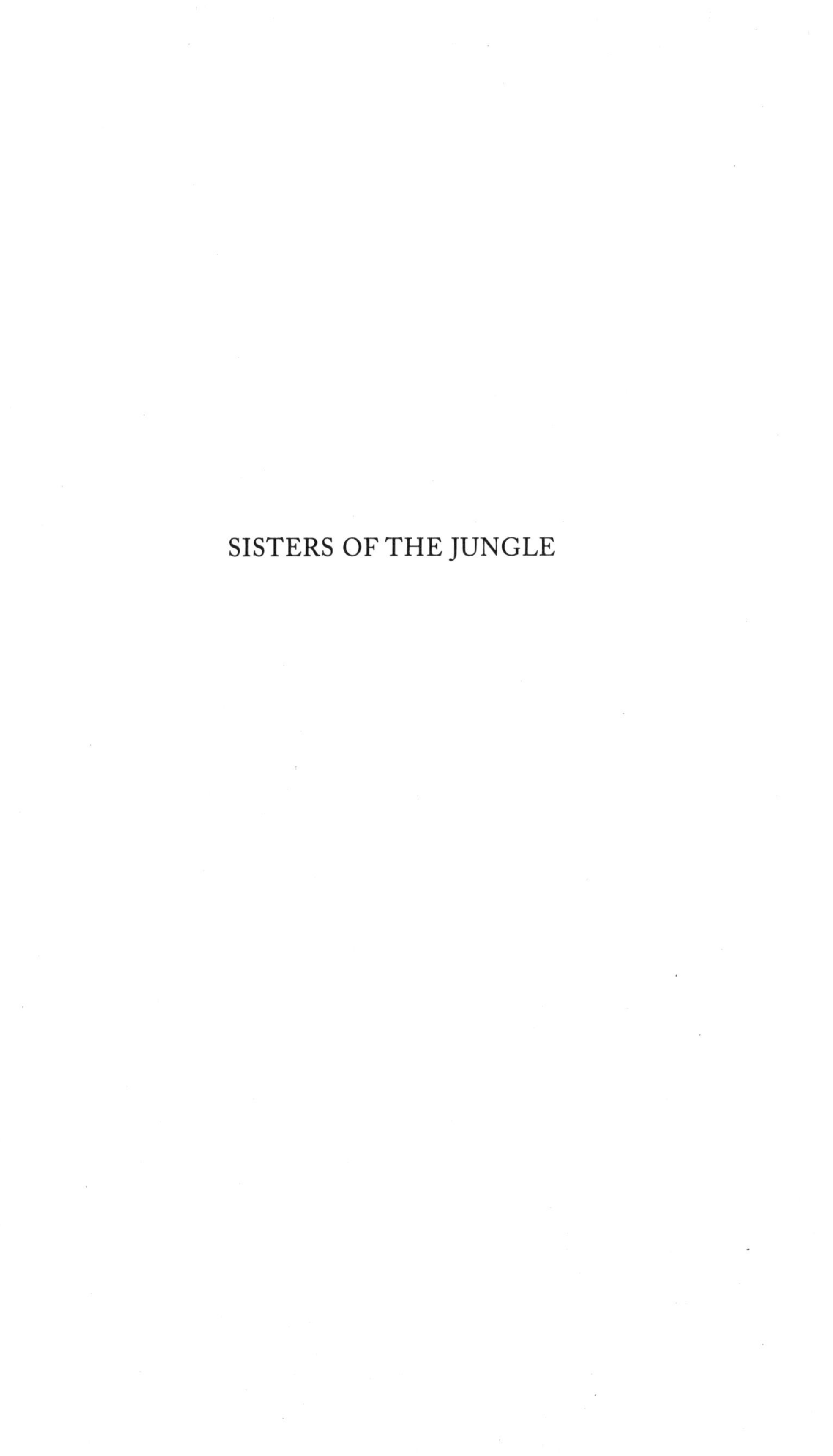

SISTERS OF THE JUNGLE

The Trailblazing Women Who Shaped the Study of Wild Primates

Sisters of the Jungle

Keriann McGoogan

Douglas & McIntyre

1 2 3 4 5 — 29 28 27 26 25

Douglas and McIntyre (2013) Ltd.
P.O. Box 219, Madeira Park, BC, V0N 2H0
www.douglas-mcintyre.com

Edited by Jen Lauriault
Dust jacket design by Jessica Sullivan, DSGN Dept.
Text design by Ruth Ormiston
Printed and bound in Canada

Canada Council for the Arts Conseil des Arts du Canada

Douglas and McIntyre acknowledges the support of the Canada Council for the Arts, the Government of Canada, and the Province of British Columbia through the BC Arts Council.

LIBRARY AND ARCHIVES CANADA CATALOGUING IN PUBLICATION

Title: Sisters of the jungle : the trailblazing women who shaped the study of wild primates / Keriann McGoogan.
Names: McGoogan, Keriann, author.
Description: Includes bibliographical references and index.
Identifiers: Canadiana (print) 20250217155 | Canadiana (ebook) 20250217171 | ISBN 9781771624459 (hardcover) | ISBN 9781771624466 (EPUB)
Subjects: LCSH: Women primatologists—Biography. | LCSH: Primatologists—Biography. | LCGFT: Biographies.
Classification: LCC QL26 .M34 2025 | DDC 599.8092/52—dc23

For my mother, Sheena Fraser McGoogan—
the woman who taught me to be brave.

Contents

Introduction ix

1 A Burning Question 1
2 Leakey's Legacy 31
3 The Chimpanzee Lady 59
4 Gorilla Girl 89
5 The Ape Lady of Borneo 135
6 The Mathematician and the Monkeys 167
7 Lady Langur 197
8 The Mother of Lemurs 229

Epilogue 263
Acknowledgements 269
Selected Sources 273
Index 284

Introduction

THE SCIENCES NEARLY LOST ME.

When I was in grade eleven, I almost failed physics. I remember it vividly. I was sitting at a carrel desk in the library with a calculator, frantically doing the math: what grade did I need on the final exam to get 51 per cent in the course? Heck, I would have settled for a 50. I'm still not sure how I pulled it off, but I passed—barely. Ever the high achiever, I felt I had cut it a little too close. I vowed never to take science again.

I know I'm not the first woman to stand at that crossroads. Women are significantly underrepresented in the STEM disciplines—science, technology, engineering and mathematics. The gender gap in STEM might be a self-fulfilling prophecy, with women avoiding STEM fields because of pervasive gender stereotypes. These ideas about the kinds of careers that are suitable for women have been around for decades, and they persist to this day.

My favourite line of evidence illustrating these stereotypes comes from a classic social sciences study that took place between 1966 and 1977. Researcher David Chambers asked more than four thousand elementary school children from Canada and the United States to draw a scientist. His purpose was to discover at what age the stereotypical image of a scientist—we're talking lab coat, spectacles, beakers—becomes ingrained in children. He found that the stereotype takes root by the second grade.

Jump ahead to 1983, when a psychologist from Northwestern University named David Miller took another look at Chambers's data. What he noticed was striking: of the nearly five thousand student drawings, only twenty-eight depicted a female scientist. And get this: not one boy drew a woman.

Many studies have demonstrated that society perceives STEM subjects as a male domain, creating a vicious cycle that contributes to a gender imbalance in these disciplines. Happily, an updated study from the United States in 2018 found that children's drawings have become more diverse, with more female scientists appearing in the images.

But, back in my teenage years, as I sat in that library carrel, I was not aware of the influence that gender stereotypes had been having on me, even though they were swirling all around. All I knew was that physics class nearly broke me.

For a while, I got away with banishing the sciences from my life. Passing physics meant I had all the credits I needed to earn my high school diploma. When it came time, I enrolled at the University of Calgary as an English major. I am the daughter of an author and I always believed I belonged squarely in the arts. I grew up in a world of books, spending my lunch hours reading Jane Austen and Charlotte Brontë.

But, somehow, the sciences caught up with me again.

As part of my bachelor of English, I was required to earn a few credits from outside of the humanities, for reasons that had something to do with ensuring we students became well-rounded human beings.

I signed up for Geology 101 ("Rocks for Jocks"), Astronomy 101 ("Scopes for Dopes") and Introduction to Biological Anthropology. That last class did not have a cute nickname, but the course description promised we would be learning about our closest living relatives: the non-human primates. A course about monkeys and apes sounded pretty good to me.

I didn't know it at the time, but if I were a superhero, enrolling in that course would have been my origin story.

The class was taught by a charismatic instructor named Brian Keating. Back then, Keating was a conservationist working at the Calgary Zoo, and the University of Calgary had brought him aboard to teach their introductory anthropology course. His voice was filled with passion as he described for us the hundreds of different primates around the world. He showed us videos of his travels and the wildlife he had encountered in faraway places. One memorable clip showed Keating being groomed by a male chimpanzee at Gombe Stream National Park in Tanzania—where he had been visiting *the* legendary primatologist, Jane Goodall. As I sat in the large lecture hall, one of about two hundred enthralled first- and second-year students, I could hardly believe that such diversity existed in nature. Where had these creatures been all my life?

After I finished that introductory class, I was thirsty for more. I turned to the course catalogue and was delighted to discover that the university offered a degree in primates—a bachelor of science in primatology. Without hesitation, I switched my major and signed up for every course on primates I could find.

As I took more and more classes, I began to notice an interesting pattern.

"You know, it's strange, but my classes are almost all women," I said to a friend who had just asked a probing question about my love life. "Not too many guys to choose from."

My friend, who was enrolled in the engineering program, laughed. "You should come to engineering—it's quite the opposite there!"

We had a good chuckle, but I still found it puzzling. I knew that women are significantly underrepresented in the STEM disciplines. Yet primatology—the science of primates—shatters this pattern. Why *were* there so many women in my courses? And why were so many notable primatologists also women?

I was not the first to notice this trend or wonder why it existed. One of the courses I took during my undergraduate degree was on the history of primatology. As part of the course, I read an article in an academic journal by primatologist Linda Fedigan titled "Science and the Successful Female: Why There Are So Many Women Primatologists." Fedigan had noticed that many of her colleagues were female, that primatology conferences were filled with women and that many of the high-profile researchers in primatology were women. In the article, which was published in 1994, she noted that there was a wealth of research on the gender imbalance in STEM disciplines, but her exploration was on the opposite imbalance in the field of primatology: when she compared the number of males and females working in primatology to general biology disciplines, she found that primatology had significantly more women.

The numbers have grown over the years. In the 1970s, women made up less than 20 per cent of the membership in professional primatological societies. By 1991, women comprised 58 per cent of the American Society of Primatologists and 38 per cent of the International Primatological Society, compared to the average of 25 per cent female membership in analogous biological disciplines. A 2002 survey of the American Association of Physical Anthropologists (now the American Association of Biological Anthropologists) membership revealed that 51 per cent were female, and that rose to a whopping 70 per cent when looking at student members. In 2008, women outnumbered men in the International Primatological Society at 57 per cent. In a search of all articles published in the *American Journal of Primatology* in 2009, 59 per cent of the first authors were female (when assuming gender could be deduced by the author's name).

Why is it that the field of primatology topples all expectations when it comes to gender balance? And how has the predominance of female primatologists influenced what we know about our primate cousins? In this book, I attempt to answer these questions through the stories of many of the intrepid women (and some men) who studied non-human primates in the early years of primatological research. These stories demonstrate how women have excelled in primate field research, uncovered new truths, contributed to the conservation of our closest living relatives and ultimately shaped an entire scientific discipline.

But first, what is it that fascinates us about primates of the non-human variety? Who are these primates, and why do we study them?

Primates, which include lemurs, monkeys, apes and humans, are the most ecologically diverse, socially complex and broadly distributed mammalian order. Primates exhibit several traits—referred to as the "primate pattern"—that characterize them as a group, including a short snout and reduced sense of smell; eyes at the front of the face and an enhanced sense of sight; five digits on the hands and feet, with nails instead of claws; opposable thumbs; and large brains relative to body size. Despite these shared traits, the diversity among primates is striking. There are approximately five hundred species of primates worldwide.

During my degree in primatology, I learned about how primate species are grouped, and later, when I became a course instructor, I taught these concepts to my students. Broadly speaking, the order Primates branches into two major groups—one includes the tarsiers, monkeys and apes, and the other includes the lemurs and lorises. Primates are generally found in tropical regions (with a few notable exceptions, like the famous snow monkeys in Japan) in Central and South America, Africa, southern and eastern Asia, and Madagascar.

One of the most familiar primates—from the large-bodied, big-brained group classified as great apes—is the muscular, black-haired chimpanzee. The chimp, for better or worse, has been made famous by films like the *Planet of the Apes* franchise and by chimp-owning celebrities like Michael Jackson. (Curious George was also a chimp: he's called a "little monkey" in the books, but the lack of a tail is a dead giveaway that he's an ape, not a monkey.) Chimpanzees have long fascinated human primates because we are so closely related. Humans and chimpanzees share roughly 98 per cent of our DNA, having descended from a common ancestor about six million years ago. Studies of these apes have shown that they use tools and live in complex family groups, complete with intricate politics shaping their behaviours.

The highly diverse monkeys, meanwhile, are split into two groups, distinguished by their nostril shape and location. The Platyrrhines (also referred to as New World monkeys) from Central and South America have broad, sideways-facing nostrils. The Catarrhines (Old World monkeys) from Africa and Asia have narrow, downward-facing nostrils. Among the Platyrrhines, I have a special affinity for the howler monkeys, because I studied them for my master's degree research in Belize in Central America. These primates are the loudest in the world. They have a specialized bone in their throats, called the hyoid bone, that amplifies the low, guttural roars they use to maintain group spacing and avoid competition for food. The first time I heard their calls in the wild, I thought there might be some kind of alien ship getting ready to descend from above. As for my favourite Catarrhine, like many, I've always been enthralled by the Japanese snow monkeys—those shaggy-haired, pink-faced macaques that are native to Japan and are known for soaking in hot springs. I've watched hours of footage of these monkeys leaning back in the hot water with their eyes closed, and it's striking how much they remind me of the humans at my local YMCA.

Baboons, another Catarrhine, are among the most well-studied primates. There are six species of baboon, and they are relatively easy to observe roaming in their open savanna habitat in sub-Saharan Africa. Humans are enthralled by baboons. In the 1960s, researchers argued that these primates were the perfect living model of human evolution because they lived on the ground and evolved in the African savannas.

And then there are the lemurs. There are more than one hundred different species of lemur, all found in Madagascar—and nowhere else on the planet. The largest living lemur is the indri, which can weigh up to ten kilograms. Indris are comical looking—black and white with fluffy round ears, a puffball tail and a face that looks constantly surprised. This species is well-known for its loud, trumpet-like "songs"—melodic, undulating cries that carry over several kilometres.

I could go on. The diversity within the Primate order sparks a natural curiosity to learn more about these species—it certainly did for me. But our fascination with our close primate relatives goes beyond mere scientific curiosity. Early primate studies demonstrate that our interest is deeply rooted in a desire to better understand ourselves.

Edward Tyson, an English scientist and physician, is widely considered the founder of modern comparative anatomy—and his look at primate anatomy has been called the starting point of primatology. In 1698, Tyson dissected the cadaver of a juvenile chimpanzee and compared its anatomy with humans, Barbary macaques and other monkeys. The skeleton of that chimpanzee is preserved at the Natural History Museum in London.

Cut to 1758, when Carl Linnaeus, a Swedish botanist, zoologist and taxonomist, published the tenth edition of his book, *Systema Naturae*, in which he attempted to organize the diversity of life on earth—the system of nature—by creating a naming scheme that would keep it all straight. Linnaeus famously categorized the genus *Homo*, to which we humans belong, within the mammalian order of Primates, right alongside monkeys, lemurs and lorises. This decision did not go over well with many of his contemporaries and successors, notably the French naturalist Georges-Louis Leclerc, Comte de Buffon. Buffon and many others refused to accept Linnaeus's classification regarding the human species, viewing humans as superior and deserving of a group of our own.

Despite resistance to grouping humans with the other primates, there remained a fascination with understanding these creatures that undeniably reminded us of ourselves. In his 1871 book *The Descent of Man, and Selection in Relation to Sex*, naturalist Charles Darwin noted the physical similarities between humans and the African apes, suggesting that humans first evolved in Africa. He also proposed that humans and apes likely shared a common ancestor. Following Darwin's work, there was much interest in studying non-human primates to understand human behaviour.

Despite this early interest in primates and their behaviour in the natural setting, most primatologists would argue that primatology as we know it—the discipline characterized by comprehensive, objective research on the behaviour, social dynamics and evolution of primates—did not develop until after World War II.

In their book *Primate Encounters: Models of Science, Gender, and Society*, Linda Fedigan, the primatologist I introduced you to earlier, and her colleague Shirley Strum provide a brief history of their discipline. They characterize the period between 1950 and 1960 as the revival of primate field studies and the beginning of North American primatology. Fedigan and Strum note that there are many "primatologies," with branches in Europe, Japan and Brazil, among other places. They situate themselves as descendants of "North American anthropological primatology," which traces its roots to the legendary American anthropologist

Sherwood Washburn, and note that their history is just a point on an "increasingly complex map."

I, too, am a product of North American primatology, having studied first at the University of Calgary and then at the University of Toronto. For my master's degree, I lived in Belize for six months, waking to the haunting calls of the howler monkeys in the distance. I kayaked Belizean rivers and strapped on Kevlar snake leggings to wade through flooded forests, searching for monkeys. I endured swarms of mosquitoes and biting fire ants to gather the data that would help me understand what had happened to the monkey population after a major hurricane.

Following my master's research, I was accepted into the PhD program at the University of Toronto. As part of that research, I travelled to Madagascar to study Coquerel's sifakas, medium-sized lemurs with a striking white coat that practically sparkles against the maroon patches of fur on their chest and limbs. According to the International Union for Conservation of Nature, Coquerel's sifakas have been designated "Critically Endangered" due to habitat loss and hunting.

My project was designed to understand how this lemur species responds to habitat loss, particularly at the forest's edges—the transitional areas between the forest and non-habitat zones cleared by human activities like livestock grazing and charcoal production and the resulting erosion. I wanted to know how these edge areas influenced the behaviour of Coquerel's sifakas and, more importantly, how we could use this information to contribute to their conservation. Lemurs have the tragic distinction of being the most endangered group of animals in the world. If lemurs go extinct in Madagascar—the only place in the world where they are found—they are gone for good.

My primatological roots, like Linda Fedigan's, can be traced back to Sherwood Washburn, who spearheaded the study of primates in their natural habitat. I recognize that there are other histories of primatology to be told. Here, I will focus on the history I am most qualified to tell.

During the primatology revival of the 1950s, the North American field established itself within academia as part of anthropology. The term "anthropology" comes from the Greek words "anthropos," meaning human, and "logos," meaning thought or reason. The fact that primatology began and remains situated within anthropology provides a clue as to the discipline's driving force: to answer the burning question "What does it mean to be human?"

The drive to understand human nature characterized the studies of the earliest primatologists. With genetic advances, we now know that the similarities between human and non-human primates go well beyond shared physical or behavioural features. Primates are the closest living relatives to humans, first appearing in the fossil record roughly fifty-five million years ago. The fascination with understanding our closest living relatives and making extrapolations to understand ourselves remains central to primate research.

Between 1965 and 1975, the discipline of primatology experienced another shift. As researchers returned from the field, having studied myriad species in a variety of locations, they noticed not just the similarities with humans but also the vast differences between species. Scientists realized that, before extrapolating from primates to our earliest ancestors, they needed to understand this variability. Field studies of primates exploded in number, with researchers reporting an overwhelming variety in social systems.

From 1975 to 1985, primatology entered what Strum and Fedigan call the "sociobiological era." Sociobiology is a field of study that focuses on understanding the biological basis of social behaviour. In primates, there was a great deal of interest in how evolutionary strategies related to reproduction influenced the overall social behaviour of individuals and groups. During this time, primatologists examined species through new lenses, often returning to Darwin's concepts of species fitness in their approach.

It was also during this time that, as Strum and Fedigan put it, a "provocative" pattern emerged: women arrived on the scene in large numbers.

My goal here is to shine a light on a scientific discipline where women take the lead by telling the stories behind their research. Against the backdrop of my own journey as a field scientist studying wild primates in Belize and Madagascar, I explore the lives of the many women who came before me. These women broke boundaries, made remarkable discoveries and shaped our understanding of our closest living relatives.

I begin with the pioneering Linda Fedigan. Fedigan emerged on the primatological scene in the 1970s, living in an RV and studying a captive colony of Japanese macaques—in Texas, of all places! Through her research on macaques and later the oh-so-intelligent capuchin monkey in Costa Rica, she highlighted the significant role of the female within primate societies, challenging the longstanding view that males are central to all primate groups. But even more important to this book, Fedigan used a scientific approach to explore the role of gender and feminism in the discipline of primatology, outlining several hypotheses for why women are drawn to the study of primates.

The next chapter, "Leakey's Legacy," may spark some debate. Your mind is not deceiving you: one of the chapters of *Sisters of the Jungle* concerns a man. Hear me out. This chapter explores one hypothesis for why women have been successful primatologists: the "goodwill of powerful men" who encouraged and supported female academics in scientific disciplines. To dig into this hypothesis and set the stage for the stories of three exceptional female primatologists who advanced our understanding of the wild apes, I need to introduce you to archaeologist Louis Leakey.

Raised by Scottish missionaries in Kenya and growing up among the Kikuyu tribe, the charismatic Leakey obsessively sought to uncover the origins of our earliest ancestors. He also famously believed that women would make better observers than men and, in his quest to understand human origins, championed three women to study the great apes in their natural environments. Although Leakey was a controversial character—various sources have referred to him as a womanizer—his contributions to primatology and his support for women in the study of wild primates offer important insights into the role of women in the field.

The women sponsored by Leakey—Jane Goodall, Dian Fossey and Biruté Galdikas—are the focus of the next three chapters. These three women are widely known as "the Trimates," a nickname believed to have been coined by Leakey.

The accomplishments and successes of Goodall, Fossey and Galdikas extend well beyond Leakey's influence. These women self-selected—each approached Leakey of her own accord, driven by a desire to learn more about the apes and contribute to our understanding of them and how to conserve the species at risk. While Leakey played an important role by providing funding, facilitating logistics and advocating for them, these women were also independent, strong and passionate. They became important role models for other women interested in studying wild primates.

Jane Goodall, driven by a deep love of animals and the natural world, travelled by steamer ship to Gombe Stream National Park in 1960 to study chimpanzees in their natural habitat. In Gombe, she observed chimps using twigs to fish for termites (the first evidence of tool use in non-human primates), overcame malaria and even found romance. As I write this, she is ninety years old and continues to tour the world, advocating for chimpanzee conservation.

Next, we travel to Rwanda alongside Dian Fossey, whose story is complicated and tragic, ending with her murder in 1985. Fossey felt a kinship with the mountain gorillas, often referring to them as friends. When she realized these apes were endangered due to poaching, she took it upon herself to engage in questionable conservation tactics, once even kidnapping a local child. Still, her early research provided insights into primate social dynamics. Her unrelenting love for the gorillas continues to inspire many to contribute to conserving these gentle giants.

The third of Leakey's Trimates, Biruté Galdikas, took on perhaps the most difficult field study of the great apes—the orangutans in the swampy forests of Indonesia. Galdikas and her then-husband, Rod Brindamour, documented the behaviour of the red-haired arboreal apes, observing solitary group structure and forced copulations. Galdikas and Brindamour also adopted and rehabilitated orphaned orangutans—victims of the pet trade—and helped establish their research area as a national park.

Next, I introduce two women who greatly contributed to our understanding of monkeys. Jeanne Altmann and Sarah Hrdy made discoveries that shifted the perspective from a generalist view of primate societies rooted in aggression, domination and hierarchy with males at the centre to a vision of complex and nuanced societies where female primates also play important roles. Altmann and Hrdy fundamentally changed how we understand primate societies.

Altmann, a trained mathematician, made a name for herself in the 1970s with seminal work that refined the sampling methods for primate behaviour. She also studied the daily lives of female baboons in Kenya—now one of the longest-term studies of wild primates—contributing to our understanding of motherhood in our primate relatives and, ultimately, in ourselves.

Through Sarah Hrdy's story, we travel to South India, where she studied a tree-dwelling, leaf-eating monkey species—the Hanuman langur. A revolutionary in the fields of primatology and evolutionary psychology, Hrdy contributed groundbreaking research on infant killing in primates, including humans, and how female primates adapt behaviourally to save their infants through practices like cooperation and promiscuity.

Finally, I tell a story that is very close to my heart as a lemur researcher. The "Mother of Lemurs," Alison Jolly, went to Madagascar to study the animals in their natural habitat and made huge discoveries, including evidence that many species of lemur are female-dominant. Jolly was also one of the first to recognize the conservation issues in Madagascar—a country where biodiversity is on the brink of collapse and the human population suffers immense poverty. She adopted an approach called community conservation, which considers the needs of both humans and animals to find mutually beneficial solutions.

Throughout this book, I draw from my own experiences to understand how these women entered primatology. More importantly, I examine their influence on this science and their impact on our world. Each woman in this book had a distinct journey—they came from different places in the world and had different backgrounds—yet their choices led them all, somehow, to the path of studying primates. Each faced adversity, but each persisted. Their collective years of effort have changed our understanding of primates—their behaviour, their conservation—and of human evolution.

CHAPTER ONE

A Burning Question

WHY ARE THERE SO MANY WOMEN PRIMATOLOGISTS?

The question struck Linda Fedigan as strange. Yet, as a young woman studying primates, she heard it again and again.

At first, she didn't think there was an unusually high number of women in primatology. She believed it was a misconception.

After all, her PhD supervisor was male, and many of her fellow graduate students were male. Her collaborators, mentees and colleagues? Male, male and male.

Fedigan, short with a slim build and blonde hair, was quiet and reserved—a self-described introvert. But she did not lack opinions. She would challenge those who asked her that question by flipping it back to them: "Why are there not more women in *your* discipline?"

Each time, she would bat the question away, but, like a boomerang, it would make a sharp turn midair and barrel straight back at her.

At first, she chalked up the persistence of this nagging question to what has been called the "National Geographic effect." Jane Goodall, Dian Fossey and Biruté Galdikas—three women who studied great apes—had made their way into the popular media starting in the 1960s and '70s. These women were featured on newsstand covers, including *National Geographic* magazine, as well as in newspapers and on talk shows. Their lives had been documented on film. They rose to fame as the faces of great ape research—research that shone a light on human origins.

Fedigan thought that perhaps the fame of those three women had created a false impression that primatology was a "female discipline." For a while, she continued to shrug the question off, but something about it began to haunt her.

Perhaps it was worth a second look.

Suddenly, she could see the prevalence of women at conferences. They were the authors of the academic papers she read. They were the ones who were prominent in the field. As a scientist, she turned to the data and found that the numbers backed it up. There were significantly more women in primatology than in other biological sciences.

Fedigan felt compelled to find out why.

When Linda Fedigan—then Linda Wood—was ten or so, her military father brought home a book. It had a black cover and large, gold lettering that read *Gods, Graves and Scholars.*

The book, authored by German writer C.W. Ceram, promised to provide readers with a history of archaeology. More than that, Ceram brought archaeology to life through stories of adventure and romance. Writing in 2000 in the *American Journal of Physical Anthropology*, Fedigan recalls her father reading her passages from the book out loud and inspiring in her a passion for understanding our past.

After that, young Linda decided she would one day become an archaeologist.

Linda Wood was born in 1949 in Enid, Oklahoma, the wheat capital of the state and home to just under fifty thousand people. Her mother was a German-Italian war bride, and her father was a member of the United States Air Force. Linda spent her toddler years near her father's family in rural Georgia while he was serving in Korea. After he returned, "military brat" Linda moved with her family from place to place as her father was sent to different stations. She spent some years in Germany, near her maternal grandparents, where she learned to speak German.

During the Cold War era, Linda's family was living in San Antonio, Texas, where she attended junior high school on the military base. This was during the Space Race, when the US and the Soviet Union sought to dominate space exploration. In 1957, the USSR launched the satellite Sputnik, beating the US into space and demonstrating their advanced rocket technology—technology that many believed could be strong enough to launch nuclear bombs at the US.

American leaders decided they needed to act fast against the security threat. One area of focus was education. The US education system underwent an overhaul, with a new curriculum focused on science. The goal was to foster future scientists who would be capable of overtaking the Soviet Union.

Linda was a guinea pig for the new curriculum—a future scientist, like it or not. Fortunately, she liked it. Consistently at the top of her class, young Linda received a scholarship to attend a private school that focused on science and had small classes, enabling the high-achieving, studious teenager to thrive.

At sixteen, Linda relocated with her family to a German military base. Counsellors at the high school there noticed how far ahead Linda was academically compared to the other students in her grade. They recommended she skip the twelfth grade and move to France to attend the American College of Paris. Wanting to protect her young daughter, Linda's mother insisted she stick it out one year, waiting until she was seventeen to leave home and embark on her higher education experience. Her mother also stipulated that Linda was to live in an all-female dormitory run by Polish nuns.

When she eventually arrived at the American College of Paris, Linda immersed herself in French culture. She eagerly took advantage of every learning opportunity, including an introductory anthropology course, which whetted her appetite for learning more about other cultures and languages. With her international experience, interest in other cultures and language skills, she was on track to become a translator or to pursue a scholarly discipline like linguistic anthropology.

Then, another pivotal moment. Another book.

Linda read *Village in the Vaucluse*, an ethnography by Laurence Wylie, first published in 1957. Wylie, an American professor, had moved with his wife and two sons to a small village in Provence, France, immersing himself in the community for a year. Young Linda was fascinated by Wylie's anthropological take on the small French village, particularly his descriptions of how women interacted with men.

She thought about pursuing a career in ethnographic anthropology.

Amid all her soul-searching, Linda met Larry Fedigan, an Irish citizen who was teaching English as a second language in Paris, and they married when she was nineteen. Shortly after, the couple relocated to Texas so she could study anthropology at the University of Texas at Austin and he could work on his doctorate in teacher education.

Inspired by Wylie's ethnography, Linda Fedigan chose to focus on sociocultural anthropology. In addition to her courses, she worked as a research assistant for a graduate student, interviewing women who read romance novels. These interviews involved asking the women about their personal lives, which Fedigan found uncomfortable.

At the same time, she was taking an introductory primatology course taught by physical anthropologist Claud Bramblett. For that course, she conducted observations of gelada baboons housed at the San Antonio Zoo. Fedigan soon realized that with non-human primates she could be a silent observer and still learn about the complexities of primate social systems and the relationships between the sexes. She loved animals, so switching to primatology seemed a natural fit.

"I was a lot better observing than interviewing, frankly," Fedigan told me when I spoke to her for this book.

In 1970, she landed a part-time job as a lab technician in Austin at the Balcones Research Center (now the J.J. Pickle Research Campus), where Bramblett housed captive groups of monkeys, including the silver-grey vervets and colourful guenons. Fedigan was tasked with cleaning the monkey cages and collecting behavioural data. She took a shine to the vervets and focused her master's research on these delicate, black-faced East African primates.

During her master's program, Fedigan began teaching an introductory course in primatology and developed an interest in the history of primatological research. She noticed a stark contrast between the descriptions of male-dominated baboon societies and the vervets she was studying. In the vervets, Fedigan observed males placing a hand on the hips of the females. She noticed that in response to this sexual invitation, the females would either stand still and receive a mount willingly, or they would turn and threaten the male, scaring him off.

Fedigan concluded that the vervet females appeared to be in control—that they had a choice rather than being merely a resource for the males.

When Linda Fedigan read the early primatological publications, she did not take them at face value. In learning about the social life of hamadryas baboons, for example, she noticed that scientists referred to groupings as "harems," meaning a group of females that mate with one male. Dominant male baboons were said to have priority of access to receptive females.

One of the stories Fedigan almost certainly would have encountered at this time was Solly Zuckerman's account of the baboons of Monkey Hill, which he details in his 1932 book, *The Social Life of Monkeys and Apes*.

Monkey Hill was supposed to be the London Zoological Society's crown jewel—the zoo's first outdoor exhibit where monkeys could live as though in nature. This new enclosure would be a departure from the rest of the zoo. In the 1920s, most animals in the zoo were kept in dark, indoor cages, and the animals were dying from diseases like pneumonia and vitamin D deficiency. To make matters worse (at least in the eyes of the zoological society), zoo visitors were starting to notice.

Monkey Hill, proposed in 1924 and modelled after the Hagenbeck Zoo in Stellingen, Germany, was intended to showcase the benefits of outdoor living for zoo animals. When it was completed in 1925, the exhibit was, by all appearances, idyllic. The oval-shaped, open-air enclosure was equipped with shelters, heaters and UV lights, and a twelve-foot-deep outer wall that mimicked a cliff face gave visitors a panoramic view of the animals.

The residents of Monkey Hill—ninety-seven hamadryas baboons—had been shipped to London by boat from the Horn of Africa. The zoo had specifically requested all male baboons because the males were large-bodied and sported an impressive set of canine teeth, which they figured would captivate zoo patrons.

The London Zoo's trouble began when six female baboons somehow slipped into the shipment. The zoo opted to release the males first, and later added the females. What ensued could be described as a massacre.

Based on what we now know about primate social systems, the zoo's decision to create a group of male baboons and then release a few females into their midst was beyond foolish. Evolutionary theory, when applied to primate sociality, tells us that social groups and interactions between individuals in such groups are shaped by ecological factors. Males and females show different social behaviours in response to various pressures that might influence their ability to reproduce in their environment—also called evolutionary fitness.

For females, reproduction—birth, lactation and parental care—requires a great deal of energy, and the limiting resource is food. Competition among female group members centres on access to food resources. For males, reproduction is limited by access to receptive females, which is why much of the competition within a primate group occurs between males over females.

Of course, in 1925, the London Zoo did not understand primate social life and the evolutionary pressures shaping group dynamics. We now know that hamadryas baboons in the wild live in societies with multiple females and only a few males. Zookeepers did not know what would happen when they released the female baboons—in short supply and in a small space—amid a group of large-bodied males.

It was like *The Hunger Games*: kill or be killed. The male baboons fought to the death for access to the females, and sometimes females got caught up in the clashes and were injured. A year into the exhibit, twenty-seven baboons were dead, either directly or indirectly, because of the aggression between individuals. Many died from strangulation. Just two years after the exhibit launched, the group had dwindled from nearly one hundred individuals to only fifty-six.

In a futile attempt to keep the exhibit alive, the zoo introduced thirty additional adult females and five immature males. Within only a few weeks, fifteen of the females were killed. Baboon carcasses littered the cliff face, as it was too dangerous for the zookeepers to enter the enclosure and clean up the casualties. In stark contrast to the chaos inside the baboon enclosure stood Solly Zuckerman, the reserved zoologist the zoo had hired to study the monkeys of Monkey Hill. Zuckerman immediately noted the male dominance among the hamadryas baboons—oh, and all the sex.

Zuckerman's thesis, which was published as *The Social Life of Monkeys and Apes* and was based on observations of the dysfunctional Monkey Hill groups, emphasized the overt behaviours he observed, like sex and aggression, and dismissed the subtleties (such as what was going on between the females in the group). He noted that male-dominated hierarchies were maintained through the deathly battles. According to Zuckerman, the females would defuse the aggression by offering sex.

He wrote: "The continuous sexual activity of the primate is probably the main reason underlying the permanent association of the two sexes, for unlike most mammals, the sexes never separate." Zuckerman concluded that sexual relations were the key to social life, calling them "the fundamental mechanism of society." Sure, he conceded, there were other factors, such as interactions between mothers and their infants, but these weren't driving the social groups—these kinds of interactions were merely consequences of sexual relations, he believed. Males were central and dominant, while females were peripheral and submissive.

Although Zuckerman noted in his book that his conclusions about the baboon society should only be applied to non-human primate behaviour, it didn't stop his readers from applying his theories to primates of the human variety. Many interpreted Zuckerman's theory in the context of humanity, using it to justify male dominance in humans and to depict humans as having a natural tendency toward war.

I can imagine Linda Fedigan, as a pensive undergraduate student, quickly snapping her textbook shut after reading this. I know I would have needed a breather—some space to reflect on these sweeping conclusions.

Understanding the role of females in primate groups and their interactions with males became a strong interest for Fedigan as she navigated her academic career. Early in the 1980s, fresh out of her PhD, she published *Primate Paradigms: Sex Roles and Social Bonds*, in which she shone a light on the often-overlooked role of female primates in social groups and highlighted their significance to species evolution. The book, written for a broad audience, sought to correct an imbalance that Fedigan felt pervaded the primate literature. She critiqued widely accepted theories on male and female behavioural patterns in non-human primates and emphasized that female choice could be as influential as male competition in shaping sexual dynamics within these groups.

To this day, *Primate Paradigms* is considered a seminal publication—influencing both science and women's studies. Although Linda Fedigan herself is quiet, her academic voice within the field of primatology is powerful. From the outset, she challenged ingrained perceptions and prevailing theories with curiosity and passion. Her balanced and objective approach was important to the trajectory of primate studies, as she devoted equal attention to non-human primate females and males.

In 1972, the Fedigans pulled up to a swath of undeveloped brushland fifty kilometres north of Laredo, Texas—their large motorhome kicking up dust as the tall electric fence surrounding La Moca Ranch came into view. Linda Fedigan knew that beyond the fence was a large group of Japanese macaques, muscular monkeys with soft pink faces and light-brown, sometimes unruly hair. Perhaps her heart fluttered a little as she thought about spending the next two years studying the group for her PhD research.

She had no idea as she sat with her then-husband in their motorhome that she would one day become a project director at this research site, spending her downtime over a full year clacking away at a typewriter in the back room of a trailer, writing a book born out of passion and curiosity while the monkeys traipsed by outside her window.

But on her first arrival, Fedigan wasn't the only newbie at the Texas research station. The monkeys themselves had been released just six weeks before. Named the "Arashiyama West" group of macaques, these were descendants of the Arashiyama monkeys of Japan, a group of thirty-four monkeys that had ranged in a forest on a mountain peak that was a twenty-minute train ride from Kyoto.

This group was famously studied by a team of Japanese researchers in 1954. Facing initial struggles to see the monkeys up close, the scientists provisioned the group, providing sweet potatoes to entice them in so they could get close enough to watch their behaviour. Soon, the scientists could observe the groups in the open at close range.

Provisioning had another impact on the monkeys: the well-fed population exploded to 163 individuals. At that point, the group broke, or "fissioned," into two distinct groups divided by kinship and dominance lines—Group A and Group B. Fissioning in primate species is an adaptation that has evolved to avoid competition within a group for food or mates. Competition is costly when it comes to the ability to survive and reproduce.

In 1966, John Emlen, a biologist from the University of Wisconsin, travelled with his research team to Arashiyama to study vocal communication and mating behaviour among the macaques as part of a cooperative project with Kyoto University. Syunzo Kawamura, one of the original scientists studying the Arashiyama groups, was there to help with research-related business. During Emlen's visit, Kawamura explained that Group A had become a nuisance.

The trouble was that the site was just eight square kilometres in size, and the two groups of monkeys, still being provisioned, had continued to grow. The habitat and food resources could only support so many individuals, even with provisioning. As a result, the monkeys had begun ranging outside the Arashiyama forests, disturbing the locals who ran farms and had homes in the nearby suburbs of Kyoto. The research team, much to their dismay, started getting complaints from the local residents.

Conflict between humans and primates is a huge conservation challenge, particularly as humans expand into primate habitats. Macaques represent an interesting case because they occupy the broadest geographic range of any primate (aside from humans), spanning from North Africa to India, southern China, Southeast Asia and Japan. This wide range is due to their ability to survive in diverse habitats, from mangroves to tropical forests to grasslands. And yes, they can even survive in urban habitats right alongside humans.

The problem with that ability to live in urban areas is that the macaques can quickly become "pests." Driven by food availability, they seek out and steal crops from farmers, which tend to be higher-energy resources than what they find in the wild. This behaviour can be problematic for humans as it damages their crops and affects their income. Macaques can also pose a physical threat by stealing items directly from people and rooting around in the garbage.

My partner and fellow primatologist Travis Steffens and I experienced this human-primate interface firsthand during a trip to Thailand. We had travelled there to get married in Chiang Mai. Leading up to the big day, we toured around, visiting markets and various temples. It was at one of the temples that Travis had his run-in.

The temple is a popular tourist destination, not only for its striking architecture but also because macaques like to hang around. Many tourists feed the macaques, so when they see a person, they know they have a shot at getting some snacks.

Being responsible primatologists, Travis and I had no intention of feeding the monkeys—we just wanted to see the temple, watch the monkeys up close and take a few pictures. The monkeys had other ideas. The adult macaques approached us, watching us carefully to see if we had anything of interest. At one point, while I stood at the entrance to the temple, I watched three monkeys hop into the back of someone's truck and rifle through their grocery bags, throwing rolls of toilet paper everywhere.

Then it happened. Travis had just snapped a photo of a juvenile macaque when an adult monkey leapt down from above and landed squarely on the worn brown backpack he was wearing. Wasting no time, the monkey began grabbing at the water bottle in the side pouch of Travis's pack. I could hear the crunch of the plastic bottle as the monkey gripped it with both hands and yanked.

"Keriann!" Travis yelped, startled by the dive-bombing monkey. His hands were full with his camera equipment. He looked at me. "Do something!"

I froze, mesmerized by the monkey, its head down, so intent on freeing that water bottle. Did I dare reach out and push it off the pack? Would I lose a finger in the process?

"What can I do?" I asked.

"Something... anything!" A pause. "You're a primatologist!"

In a desperate move, Travis tried rapidly shifting his body from right to left and was able to flick the monkey off his backpack in a smooth motion. His water bottle—and my fingers—were still intact. Crisis averted.

Back in 1966 Japan, the Arashiyama monkeys were also running rampant. Kawamura needed a solution to the Group A problem. The idea of culling the population was unappealing: the monkeys originated from an iconic research group dating back to the early stages of primatology and were a living testament to the origins of

Japanese primatology. Researchers had studied this group extensively and had learned a great deal about primate social behaviour, including that groups are composed of related females, and that understanding female kinship was the key to understanding the social dynamics of the group.

Not wanting to destroy the monkeys, Kawamura was toying with the idea of relocation. He told Emlen that he would be willing to gift the group to American scientists if there was interest in moving the monkeys to the US to set up a captive colony there.

In 1968, ten American scientists began working through the logistics of this monumental task. The researchers agreed on two crucial points: the monkeys needed a place where they could be kept together as a group, and they should not be caged. They determined that they needed an area that was both hilly and forested, with a moderate climate. They knew, too, that there needed to be a mechanism in place to contain the monkeys—a large fence of some kind. To facilitate research, the site needed to be close to a university centre but also far enough away from other humans so as not to be disturbed. The team investigated sites in Michigan, South Carolina, Georgia and Hawaii, but none were suitable.

Emlen needed to broaden his search, so he put feelers out to other scientists across the country. One researcher he contacted in his search was Claud Bramblett. Later, while teaching a course at the University of Texas at Austin, Bramblett mentioned the macaques who needed a home. One of his students was the daughter of a Texas rancher named Edward Dryden Jr., and she relayed the request to her father, who stepped up with an undeveloped forty-four-hectare section of his ranch.

To Dryden, the macaques represented a business opportunity. He had his sights on raising and selling any "surplus" monkeys bred at the site to zoos and research institutes while maintaining the core group on his ranch. In all, 150 monkeys were captured, examined by Kyoto University's Primate Research Institute, tattooed for future identification and flown from Osaka to Hawaii and then to Laredo.

Since Fedigan was one of Bramblett's PhD students, Arashiyama West was a natural site for her primate studies. When she arrived in 1972, she was met by Tetsuzo Mano, a Japanese primatologist who had studied the monkeys in Japan before they were relocated. In her review article "My Path to Primatology," Fedigan described how Mano showed patience and care as he trained her on how to tell the monkeys apart, document their behaviours, and understand their social systems.

Each monkey had been given a name and number, and Mano filled Fedigan in on their personalities and history within the group. It was with the Arashiyama West colony that Fedigan was exposed to a collaborative approach to research.

She wrote that the Japanese primatologists were generous in sharing their knowledge and data for her to review. Mano explained that this was how they operated at Arashiyama—with senior researchers acting as mentors for junior members of the team. Fedigan credited the Japanese influence as the inspiration for her research approach, which emphasizes long-term data collection as well as mentorship and collaboration among colleagues.

I am lucky to have experienced Linda Fedigan's mentorship directly. She joined the University of Calgary while I was there completing my master's research. I remember it was a big deal: she had been awarded a Canada Research Chair, a position held by Canada's preeminent researchers, and the fact that she was coming to Calgary would bolster the growing primatology program. I remember meeting her for the first time, butterflies in my stomach, as I shook hands with primatology royalty. I learned quickly that she did indeed practise science with immense generosity and cooperation.

I only took one course with Linda Fedigan, but it was one that, I believe, showcased her work as a mentor. It was called

"Professional Skills" and it covered topics meant to prepare graduate students for academia, ranging from presentation skills to scholarly publishing to shaking hands at conferences. I still implement the lessons I learned in that course in my professional life, and each time I do, I think about Linda and how fortunate I was to have the opportunity to learn from her.

In Texas, Linda Fedigan's focus was on collecting data on the macaques' life histories. She explored the population dynamics and was particularly interested in female dominance and reproduction. She wanted to know why some females had more reproductive success than others.

Not long after obtaining her PhD in 1974, Fedigan landed a tenure-track position at the University of Alberta, where she continued her research with the Arashiyama West colony. Mary Pavelka, one of Fedigan's graduate students during this time (and later my master's supervisor), studied female old age and end-of-life reproduction in the Arashiyama West macaques. Together, Fedigan and Pavelka published a series of ten papers comparing the end of reproduction in Japanese macaques versus human females.

Two years after the macaques landed at La Moca Ranch, Edward Dryden passed away. His widow continued to finance the monkey colony but did not have the same passion for the task as her deceased husband. The monkeys needed a new home. In 1980, Bramblett and one of his students, Louise Griffin, coordinated a move to some land near Dilley, Texas. The monkey population thrived and soon began to outgrow their new enclosure. It also became difficult to fund the colony.

In 1999, the Animal Protection Institute, an animal advocacy group, purchased the land where the monkeys resided and took over Arashiyama West. The institute implemented birth control to curb the population, which meant naturalistic studies of life history and reproduction had come to an end. It also changed the focus of the site, relaunching it as a sanctuary rather than a place for science.

In the late 1970s, after the research with the Arashiyama West monkeys had come to an end, Fedigan began envisioning a long-term field station. Studying female primate life histories requires long-term research because primates are long-lived, with many monkey species living up to twenty-five years or more. For researchers to fully understand their lives from birth to death, the primates need to be examined over decades, not months. Early primate researchers only studied primates for short periods, with some of the longest studies spanning just one year. Fedigan was one of the first to recognize the importance of long-term research for our understanding of primate social lives.

She compiled a wish list of qualities for her ideal long-term field site:

- The site should have primates that are free-ranging in their natural habitat.
- The primates should live in multi-male, multi-female social groups.
- There should be minimal human impact.
- The site should be a safe place for students to conduct their research.

Fedigan's colleague, Ken Glander, who had also worked with Claud Bramblett, suggested Costa Rica as a potential site. At the time, Fedigan was on St. Kitts, an island in the West Indies, overseeing a study of the black-faced, light-brown vervet monkeys that had lived there for roughly three hundred years. Like the Arashiyama West macaques, the vervets weren't native to St. Kitts and had likely been brought over in the seventeenth century along with early settlers as exotic "boat pets."

St. Kitts was Fedigan's third attempt at finding a suitable place to conduct long-term research. So far, it wasn't looking promising.

She was happy with the level of safety in this popular tourist destination—the island is known for its picturesque, forested mountains and black sand beaches—and the scientific studies were going well, but she was struggling with an ethical question.

By habituating the monkeys to the presence of researchers, she realized, she was putting them at risk of capture and harassment by the local human population. As with the Arashiyama macaques in Japan, the vervets of St. Kitts shared their habitat with humans and already had a reputation as pests, often raiding farmers' crops. Fedigan worried that by staying and conducting research on the monkeys—getting them more and more accustomed to humans—the monkeys might grow bolder, leading to further conflict between them and the frustrated humans.

St. Kitts was just one of many false starts for Fedigan. After her research at Arashiyama West ended, she thought she'd try studying the brown, wispy-furred Barbary macaques, famous for being tailless, in North Africa. She had even received a grant to fund her research there, but it all fell apart when she was unable to obtain a visa.

In 1977, Fedigan considered switching gears and doing some research on a New World monkey—the long-limbed, black-and-grey spider monkeys that lived near the Mayan temples in Tikal, Guatemala. She set up a site, sent some of her students there to do research and successfully produced student theses and publications, but it quickly became clear that the Guatemalan government was unstable. Things came to a head when one of her local team members disappeared. Fedigan knew she could not in good conscience send her students to an unsafe site.

After Guatemala, Fedigan tried a colony of non-provisioned macaques on a southern island of Japan, but her own health issues meant she had to return home unexpectedly.

In 1982, Fedigan finally took Ken Glander's advice and gave Costa Rica a go. She and her husband set out on a visit to survey potential research sites. She was taken with the country from the start, struck by the many natural reserves and parks where research was a very real possibility. Ultimately, she selected Santa Rosa National Park in Guanacaste, on the northwestern tip of Costa Rica. Santa Rosa ticked all the boxes and was a safe environment for both primates and researchers. It was there that she set up her longest-running field site to date.

When Linda Fedigan arrived in Santa Rosa National Park on her reconnaissance trip, she was thrilled to find three different species of monkeys living in the park. The forest canopy was alive with activity. The black-bodied, white-faced capuchins leapt gracefully from tree to tree, with mothers carrying infants on their backs as they carefully navigated gaps in the canopy. The black howler monkeys roared and barked to maintain space from other groups, avoiding competitive interactions. The lanky spider monkeys used their long arms to swing through the treetops like children on monkey bars at a playground.

Santa Rosa protects roughly one hundred square kilometres of land and marine waters, including a mosaic of deciduous, evergreen, semi-evergreen and regenerating forests. The biodiversity is astounding, encompassing thousands of insects and hundreds of plant, mammal, bird and reptile species.

Fedigan quickly learned that Santa Rosa was just one sector of the broader Area de Conservación Guanacaste, established in the 1970s and '80s by evolutionary ecologist and University of Pennsylvania professor Daniel Janzen. During his research there, Janzen witnessed the destruction of forests through human activities like farming, setting fires, logging and hunting.

Unable to sit idly by, Janzen spearheaded the Guanacaste project, which sought to expand forest fragments to benefit the region's biodiversity. Along with Costa Rican conservationists, he implemented fire prevention, forest regeneration and conservation education programs to bring the forest back to life. He worked with the Costa Rican National Park Service to merge Santa Rosa with several nearby parks and reserves, creating one cohesive protected area. He also started the Guanacaste Dry Forest Conservation Fund to raise money to purchase surrounding ranches. Today, Santa Rosa is a UNESCO World Heritage Site. It extends over a vast range of ecosystems, from lowland forests on the Pacific coast of Guanacaste to the dry forests of Santa Rosa, and stretches over volcanic mountains to the cloud forests and rainforests on the eastern slopes.

Santa Rosa appealed to Fedigan as a long-term field site because it afforded the opportunity to ask a multitude of questions and to try to answer those questions by studying a variety of different primate species. She did not hesitate to apply for her research permit to work at Santa Rosa, and her research there officially began in 1983. She was permitted to study the behaviour and life history of the monkeys. At the same time, the National Parks Service asked Fedigan if she would conduct a census of the three species to get a sense of how the populations were doing in this recently protected area.

Her census work inspired her to focus primarily on the capuchins. She was interested in these monkeys because not much was known about the species in the wild. Not only that, the capuchins were also female-philopatric, meaning the females remained in the groups they were born into throughout their lives, while the males emigrated. The deep female social relationships fascinated Fedigan.

The capuchin monkey is a medium-sized monkey, recognizable by its black body and white upper chest and shoulders, black cap on top of its head, and long, grasping tail. Capuchins are known as the "organ grinder monkey" because they were trained to work alongside those Victorian street musicians. Due to their high intelligence, they are often trained for use in the entertainment industry. Marcel, Ross's monkey on the popular '90s sitcom *Friends*, was a capuchin.

Crystal the Monkey is another capuchin that has done the rounds in Hollywood, having appeared on television shows including *Animal Practice* and *Community* and in movies like *We Bought a Zoo*, *Zookeeper* and *The Hangover Part II*. She was even a nominee at the 2011 Teen Choice Awards. Crystal also played Dexter, the cheeky, slap-happy monkey in *Night at the Museum*, a role that tormented me to no end as a primatologist because the capuchin, which is from South America, was found in the "Hall of African Mammals" in the movie. Facepalm.

Several other species of primates, including gorillas and chimpanzees, have been used in television and film since the early days of Hollywood. Moviegoers have delighted in seeing our cute, cuddly primate relatives dressed in clothes, getting up to no good and "smiling" on the big screen. What most people don't realize is that a bared-teeth display from a non-human primate is often a signal of fear or submission.

There is also a lack of understanding surrounding primate welfare and conservation issues in the entertainment industry. Many of the primates depicted in movies and television are infants, as they are easier to control than muscular, strong adults. In many cases, the primates are taken away from their mothers shortly after birth, which can lead to psychological issues. They are sometimes trained using negative techniques, and proximity to humans means a high risk of disease transmission.

Featuring primates in TV shows and movies can also create misconceptions about their conservation status, leading people to mistakenly believe that the species commonly used in entertainment are not endangered. People may also think that having a primate as a pet would be a good idea. In fact, primate pets are known to be highly difficult to manage, often destructive and even downright dangerous.

Hollywood is beginning to update its thinking on these issues. The recent *Planet of the Apes* movies all used CGI rather than live primates, and in 2012, Walt Disney prohibited the use of great apes as performers in its productions.

While there has been some progress for the great apes, capuchin monkeys are still frequently used in the entertainment industry. This ongoing practice is problematic when it comes to public perception: in a 2015 survey of more than one thousand visitors to the Lincoln Park Zoo in Chicago, nearly one in five said they would consider a primate as a pet.

Linda Fedigan's experience with wild capuchins demonstrates how disruptive human intervention can be for these monkeys. During her research in Santa Rosa, she struggled with distinguishing between the monochromatic howler monkeys and following the spider monkeys, who moved far and fast. For those reasons, she set about darting, marking and releasing the monkeys so she could more easily track them over their lifespans.

In 1985, with the help of Ken Glander, she captured and marked fifty-four monkeys—both capuchins and howlers—using a blowpipe and CO2 gun. The drugged primates fell from the trees, where a team member waited with a large hammock to catch them. The scientists then weighed, measured and marked the animals before returning them to the wild.

Fedigan noticed the capuchins were not taking well to the capturing regime. Of the fifty-four monkeys captured, just eight were capuchins. The capuchins were highly agitated by human intervention, and pragmatic Fedigan decided it was detrimental to the monkeys' well-being to continue attempting to capture them. She also realized she could study the monkeys' appearances to tell them apart.

With the help of local field assistants, Fedigan began tracking the monkeys and spending time with them to get them used to the presence of humans. By the end of 1985, she was finally ready to begin her research. She established five study groups that were easily accessed from the park's housing, and she and her students began collecting life history data. As her dataset grew, Fedigan could begin to answer the questions that had always fascinated her, including questions about female reproduction and social interactions with males.

The female capuchins in Fedigan's study had between zero and eleven offspring during their reproductive years. Fedigan and her students explored the factors affecting female reproductive success further and found that although the capuchins had strong, linear dominance hierarchies, these hierarchies did not predict reproduction or infant survival. What did appear to predict better reproductive success for the female capuchins was group composition: females living in a group with a higher adult male-to-adult female ratio and a stable male membership tended to have more infants, and those infants were more likely to survive. Additionally, having infants in a group with close female kin meant others were available to help with rearing the infants and forging alliances in the face of competition.

Climatic patterns also played a role: more rain meant more food and water, and better chances for infant survival. The long-term nature of Fedigan's work also showed that females reproduced until the end of their lives, so the longer they lived, the more offspring they had.

Fedigan's work with the capuchins meant she could explore the relationships between males and females in the group and examine how they affected the females' reproductive success. Her observations uncovered a range of interactions between adult males and infants, including protective behaviours as well as aggression. When males entered a new group, they typically took an aggressive approach, injuring resident males and attacking females and their infants. Infanticide is a major cause of infant mortality.

Linda Fedigan's work at Santa Rosa is the epitome of a long-term research site. There, she grew as a mentor, overseeing more than thirty graduate students from twelve universities as they conducted research and contributed to the data collected at the site.

That burning question just wouldn't go away.

Fedigan had spent years studying the Arashiyama West macaques. She had landed a tenure-track position, published her influential work on female primates and their role in society, and set up a long-term research site in Costa Rica. Yet still, people continued to ask her: "But *why* are there so many women anthropologists?"

After some reflection, it occurred to her that the heart of this question related to the interactions between and coexistence of males and females. *This was the very question she had always set out to ask about non-human primates.* She was inspired to tackle the question scientifically—first, to check if there were indeed more women than men in primatology, and then to dig into the reasons why.

Although she sometimes viewed her work in this arena as an extracurricular pursuit, Fedigan acknowledged in her writing that this question was brought to her because she was the right person for the job.

So, what did she deduce? Fedigan outlined her thinking in her 1994 article "Science and the Successful Female: Why There Are So Many Women Primatologists."

First thing first: she dispelled an insulting stereotype.

Fedigan knew there was a widespread belief that women study primates because they are cute and cuddly—what she termed the "big brown eyes hypothesis." She balked at this suggestion, stressing that primate fieldwork is hardly romantic and that non-human primates can be downright nasty. Fedigan pointed out that this idea, perpetuated by the popular media using infant primates for television shows and movies, couldn't be further from the truth.

She provided the example of the capuchins she studied in the wild eating adorable coati pups (a South American member of the raccoon family) alive. We know that chimpanzees, too, hunt and eat meat—feeding on bush pigs, red colobus monkeys and baboons.

In her book *In the Shadow of Man*, renowned primatologist Jane Goodall describes her experience with the not-so-cute side of chimpanzee behaviour. One morning, while watching the chimps near her camp in Tanzania, she saw a baboon troop pass through the area. The chimps rose and silently stalked the monkeys. Goodall quietly followed. "As I rounded the building," she recalled, "I heard the sudden screaming of a baboon and a few seconds afterward the roaring of male baboons and the screaming and barking of chimpanzees."

Goodall broke into a run, ducking into some thick bushes. She watched, wide-eyed, as a male chimpanzee lifted a juvenile baboon by the leg, hoisted it above his head and slammed its head into the rocks.

How's that for cute and cuddly?

With the big brown eyes hypothesis put to rest, Fedigan next suggested in her paper that the trend of women in primatology may have to do with the time in history that the discipline emerged. By the 1960s, primatology was flourishing, with studies on captive and wild primates taking place around the world and researchers seeking to understand primate behaviours and society. By the end of that decade, international primatology conferences and journals had been established, providing the discipline with forums to announce discoveries.

The 1960s and '70s also marked the era of the women's movement in North America and Europe, and the second wave of feminism. As primatology grew as a scientific discipline—one that offered opportunities to seek answers to new questions and travel to far-off places—so did women's independence and the desire for equal rights and opportunity. It should come as no surprise, then, that the 1960s saw the rise of some of the most prominent female scientists in the field.

Linda Fedigan reflected in her writing that she was attracted to primatology in the late 1960s because, as a burgeoning discipline, there was a great deal of opportunity for scientific discovery.

In 1989, feminist scholar Donna Haraway published *Primate Visions*, a comprehensive analysis of the history of primatology. In it, she argued—much to the chagrin of some primatologists—that primatology had undergone a shift toward becoming a feminist science. As the women's movement peaked in North American society, Haraway said, we began to see feminist perspectives taking root within the discipline.

The book received mixed reviews. Some primatologists called it "infuriating," though it was well-received by scholars working in the history of science and feminist theory.

In a particularly memorable review, primatologist Alison Jolly and her daughter, cultural studies professor Margaretta Jolly, published their opposing thoughts in the form of letters to each other. Alison Jolly wrote that Haraway "gets us primatologists wrong," taking issue with Haraway's assertion that the scientific knowledge generated from studies of wild primates is subjective—socially constructed based on the observer's personal agenda.

In her response, Margaretta Jolly wrote that science is like anything else in that it is "embodied in narrative" and that Haraway was merely pointing out that the wider social landscape plays a role in shaping science and the scientist.

In a 2001 article, Linda Fedigan explored whether primatology could be considered a feminist science by examining it through the lens of history of science professor Londa Schiebinger's "tools of gender analysis." These tools involve analyzing how gender fits within the priorities of a scientific study and decisions regarding how populations are chosen for a study.

Using this method, Fedigan provided numerous examples of how primatology fits within the feminist framework. She argued that primatologists have shifted their research over the years to explore gender-related issues, asking questions about female primates' behaviour and testing hypotheses about male aggression and sexual coercion, and the repercussions for females. Observation methods have shifted as well—standardization now means researchers watch all members of a group rather than focusing on the overt behaviours often exhibited by males. Researchers explored new species—not just the male-dominant savanna baboons but also others, like lemurs, where females are in charge.

Fedigan pointed out that feminism can influence science by creating more opportunities for women to enter and succeed in science, increasing gender awareness and altering the dynamics. She views primatology as a discipline where women's influence will improve the science.

Yet, she wrote, just a handful of primatologists would go so far as to call themselves feminists. She noted that this paradox is important to understand because it sheds light on how primatology has shifted over time.

She also asked why so many primatologists distance themselves from feminism. She proposed that there is a fear that disciplines that are viewed as feminist are at risk of being devalued. There is also a perception that integrating politics into the discipline conflicts with the idea of objectivity and the scientific method. There is a perception, she argued, that science exists outside of all other human activities and is pure and free from bias.

Fedigan suggested that the goals of feminists and scientists actually dovetail, and the result is an inclusive science that encompasses the perspectives of both the primatologists themselves and their study subjects.

I pause here to note that although primatology may be inclusive, important questions remain. A 2017 article about the representation and experiences of women in biological anthropology noted that at annual conferences, men give more talks, while women present more posters (generally perceived as less prestigious). In male-organized symposia, there is a lower proportion of female first-author presenters than in female-organized symposia, a surprising bias given that females outnumber males in this discipline. Notably, women are still underrepresented in senior academic positions, which indicates that a glass ceiling remains.

The International Primatological Society has a predominance of female members at the graduate student and assistant professor levels, but the opposite trend occurs when it comes to full professors, even though there is an abundance of female students and high-impact publications from professional women.

Still, there is a prevalence of women within the discipline of primatology.

Fedigan suggested that the discipline's ties to the life sciences could also be a factor. Graduate enrolment of women is higher in the social sciences, psychology and life sciences, while men tend to be concentrated in engineering. Primatology is often housed in social science departments built around psychology and anthropology—fields where female enrolment tends to be higher.

She offered another hypothesis for the large proportion of women in primatology: could it be that the primates themselves attract women researchers? She argued that many primate species are female-bonded, meaning females spend their whole lives in the group where they were born and have strong relationships with one another. Not only that, in some primate species, females play important roles in their group, and in some cases, females are dominant over males.

Fedigan's hypothesis also suggests that female scientists may be more drawn to a science that focuses on understanding what it means to be human. She points to a 1988 publication that argued women are more attracted to disciplines where they can examine human nature and study subjects that relate to the human experience, as opposed to hard abstractions more commonly found in physics or chemistry, for example.

Another explanation Fedigan offered for the preponderance of women in primatology is that the field has a tradition of strong female role models. I wonder if she had any inkling while she explored this hypothesis that she would go down in history as one of those role models herself. She certainly has been a role model for me.

Research shows that one way to challenge the stereotype that women are not cut out for STEM disciplines is through the presence and support of female role models. When young women see other women forging a path in science, they are more likely to pursue it themselves. In primatology—especially today—we find a seemingly endless list of successful female primatologists. Women have long held prestigious roles within the discipline; for example, the first female president of the International Primatological Society took office in 1992, and five of the eight recipients of the organization's lifetime achievement awards are women. Strong role models can be famously traced back to the 1960s and "the Trimates"—Jane Goodall, Dian Fossey and Biruté Galdikas—the three women who ventured into the wilds to study the great apes in their natural habitat and made waves in the discipline.

The Trimates also embody another hypothesis: that women are attracted to primatology because of the media coverage of women in this discipline. The "National Geographic effect," says Fedigan, can explain some women's initial attraction to primatology, but it is unlikely to explain why women put in the years of effort needed to become successful scientists. Aside from being strong female role models and National Geographic icons, the Trimates exemplify another of Fedigan's hypotheses about why women are attracted to primatology: the influence of powerful male mentors who actively support female academics. The best-known example supporting this hypothesis is Louis Leakey. Leakey, a well-known archaeologist, sponsored Goodall, Fossey and Galdikas in their primatological pursuits. He famously believed that women made better observers in the field than men because they were more patient.

I have some thoughts about generalizations like that, but regardless of whether there is any truth to Leakey's belief, in his commitment to it, he may have changed the face of an entire discipline.

How did that happen? To answer that question, we turn to the man himself.

CHAPTER TWO

Leakey's Legacy

"**YOU HAVE A PHONE MESSAGE**," Biruté Galdikas's mother said.

It was March 1969, and twenty-three-year-old Galdikas had just returned from famed archaeologist Louis Leakey's visiting lecture at the University of California in sunny Los Angeles. During his talk, the charismatic Leakey—who Galdikas described in her book *Reflections of Eden: My Years with the Orangutans of Borneo* as having "bright eyes a tiny bit too close together, and a short mane of white hair"—regaled the undergraduates with stories of finding fossils of our human ancestors and spoke passionately about the importance of studying living primates to better understand human evolution. He told the crowd about Jane Goodall, who had embarked on a study of wild chimpanzees in Tanzania, and about Dian Fossey, who was in Rwanda learning all she could about the majestic mountain gorillas.

After the lecture, Galdikas rushed to approach Leakey, where she told him of her desire to be the first to conduct a long-term study on another of the great apes: the orangutans of Indonesia. She remembers leaving the lecture hall "in a daze" after talking with him.

Back at home, much to her delight, that phone message had been from Louis Leakey himself. Galdikas had been invited to pay the archaeologist a visit to talk more about the orangutans.

When she arrived the next morning, Leakey tested her with a brain teaser. "Which ones are red and which ones are black?" he asked as he gestured to the deck of cards he had spread face down on the coffee table. Galdikas looked at the deck—the backs of the cards all had an identical pattern. How could she possibly distinguish the colour? She stared at the deck.

Suddenly, she noticed something: "Well, I can't tell you which are which, but I can see that half of the cards are slightly bent."

She sat up and looked Leakey in the eye, triumphant that she had caught him in his trick.

He smiled and his eyes twinkled. "You know, all the men I have given this test to failed. Jane Goodall and Dian Fossey, like you, easily passed."

Louis Leakey then launched into his views on men and women, which Galdikas would hear time and again over the years. Leakey believed women were superior to men at studying animal behaviour. They were more patient and less threatening to wild animals. They were better observers, as Galdikas had just proven with the deck of cards—they could see the details. Women, Leakey firmly believed, were more perceptive.

I cannot abide by this overgeneralization. I will use myself as an example. Sure, I can claim patience—that I have in droves. Grit and determination: yes. But in my everyday life, I, a woman, am the least perceptive person on this planet. I could be walking down the street and pass a clown on stilts juggling and I might miss it. I am so often in my own head—perhaps that is the writer in me. I had to actively work on my observational skills when I studied primate behaviour. I spent hours watching every move the primates made and writing it down carefully. I practised using my binoculars to see how they moved their bodies, to watch their mouths as they chewed on leaves and fruits. I got there, but none of it came naturally to me.

However, whether or not I agree with Leakey's assessment of women is not the point. Leakey believed women would make better observers of primates in their natural habitat than men, and—like it or not—that belief played a role in shaping the trajectory of primatology as we know it today.

Driven by his beliefs, Leakey championed three women over the years to travel to remote regions of the world to study the great apes. In Jane Goodall, Dian Fossey and Biruté Galdikas, he had found his proteges.

He may not have known it, but Leakey had probably spotted in Jane Goodall and the others the kind of personality required to study the great apes in their natural habitat—someone with a deep passion for animals and a desire to learn. As Goodall writes in her book *In the Shadow of Man*, Leakey "wanted someone with a mind uncluttered and unbiased by theory who would make the study for no other reason than a real desire for knowledge; and, in addition, someone with a sympathetic understanding of animals."

These three women have been given many nicknames over the years, including "Leakey's Ladies," "Leakey's Angels" and, of course, "the Trimates." The cutesy and perhaps most offensive of the names, "Leakey's Angels," conjures images of the trio of 1970s female TV detectives of *Charlie's Angels*, feathered bangs and all.

"Leakey's Angels" is often attributed to Biruté Galdikas, but that is an example of the media running rampant. In *Reflections of Eden*, Galdikas wrote, "Leakey found many of his angels in the city of angels." She was not referring to herself or to Goodall and Fossey, but rather to the emergence of the L.S.B. Leakey Foundation (now the Leakey Foundation) in Los Angeles in 1968, which provided sponsorship for Leakey's endeavours to understand human origins. But the media could not resist—the name took on a life of its own and shaped public perception of the three scientists.

Personally, I prefer "the Trimates"—grounded in science, this nickname recognizes these trailblazing primatologists through the species that they studied: the chimpanzees, gorillas and orangutans. I also like how the name acknowledges that humans are primates—a fact that is too often forgotten.

Louis Leakey's interest in women went beyond field science. Growing up, he preferred spending time with the opposite sex and had few male friends. As he grew older, he collected female proteges—his "harem," as some whispering onlookers used to say, according to Virginia Morell, author of a 1995 biography of the Leakey family called *Ancestral Passions*—most of whom were in their early twenties. Leakey's admiration of women led him to engage in affairs and chase after women who worked for him.

Whether or not I agree with Leakey's opinions and treatment of women, his actions may help explain why the discipline of primatology has been shaped by so many female scientists. Leakey's story aligns with the "goodwill of powerful men" hypothesis, and his efforts, along with those of the women he trained, set us on the path that brought us to our current understanding of living primates and our earliest human ancestors.

"Hello?" the woman said softly into the receiver. Her voice was smooth, and in her British accent, she enunciated each syllable to perfection. Ordinarily, she was quite shy, but for this call, she was mustering all her strength. "I would like to make an appointment to meet Dr. Louis Leakey."

There. The words had come tumbling out, and this woman, a young Jane Goodall, waited expectantly.

A pause. Then a gruff voice said: "I'm Leakey. What do you want?"

Leakey wasn't trying to be rude, but he did have a distaste for telephones.

This was the spring of 1957, and fifty-three-year-old white-haired and moustached Louis Leakey was the curator of the Coryndon Museum (now known as the National Museum of Kenya) in Nairobi. He had been making waves in the field of paleoanthropology after decades spent working to prove the origins of the earliest humans in Africa. In 1929, when Leakey began his work, most scientists believed that humans originated in China. At a site called Zhoukoudian near Beijing, researchers had just discovered the skull of Peking Man, which we now know was a specimen of *Homo erectus* (dated to roughly 750,000 years ago).

In 1948, however, Leakey and his second wife, Mary, had made front-page news with a discovery: they'd found the complete fossil skull of an 18-million-year-old ape called *Proconsul* while on an expedition to Rusinga Island in Lake Victoria, Kenya. The specimen included both the upper and lower jaw, with a complete set of teeth and a large part of the cranium. The skull was distorted, but Leakey noted the humanlike shape of the forehead, the eye sockets and the jaw.

Recent reconstructions have shown that this ape-like species had a larger brain than living monkeys of similar body size. Since the Leakeys discovered that first *Proconsul* skull, more and more specimens from almost every part of the extinct animal's skeleton have been found and studied. In the early days, Leakey proposed *Proconsul* as the ancestor to both apes and humans—potentially representing the "missing link" scientists had been looking for, and in Africa to boot. There is still a great deal of debate, however, about *Proconsul*'s place in human evolutionary history—whether it is linked more closely to the great apes or is a near ancestor to the earliest humans.

Riding high from their *Proconsul* find, Louis and Mary Leakey had shifted their focus to a site called Olduvai Gorge, about four hundred kilometres south of Nairobi in Tanzania's Serengeti Plain. In this steep and dusty ravine, the couple had already uncovered much evidence of humans, including stone tools.

Many more discoveries were to come, but Leakey did not know it as he answered the phone that spring day in 1957. On the other end of the line, the young woman explained her interest in meeting with Leakey to talk about animals. A friend had recommended she call.

As Jane Goodall spoke, Leakey might have been thinking about another goal: finding someone to study living apes in their natural habitat. He knew he could learn a lot from fossils like *Proconsul*: he could estimate dates to know when species emerged in human history, look to the anatomical features to understand how early humans moved and even reconstruct their diet by examining nearby animal remains. But he knew that fossils alone could never tell the whole story of early human social groups and behaviours. To get that information, he needed to turn to humans' closest living relatives: the great apes.

Could he have sensed, as he agreed to meet with Jane Goodall, that everything would change—for him, for Goodall, and for our understanding of humans and primates?

The first woman in Louis Leakey's life was his mother, Mary "May" Leakey. She gave birth to Louis Seymour Bazett Leakey in 1903 in a mudwalled hut in Kenya. Louis had come early. With the help of Mrs. Watson, a midwife and the wife of the minister of the Church of Scotland Mission, May Leakey managed the difficult birth. To keep the baby warm, Mrs. Watson and Reverend Harry Leakey, Louis's father, transformed the hut into a makeshift incubator by lighting a charcoal fire and tightly closing the bedroom doors and shutters. A young Kikuyu boy—a member of the

Bantu-speaking community from Kenya—stayed by the fire, continuously stoking it. Meanwhile, Harry Leakey and the midwife wrapped baby Louis in layers of cotton and wool and placed him beside his mother. Miraculously, little Louis survived.

Louis was the third son born to the Leakeys, who were Anglican missionaries who had travelled to Nairobi, Kenya by steamer ship and rail, in service of the Church Missionary Society. Harry Leakey was slim, with short dark hair and a full beard. In Virginia Morell's 1995 biography, she describes May more simply as pretty, as well as serious and quiet but strong-willed. The couple was living their dream in Kenya, spreading the word of God among the Kikuyu people. The Kikuyu lived in the highland forests above Nairobi, raising cows and goats, tending to beehives, and growing millet, beans, sweet potatoes and sugar cane.

Louis split his childhood between Kabete Mission Station in central Kenya, with its mud huts and canvas tents, and Reading, England, a growing town that opened its first cinemas in 1909 and built council houses in the 1920s. The family returned to England when Louis was two years old because Harry had begun suffering insomnia, dizzy spells and ringing in the ears. They lived in Reading for two years while he recovered from what his doctor diagnosed as a "nervous disorder brought on by overwork."

But Harry would not be deterred. He had a mission, and he intended to see it through. In 1906, just before Christmas, the Leakey family travelled back to Kenya, where they were delighted to find an upgrade from their mud hut: the Church Missionary Society had built them a stone bungalow with a corrugated iron roof. Harry and May set about organizing their new home, and May gave birth to her fourth child. Meanwhile, Louis was growing up, learning traditional stories from his Kikuyu nurse, a woman named Mariamu, and speaking and dreaming in the Kikuyu language.

Louis Leakey's life spanned two worlds: the Kikuyu culture and his family's Victorian customs. He later wrote that he felt "more Kikuyu than English." His 1977 book, *The Southern Kikuyu Before 1903*, documents the Kikuyu way of life before and during British colonialism and gives clues about the origin of his attitudes and behaviour toward women.

Leakey describes the Kikuyu tribe as originally having a matrilineal society where women influenced the identity and inheritance of their offspring. Women took husbands (as opposed to men taking wives), farmed the land and led most of the trade between tribes. However, between 1890 and 1963, the Kenyans were under British rule. As the British redistributed the land, Kenyan women lost ownership, thrusting them into economic dependence on men and shifting Kikuyu society toward patriarchal values, which are still prevalent today. Some have speculated that Louis Leakey's Kikuyu upbringing led to him embracing patriarchal norms, acting as a Kikuyu elder would by surrounding himself with women to demonstrate his power and influence.

Young Louis studied hard in his lessons and hoped to one day follow in his father's footsteps by studying theology and ornithology at Cambridge University. In 1914, when Louis was eleven, he met a slim young zoologist named Arthur Loveridge, the first curator of Nairobi's Natural History Museum. Louis was captivated by Loveridge from the start: he knew all the Latin names for animals and plants and spent his days in the forests and in the Kabete area, where he stayed with the Leakeys. Recognizing a spark in the young boy, Loveridge took Louis under his wing, teaching him how to classify the birds and prepare museum specimens.

In 1916, there was another life-altering event for Louis Leakey: a cousin sent him a book called *Days Before History* as a Christmas gift. It was a story of adventure about the "Stone Age men" of Britain, filled with descriptions and drawings of stone tools like arrowheads and axeheads. Young Louis was inspired. He began picking up rocks that he found at the bottom of roads and slopes, which he proudly showed to his parents. His father dismissed his finds, calling them "just pieces of broken glass." Louis was deflated but hung onto the shards just the same, stashing them away in his collection.

One day, he worked up the courage to bring them out again, and this time, he showed his collection to Loveridge. Loveridge confirmed that the finds were much more than glass: they were worked obsidian. Jet-black in colour with a glassy shine, obsidian is a natural volcanic glass formed by the rapid cooling of lava. The pieces Louis had found were tools or weapons belonging to our early human ancestors.

Loveridge taught Louis how to catalogue his finds. This was a pivotal moment for Louis. He was determined to learn all he could about the early humans of his home in East Africa.

The dark-eyed young woman emerged from the back of the auditorium in Louisville, Kentucky. It was a full house, and she had grabbed the best seat she could find.

It was March 1966. By this time, Louis Leakey had made a name for himself. He had established a connection with the National Geographic Society, and his work studying human origins had made him something of a celebrity, even beyond scientific circles.

Clutching three articles she had penned for the *Louisville Courier Journal* about her recent African safari, the young woman took a deep breath and joined the lineup of people hoping to speak with Leakey. She wondered: would he remember her?

She reached the front of the line. It only took a moment before a flash of recognition and a smile lit up Leakey's face. He reached for her hand and squeezed it firmly. Her heart soared, and she excitedly thrust her wrinkled papers into his hands, hurriedly explaining that she had written an article about her visit to Olduvai that he might wish to see.

"Miss Fossey, isn't it?" Louis said warmly. "Please wait here until I've finished with all these people."

Dian Fossey had met the famous Louis Leakey in 1963 on her first trip to Africa—a safari she had used her life savings and a bank loan to fund. She had heard about the Leakeys and the riches of Olduvai Gorge and had made a point of visiting Louis and Mary in Tanzania. She told Leakey that she would be visiting the mountain gorillas, and he told her about Jane Goodall's work with the chimpanzees, which was well underway by that point.

Leakey welcomed Fossey to explore Olduvai, where she ran down the slopes, hoping to see some of the fossils. Unfortunately, her enthusiasm resulted in a twisted ankle. Back at camp, Leakey made a point of personally examining and bandaging the ankle.

"How is your ankle?" Leakey asked Fossey as the two stood at the back of the auditorium in Louisville. "Has it healed properly?"

Fossey could hardly believe he remembered the incident—that he remembered her. He asked her about the rest of her Africa trip. "Did you manage to see the gorillas at Kabara?"

She filled him in. Yes, despite her twisted ankle, she had travelled to the Kabara meadow in the Democratic Republic of Congo. She had seen the gorillas in their natural habitat, and she had fallen in love with the primates.

"I'm looking to start a long-term study of the gorillas," Leakey said. "You might be just the person I need."

Like his father, Louis Leakey studied at St. John's College at Cambridge University, where he threw himself wholeheartedly into anthropology and archaeology and received his bachelor's degree in 1926. When he graduated, he won a research fellowship and received several grants from England's Royal Society, the Percy Sladen Memorial Trust and the Kenyan government to fund his first East African archaeological expedition. Along with another Cambridge graduate named Bernard Newsam, twenty-three-year-old Louis Leakey headed back to the place of his youth, Kabete Mission Station, where he set up base camp and began his quest to uncover human origins in Africa.

Leakey quickly became known in Kenya. He published articles about his excavations in the *East African Standard*, and a farmer in the Elmenteita area named Mr. Gamble asked him to investigate two caves on his property. Leakey and his team excavated the caves, finding stone tools, pottery and fragments of human skeletons.

During this time, Leakey met twenty-six-year-old Henrietta Wilfrida Avern, or Frida, as she liked to be called. Avern was completing an eighteen-month tour of East Africa with her friend Janet Forbes.

Leakey was attracted to her right away. In *Ancestral Passions*, Morell describes Frida Avern as not especially striking in appearance, but with a certain charisma—a "lively mind," a "generous smile" and "sparkling brown eyes." Leakey wasted no time, inviting Avern and Forbes to dinner one evening and the day after taking them to Lake Nakuru, one of the Rift Valley lakes known for its abundance of flamingos, for a picnic. Louis Leakey fell head over heels for Frida and could hardly contain himself. The next day, he drove to Nairobi to see the two women off and, as Frida waved goodbye through the train window, Louis exclaimed: "We should be married when I come home!"

Although Frida thought Louis was "completely mad," there was something magnetic about him. One year later, in 1928, the two married and set sail to begin his second archaeological expedition in Kenya.

Leakey's first expedition had been a success thanks to his reports on prehistoric cultures in Kenya, so he received large grants from the Rhodes Trust and the Royal Geographical Society to fund his second. With a large team of eight scientific staff,

Leakey returned to Gamble's Cave to dig deeper, hoping to find the oldest human remains in Africa. There hadn't been time to fully excavate the cave the first time, and Leakey knew there was more to uncover.

Leakey and his wife set themselves up in an abandoned farmhouse, which, according to Morell, he described as "magnificent." The thatched-roof huts meant they didn't need to buy tents, so he was saving money. The other benefit was that the house was just six miles from Gamble's Cave. But with its crumbling mud walls, earth floors, makeshift furniture from packing cases, and bats and insects crawling through the ceilings, others who later joined the expedition found the conditions atrocious.

Despite all that, the second dig was a roaring success. The team uncovered two *Homo sapiens* skeletons, many stone artifacts and the remains of several extinct animals. Just three weeks before they were to pack things up, geologist John Solomon, one of the team members, uncovered a pear-shaped hand axe—evidence of the oldest known culture, which Leakey pegged as being between forty thousand and fifty thousand years old. (We now know this tool is 500,000 years old.)

Leakey presented his paper, "An Outline of the Stone Age in Kenya," in 1929 at the British Association meeting in Johannesburg. His work inspired about sixty scientists to travel to Kenya to inspect his excavation site. Impressed by what they found, the scientists returned with praise for Leakey and his excavations. That same year, Louis and Frida Leakey headed back to England, where Louis was awarded a two-year fellowship at Cambridge.

Yet, Leakey knew he would be back in Africa soon enough. He was already planning his next expedition to Olduvai Gorge.

The energy in the room was palpable. It was 1969, and the studious young woman, her light brown hair parted down the middle, watched from the crowd as Louis Leakey regaled the audience at the University of California, Los Angeles, with stories of Olduvai Gorge and finding "Zinj," *Zinjanthropus boisei*, after years of searching. Leakey had discovered the remains of a human cranium alongside nearly four hundred more fragments. The remains comprised a nearly complete skull and were dated to about 1.75 million years ago, helping to establish the origin of humankind in Africa.

One of the young woman's professors had told her that Leakey was an eccentric genius, and she wholeheartedly agreed with that assessment as she listened to him speak. He put forth out-of-the-box and controversial hypotheses in that lecture and in his career. This man was charismatic, and the crowd was eating up his every word.

After his lecture, Leakey opened the floor to questions.

"Dr. Leakey, what are your feelings on the importance of studying non-human primates to understand human evolution?" someone in the audience asked.

Her heart soared. The apes! She knew all about Jane Goodall and Dian Fossey, and she greatly admired their work with chimpanzees and gorillas.

"Imperative!" Leakey exclaimed. He patted his shirt pocket. "In fact, Dian has just sent a telegram saying that the mountain gorillas are so used to her presence that one has even taken to untying her shoelaces."

As Louis Leakey said this, the woman in the crowd couldn't help but feel that he was looking directly at her—that he knew of her interest in the primates and in studying the orangutans. At the end of the question period, she shot out of her seat and joined the people waiting to speak with Leakey one-on-one.

"I wish to study the orangutan," she blurted out when it was her turn.

He chuckled. She could see he was only mildly interested—amused, perhaps—but she persisted.

"You hold the key, Dr. Leakey," she told him emphatically. She explained that she had written to the Malaysian government for permission to conduct research and was already taking classes in field archaeology at UCLA.

She paused, not quite sure what else to say. She stumbled over her words. "I—I've written to several researchers, including Tom Harrisson."

Tom Harrisson was a British ornithologist, explorer, museum curator and archaeologist, among other things. As it turned out, his was the right name to drop. Leakey knew Tom and his wife, Barbara, very well. Suddenly, he looked at the young woman before him with fresh eyes.

"I am leaving for Africa tomorrow," he said. But please write to me—what is your name?"

"Birutė," she replied. "Birutė Galdikas."

"Birutė," he repeated, looking at her intently. "Please keep in touch."

Birutė left the auditorium reeling. A friend approached.

"What did he say to you?"

After a brief pause, she replied, "I'm going to study orangutans."

In the early 1930s, Louis Leakey's career was skyrocketing. His Olduvai expedition in 1931 had been a roaring success in scientific circles. It had resulted in a bounty of stone tools, the preserved tusks of an extinct elephant, the skull of a strange species of hippo, the remains of a giant antelope, and bones of crocodiles, turtles and fish. Louis deduced that a horde of hunters had chowed down on that hippo, leaving their heavy tools behind. He had less luck finding human remains, so near the end of his trip, he visited a nearby site called Kanam. There, he found precisely what he was looking for, uncovering a weathered lower jaw—a human mandible that he concluded belonged to the true ancestor of *Homo sapiens*.

Leakey's Kanam jaw would later become embroiled in controversy. In 1934, prominent Pleistocene geologist Percy George Hamnall Boswell was sent to verify the age of the jaw. He found that the iron stakes Leakey had cemented to the ground to mark the fossil's location had been taken by local Luo fishermen. Additionally, one of the photographs that had been taken was of the wrong site. As a result, during Boswell's visit, Leakey could not confirm precisely where the jaw had been found. Without careful markings, the fossil could have been carried by water from one geologic location to another or found somewhere else entirely. Boswell also questioned the dates Leakey had assigned to the specimen. In a 1935 letter to the editor published in *Nature*, Boswell argued that the age Leakey had assigned to this fossil find was "uncertain" and the evidence "misleading."

But in 1932, that controversy had yet to be unveiled, and Leakey's initial announcement of the Kanam jaw garnered him a great deal of attention. The Royal Society and the British Museum of Natural History both asked to exhibit the specimen. The press wanted to interview him. And, in what turned out to be the most life-altering event, Leakey was invited to give a talk by the Royal Anthropological Institute.

It was at that event that Leakey met a shy young woman named Mary Nicol. Nicol was a burgeoning archaeologist and a talented artist, working under Gertrude Caton Thompson, an archaeologist who had worked in Zimbabwe and Egypt. Caton Thompson had brought her along to the dinner that night, where, as luck would have it, she was seated next to Louis Leakey.

The two quickly found a shared interest in archaeology and animals, and had a pleasant conversation. In Morell's biography, Nicol recalled that meeting as being "nothing special," yet it marked the beginning of their relationship. Leakey was intrigued by Nicol. That summer, his letters to her were, as she described, "perhaps more frequent than was strictly necessary."

Why? Because, at this point, Leakey was still married to Frida—who was eight months pregnant.

According to Virginia Morell, Leakey had already had several girlfriends since he and Frida had returned to England. Yes, Louis Leakey had a fondness for women. But with Mary Nicol, things were different. Leakey had fallen in love. In Nicol, he found someone he could confide in, not just about his unhappy marriage (by this time, rumours of his infidelity had emerged; some have tied the behaviour to a disconnect between Frida's desire to put down roots and Louis's unrelenting wanderlust), but also about the anthropology he was so passionate about. For her part, Nicol liked Leakey because he treated her as an equal and a colleague.

One month after Leakey's son Colin was born, in January 1934, he confessed to his wife: "I have fallen in love with Mary, and I am going to take her to Africa." Frida was horrified and hurt, but for Louis, there was no turning back. In the fall of 1934, he set about raising funds for his fourth expedition. He would revisit Olduvai Gorge and continue his work at Rusinga Island in Kenya. Nicol would join him.

Mary Nicol was enraptured by all that Olduvai had to offer and a great deal more tolerant than Frida about the realities of fieldwork. Their first journey to the site took place amid a six-week period of monsoons. Louis decided to try out a new road to Olduvai, a more direct route up the eastern slope of the 7,500-foot Ngorongoro Crater, the world's largest inactive volcanic caldera, a type of sinkhole formed by a volcanic eruption. As he and his team made their way up the volcano, they found themselves stuck in black, sticky mud. He later wrote: "On some occasions, we practically carried the car and the equipment."

Despite the challenging journey for Nicol's first time out, she was treated to a gorgeous view into the Ngorongoro Crater, complete with wildebeest, hundreds of zebras and even rhinoceroses. In *Ancestral Passions*, Morell writes that Nicol thought Olduvai was incredibly beautiful and that she was impressed by the archaeological and geological "excitement."

Frida filed for divorce from Louis in January 1936 and gained custody of their two children. According to Morell, Frida never remarried and did not ask Louis for money to help raise their children. Pricilla, Louis and Frida's daughter, noted that Frida found it easier to keep their lives separate from their father's, wanting Pricilla and her brother, Colin, to meet Louis only when they were grown up. The children honoured their mother's wishes, seeing their father again after they had each turned eighteen.

The divorce meant Louis Leakey and Mary Nicol could marry, and they did so in a registry office in the town of Ware, England, on Christmas Eve of 1936. Three weeks later, in January 1937, they headed back to Kenya.

Over the years, Louis and Mary, now Mary Leakey, were a team, though Mary made the most discoveries in the field. Meanwhile, Louis published and publicized.

It was Mary Leakey who would uncover *Zinjanthropus boisei* in 1959 in Olduvai Gorge. Louis had stayed back at the camp, nursing a bad fever, while Mary continued. She unearthed a human cranium. On further examination, there were more fragments, making up a nearly complete skull. Louis concluded that this find "represent[ed] one of the earliest Hominidae." Today, we know this specimen belongs to the robust early hominins classified as *Paranthropus boisei* or *Australopithecus boisei*, which lived roughly 2.5 million years ago.

Mary Leakey also uncovered the first specimen of *Homo habilis*—"the toolmaker." This species lived between 2.8 and 1.5 million years ago. Louis Leakey published a paper in 1964 asserting that Mary's discovery in Olduvai revealed that this species used tools and was a contemporary of *Zinjanthropus.*

Mary continued her work even after Louis passed away in 1972. In 1978, she found volcanic ash–filled footprints in mud deposits at

Laetoli in northern Tanzania. The footprints, dating from between 3 and 3.5 million years ago, were made by a bipedal hominin—likely *Australopithecus afarensis*. This find showed that bipedal locomotion evolved much earlier than previously thought.

As a woman in science, I am fascinated that Mary Leakey, who was often perceived as the woman behind the man, was directly responsible for many of the most significant fossil finds of the time. Yet, because Louis held the limelight—and, no doubt, because this was the 1950s and '60s and science was still male-dominated—Mary was overshadowed. For her part, Mary did not resent Louis for his role as the mouthpiece. She was shy and preferred not to be in the spotlight.

Mary viewed her relationship with Louis as a partnership. Without his lofty ideas, she may not have had the opportunity to uncover the fossils of Olduvai. Without her diligence, many of their discoveries would not have surfaced.

Back in 1957, Louis Leakey hung up the phone, having just made an appointment with that young woman who was so keen on animals. *What was her name?* He glanced at his appointment book. *Right. Goodall.*

Leakey set his calendar aside and returned to his current preoccupation: the fossilized bones of *Proconsul*, the primate he and Mary had discovered on Rusinga Island in Kenya.

Specimens representing 450 individual Proconsul!

Leakey later wrote that this rich ape population provided evidence that East Africa represented "the birthplace of man himself."

Rusinga Island is on the eastern part of Lake Victoria, the largest lake in Africa. Leakey first noticed the island in 1926 while aboard a steamer crossing the lake. Normally, the steamer operated at night, but on this lucky occasion, it sailed in the day.

Leakey spotted the interesting piece of land from the boat and examined it with his binoculars.

Well, this looks promising, he thought, making a note to return to the island to search for fossils. In the 1930s, Leakey did return during his third and fourth expeditions, uncovering animal fossils that placed Rusinga's deposits as far back as twenty million years, to the Miocene epoch.

In a publication about the fossil in *Nature*, Leakey wrote, "In *Proconsul*, we have a near approach to a form of ape-link creature from which the human stem eventually was evolved."

Rusinga Island also provided fossilized evidence of plants, seeds, fruits and insects, which meant that Louis and Mary could reconstruct the environment that the "missing links" had inhabited twenty million years ago.

Louis Leakey believed Rusinga had been an open forest with great rivers running into the lake and extensive open grasslands between the rivers. Subsequent reconstructions based on paleobotany, faunal analysis and geochemistry have shown mixed results, suggesting that Rusinga might have been a tropical rainforest or a semi-arid environment. More recent reconstructions indicate that Rusinga consisted of both closed forest and open areas with seasonal ponding.

This reconstruction is not far off the image in Leakey's mind. He believed the environment of our earliest primate ancestors was similar to that of the chimpanzees living on the shores of Lake Tanganyika, which is shared across Burundi, the Democratic Republic of the Congo, Tanzania and Zambia.

A colleague at Cambridge, Jack Trevor, first alerted Leakey to these chimpanzees. Trevor, while serving in the British army and stationed in Kenya, had visited a small reserve in Tanganyika (now Tanzania), home to the fascinating chimpanzees. Leakey could not help but draw parallels between these chimpanzees and the early Miocene apes living on Rusinga Island.

Shortly after learning about the chimpanzees, Leakey decided someone should study them as an analogy for the behaviour of our early human ancestors. In 1946, according to Morell, he sent a young man (whose name has never been revealed) who "failed utterly."

Leakey made a second attempt in 1956 to learn more about apes in their natural habitat, sending a Scottish-born woman named Rosalie Osborn. Louis met Osborn while working on a pig-fossil study in England in 1954. The two had an affair, and Osborn moved to Kenya in the summer of 1955 to work as Leakey's secretary at the Coryndon Museum. According to Morell, Leakey had been known to continue to have flings after his marriage to Mary, which she had learned to tolerate, perhaps repenting for the beginnings of her own relationship with her husband. But Leakey's relationship with Osborn was more serious. Mary and Louis's son Richard later referred to Osborn as "the third Mrs. Leakey."

When Leakey eventually broke things off with Osborn, he faced the awkward problem of seeing her every day at the museum. Ever the problem-solver, Leakey sent Osborn to Uganda for a four-month study of mountain gorillas. The trip was part of his larger plan to study the great apes in Africa. By sending Rosalie Osborn to Uganda, he was at once advancing his research program, providing a consolation trip for Osborn and keeping his wife, Mary, happy.

His solution was not quite as elegant as he had envisioned, however. When Rosalie Osborn's mother, who believed her daughter was safely working at the museum, found out she had gone into the bush, she demanded her daughter quit the study and return to England, which Osborn did in January 1957.

After spending just one morning with Jane Goodall, noticing her keen interest in animals featured in the museum's exhibits—even the snakes—Leakey offered her a job as his assistant secretary, replacing Rosalie Osborn.

As Goodall wrote in *The Shadow of Man*: "Somehow, he must have sensed that my interest in animals was not just a passing phase but was rooted deep." Of course, Goodall had no idea about the circumstances under which her predecessor had departed. The world is lucky she did not know, because, if she had, she may have turned down Leakey's offer.

In May 1957, Leakey asked Goodall and another young woman named Gillian Trace to join him and Mary on their annual dig in Olduvai Gorge in the Serengeti plains, this time taking care to secure Mary's approval of the two young women. Leakey had been working at Olduvai since 1931 and had already made several incredible discoveries, including stone tools. The aim of this trip was to find the toolmakers.

Jane Goodall had the time of her life on the dig, spending hours extracting the remains of creatures that had lived millions of years before. In the evenings, she and Trace were free to walk the arid plains above the gorge, spotting dik-diks, gazelles, giraffes and even black rhinoceroses.

Near the end of their trip, Leakey began to talk to Goodall about the chimpanzees on the shores of Lake Tanganyika. He believed studying these chimpanzees could provide incredible insight into our ancestors. While he had tangible evidence of what our human ancestors looked like through fossils, there was no way to know how they behaved. Since apes and humans share a common ancestor, studying ape behaviour in their natural habitat could provide important clues to our human past.

Lake Tanganyika is remote, mountainous and rugged, and studying the elusive chimpanzees that lived near its shores would require patience and determination. It might take months, or even years, away from civilization to learn all there is to know. The chimpanzee study would require grit, a passion for knowledge and a deep love of animals.

When Louis revealed to Jane Goodall that he wanted to send her, she at first did not feel qualified because she had no formal scientific training. But, as she later wrote, "Louis knew exactly what he was doing." He saw in Goodall the patience and determination he knew was required to study wild chimpanzees. He wanted someone who was fresh and unbiased. He wanted someone "who would make the study for no other reason than a real desire for knowledge." Someone "with a sympathetic understanding of animals."

Jane Goodall agreed enthusiastically.

Over time, Louis Leakey's relationships with women earned him a reputation. In *Ancestral Passions*, Morell describes how, while he was married to his first wife, Frida, Leakey sometimes stayed overnight in Cambridge or London, visiting his girlfriends. And, of course, he had met and fallen in love with Mary while he was still married to Frida.

Friends and colleagues noticed Louis's effect on women and had things to say about it. As documented by Morell:

"He appreciated women, and because of that, women responded to him."

"Women came to him like moths to a flame."

"Louis is a philanderer, you know. Always after men's wives."

Anthropologist Irven DeVore recalls the first time he and his wife met Louis Leakey. He describes Leakey as being dressed in an "awful boiler suit" with a "great shock of unruly white hair, a heavily creased face" and a "snaggle-toothed" mouth.

"Objectively, he must be one of the ugliest men I've ever met," he said to his wife.

Much to his surprise, she replied: "Are you kidding? That's the sexiest man I've ever laid my eyes on."

Louis Leakey's charisma indeed attracted women. At least one of them, Rosalie Osborn, fell deeply in love with him, according to Morell. When Osborn returned to England at her mother's request after her short-lived stint in Uganda studying gorillas, Leakey continued to support her. He found her a job at the British Museum of Natural History and arranged for her to study zoology at Cambridge University. Ultimately, Osborn moved back to Kenya and worked as a biology teacher. She never married and, according to Morell, continued to carry a torch for Leakey.

When Louis Leakey died in 1972, his son Richard, aware of his father's affair and its impact on his mother, Mary, prevented Osborn from attending the funeral. However, Osborn later secretly visited Leakey's grave often.

The Leakey family had decided to source quartzite from Olduvai Gorge for the headstone, in tribute to the stone tools that *Homo habilis* constructed. The headstone took longer than anticipated to finish, and by the time it was ready and Louis and Mary's first son Jonathan drove it to the grave, he was shocked to find that someone had beaten him to the punch. The marble headstone that was already in place read:

Louis S.B. Leakey
Wakarüigi
ILYUA
1903–1972
You live on
In the minds you inspired
In the projects you pioneered
In the lives you improved and created
In the hearts that loved you
Your influence cannot die.

When the family inquired at the church, no one could tell them who had placed the stone. Jonathan called his brother

Richard, who was also baffled—until Jonathan mentioned the cryptic acronym on the headstone: ILYUA.

Richard knew immediately that the stone was Rosalie Osborn's doing. Years before, he had discovered a packet of letters from Osborn to his father, each signed ILYUA, which Richard is quoted as saying stands for "I'll love you always."

Despite the complex feelings the gravestone must have elicited in the family, the Leakeys decided to leave it in place. Rosalie Osborn had never stopped loving Louis Leakey, and Leakey had held a special affection for her, once confiding to a friend that she had been his "great love." The headstone placed by Osborn still stands on Louis Leakey's grave today.

However, Mary Leakey was sure to instruct her sons that she should not be buried in the same cemetery. Instead, when Mary died in 1996, she was cremated, and her ashes were scattered at Olduvai Gorge, where she had made so many of her discoveries.

Osborn likely knew about and was perhaps crushed by what happened after she left her post as Leakey's secretary. After Jane Goodall settled into her role as his new secretary, it became clear that Leakey had developed feelings for her. Subtle kindnesses quickly became overt. According to Goodall's biographer, Dale Peterson, Leakey would listen in on her private phone calls and invite her on overnight camping trips, and, one Sunday morning, he arrived at her door unexpectedly with a single red rose.

Unlike Rosalie Osborn, Jane Goodall was uninterested in Leakey's romantic overtures and viewed them as childish. In a letter home, she wrote: "I begin to see why Mary has taken to the brandy."

Even after Goodall began a relationship with Brian Herne, a big-game hunter she met while at Olduvai, Leakey persisted. He continued sending roses and trying to hold Goodall's hand. Goodall was frustrated and, although she felt sorry for Leakey, she was not enjoying his advances. Eventually, as she told her mother,

Vanne, she had "thrashed it out" with Leakey until he agreed to be "merely a father" to her. It took a while, but eventually, Leakey backed off.

Leakey's advances toward Dian Fossey mirrored his behaviour with Goodall. He wrote her love letters, claiming that they were "kindred spirits." By 1968, when Fossey was ensconced with the gorillas, Leakey was sixty-seven, overweight, physically disabled and separated from Mary. Around the same time, Fossey began having severe chest pains, and a visit to the doctor in Nairobi confirmed she had tuberculosis. She needed a rest. Fossey wrote to Leakey, who asked her to come to Nairobi.

Leakey invited Fossey on a holiday, and after she was treated by a doctor, the two took off on a safari in south-central Kenya. They stayed in luxurious tents, dined on terrific food and drank fine wine. According to Farley Mowat, one of Fossey's biographers, on this trip with Leakey, "Dian succumbed to the romance of star-filled nights on the sweet-smelling savanna."

At the end of the trip, Leakey left Fossey with three letters, each gushing about the "heavenly week we had." But he didn't stop there. Even after the trip, letters filled with grand overtures and expressions of love continued to arrive.

"My dearest love," some of them began.

And within: "I love you and love you so there are no words that can describe the peace and calm" or "I love and love and love and love every bit of you and all you stand for and are."

Dian Fossey never replied to the letters, much to Leakey's dismay.

At the time, she had taken an interest in National Geographic photographer Bob Campbell, which could explain her lack of response. But it may have been more than that. Here was this man she looked up to—idolized—making the grand overtures of a teenage boy. What kind of behaviour was that for her mentor? What response could she have had? Then there was the power dynamic. How could she send a letter back turning Leakey down when he had funded and organized her time with the gorillas? She so loved the gorillas, and she was helping to save these animals at risk. If she rejected Leakey, would it all go away?

In one of her diaries, Fossey wrote: "Don't know what to do about L. God—what a mess."

In addition to his well-documented affairs with Mary Nicol and Rosalie Osborn and his behaviour with both Jane Goodall and Dian Fossey, Louis Leakey's name continues to be embroiled in rumours about affairs with other women. A particularly controversial story outlined in *Ancestral Passions* involves Vanne Goodall, Jane's mother. Louis and Vanne were close, and when he visited London, he would stay with her, spending time with her at concerts and the ballet. This relationship sparked rumours of an affair and some speculation that Louis and Vanne had met while teenagers in England. In her book *Leakey's Luck*, Sonia Cole asserts that Louis Leakey could potentially be Jane Goodall's real father. Goodall has dismissed this allegation. Vanne Goodall refused to comment, and Mary Leakey thought it was ridiculous. Yet, according to Virginia Morell, two of Leakey's sons—Richard and Colin—think the claim could be true and might explain his strong ties to the Goodall family.

Morell, however, deems it "doubtful he had time for another relationship" given the timeline—nine months before Jane was born, Leakey would have been in England, married to Frida but involved with Mary. And Jane Goodall has pointed out that she very much resembles her father, Mortimer Herbert Morris-Goodall.

Yes, Louis Leakey's proteges were women. And yes, certainly, this pattern was rooted in Louis's appreciation of women, both romantic and otherwise. Even still, the success of Jane Goodall, Dian Fossey and Biruté Galdikas went well beyond Louis Leakey. Their origin stories—how they met Louis Leakey and went on to study wild apes—demonstrate their independence of spirit, great determination, and passion for the primates.

CHAPTER THREE

The Chimpanzee Lady

TRAVIS AND I WERE SPEED-WALKING along Toronto's Front Street, on our way to Meridian Hall. We had rushed straight from work, fought the inevitable traffic along Highway 401 between our home in Guelph to Toronto, and grabbed a quick bowl of lobster bisque from St. Lawrence Market.

As we neared the theatre, we could see crowds flocking toward the entrance. Puffing a little from our swift walk, we showed our tickets to the usher and made our way to our seats.

"This way," I said.

"Really?" Travis asked as we walked closer and closer to the front of the theatre.

I grinned and nodded. I had sprung for the good seats.

We finally stopped, just five rows from the stage. I pulled off my coat and turned to hang it on the back of my seat. As I did, I paused to take in the three-thousand-seat theatre that was rapidly filling up with people of all ages. A woman behind us wore traditional African dress. Another woman had brought her golden retriever service dog with her. The two men beside us, dressed in suits, looked like Bay Street traders. I scanned the audience to see if there were any familiar faces.

"I don't see anyone we know," I said. Primatology is a small world, and it wouldn't be surprising to spot a few colleagues. I turned back around and looked at the stage, where a couch and a podium were ready for the honoured speaker. Several stuffed animals were lined up neatly on the podium.

My heart pounded in anticipation. *The* Jane Goodall would soon take the stage. This was a woman who, driven by her fascination with animals, had travelled across the world to complete the first long-term study of wild chimpanzees in Africa. She made huge discoveries that contributed to our understanding of primates and human evolution. This event was one of Goodall's first live events since the pandemic and would showcase her groundbreaking research on chimpanzees and her focus on primate conservation and climate change.

As we waited for the lecture to begin, the theatre buzzing with excitement, that burning question popped into my head: *Why have so many women been drawn to the discipline of primatology?* In that moment, one answer seemed obvious: Dr. Goodall was a role model to everyone in that theatre and to the many women who would go on to study wild primates, myself included.

I elbowed Travis.

"Do you think she'll talk about the termites?"

Those small insects with their wriggling winged bodies and large red heads turned everything upside down.

The year was 1960, and Jane Goodall, a twenty-six-year-old Englishwoman, had travelled to the mountainous Gombe Stream National Park in western Tanzania. Gombe is nestled on the shores of Lake Tanganyika, the second-largest lake in the world by volume. British explorers in 1860 described it as "an expanse of the lightest and softest blue" and "sprinkled by the crisp east wind with tiny crescents of snowy foam."

On the shores of Lake Tanganyika, with high mountains as the backdrop, this deceptively demure-looking young woman, with her characteristic low blonde ponytail, was filled with grit, determination and a passion for wildlife. She was dedicated to studying and protecting wild chimpanzees.

That morning, Jane Goodall had been up for hours, climbing up and down the valley, crawling on her hands and knees through dense undergrowth, in search of the chimpanzees. So far, nothing.

It was October and the rains had come. Her khaki field uniform—shorts and a button-up shirt—was soaked from pushing through the wet foliage. This was not the first time Goodall had come up empty in search of the chimpanzees. These primates had proven elusive. Sometimes she would hike for hours without spotting a single chimpanzee, or, if she did get lucky, they would see her, call out in alarm and flee. As a result, many of her observations were from a great distance: she would squat atop a perch on an open, rocky mountain about a thousand feet above the lake—"the Peak," as she called it.

The chimpanzees, she would later write, did not at first accept this "strange white ape who had invaded their forest world."

On that day, something caught her eye. A flash of black in the long grass about fifty metres away. Then, as though in a dream, the dark shape slowly came into view.

A black head. A long arm covered in jet-black hair.

She could see him fully now, his dark face with just a wisp of silvery hairs on the chin.

David Greybeard. Goodall had named this chimpanzee after David and Goliath, and Greybeard because of his silver chin hairs. David had been less afraid of Goodall than the others, and his presence calmed the group. Whenever Goodall spotted David, she knew she had a shot at getting up close with the chimps. "In those early days," she later wrote in *In the Shadow of Man*, "I spent many days alone with David. Hour after hour I followed him through the forests, sitting and watching him while he fed or rested, struggling to keep up when he moved through a tangle of vines. Sometimes, I am sure, he waited for me."

Now, David was sitting next to a large mound of red earth on the ground—a termite's nest—but what was he doing?

Jane Goodall pushed a stray hair back behind her ear, quietly moved closer and raised her binoculars to her face. She stood and watched, barely breathing, as David carefully poked a long stem of grass into the nest. The termites coated the stem, and the chimpanzee raised it to his mouth and hungrily slurped up the insects with his lips, chewing each mouthful slowly and deliberately. Goodall watched and waited, enraptured, as David fished for termites for an hour. She carefully observed and recorded everything she saw, and when he finally moved away, she rushed to the scene, where she examined one of David's discarded tools and tried her hand at termite fishing.

In the coming days, Goodall would observe this behaviour several more times, and with several other individuals. On a few exciting occasions, she watched as the chimpanzees prepared the twigs for use. If a leafy twig was selected, the chimpanzee would strip the leaves off. If the twig became bent in the process of fishing, the chimpanzee would break off the bent pieces. The chimpanzees were modifying the twigs in advance and with purpose.

Goodall knew that modifying a natural object for a particular purpose is the very definition of tool use. Before her discovery, scientists had regarded the ability to make and use tools as unique to the human species—a behaviour and cognitive ability that set us apart from the other primates.

Goodall sent telegrams—the text messages of the 1960s—to her mentor, Louis Leakey, sharing her observations. Leakey received Goodall's communications with wild enthusiasm. He cabled a message back to the young primatologist immediately:

"Now we must redefine 'tool,' redefine 'man,' or accept chimpanzees as humans."

Valerie Jane Morris-Goodall came into the world at 11:30 p.m. on Tuesday, April 3, 1934, in Hampstead Heath, North London. From a young age, she was fascinated by animals, befriending whatever creatures she found in her garden. By the time she was eight years old, she had decided she would one day go to Africa and live with wild animals.

When Jane was just eighteen months old, her nanny rushed to Jane's mother, Margaret Myfanwe Joseph Goodall, or "Vanne" as she liked to be called, with a problem.

"Valerie Jane's got a handful of horrible, pink, wriggling worms in her bed," said the nanny. "They're under her pillow and she is touching them. It is quite disgusting."

Jane's mother had striking green eyes, hair likened to burnished chestnut and a warm, confident smile. Although she had worked as a secretary in London, Vanne's true passion was writing. She also loved music and played the violin. After she married, Vanne quit her secretarial job and embraced her role as a full-time wife and mother.

At the sight of the worms, Vanne did not scream. Instead, she reasoned with Jane that perhaps it was too hot and stuffy beneath the feathers of the pillow. That if she kept the worms there, they might suffocate before morning. Together, mother and daughter gingerly carried the worms out to the garden, dug a small hole and put them back into the earth.

Young Jane also cherished a stuffed chimpanzee named Jubilee, a gift from her father on her first birthday. Jane's father, Mortimer, was a race car driver, handsome and charming but restless, obsessed with racing, and an absentee father. As Goodall later recalled, Mortimer touched her only once when she was a child.

Dale Peterson, Jane Goodall's biographer, concludes that Mortimer's influence on young Jane and his other children was "more of nature than of nurture." To Jane, Mortimer gave his "good eyesight, high energy, a natural and happy competitiveness, a capacity for intense and extended concentration, a surprising attraction to risk, and an unusual tolerance for physical stress and oscillatory motion." And, importantly, Mortimer was responsible for that stuffed chimpanzee.

The toy commemorated the London Zoo's first captive-born female chimpanzee, named Jubilee. The stuffed animal was nearly as large as one-year-old Jane; it was covered in scraggy dark-brown fur, with floppy pale-brown hands and feet. When Jane pressed its stomach, she was delighted to find that it played music. Mortimer had come across the toy in Hamleys toy shop on Regent Street in London while on the lookout for a birthday present for Jane. He had no idea the impact that this gift would have on his daughter.

Besides falling in love with that stuffed chimpanzee, young Jane was inspired by stories of Doctor Dolittle and Tarzan. In her 1988 book *My Life with the Chimpanzees*, Goodall recalled borrowing the first in the series of Doctor Dolittle books from her local library as a child: "I read it all the way through. Then I read it through again. I had never before loved a book so much."

Jane's love of animals and nature manifested in many ways. On one memorable afternoon, while Vanne was out volunteering for the war effort, five-year-old Jane wandered off, ostensibly to visit the horses in the stables. But that afternoon, Jane had other plans. She wound her way to the henhouse and hid inside, crouching among the straw. Her aim? To watch a hen lay an egg. She wanted to see how egg-laying worked. The process took five hours, but Jane did not lose patience.

"If I moved, I would spoil everything. So I stayed quite still. So did the chicken," Jane wrote. "I saw a round white object gradually protruding from the feathers between her legs. It got bigger.

Suddenly she gave a little wiggle and—plop!—it landed on the straw."

Jane was so enthralled by the hen that she didn't realize how long she'd been gone. Back at the house, Vanne, having returned from volunteering, had grown so worried about Jane's whereabouts that she enlisted some nearby soldiers for help. After searching and coming up empty, someone eventually called the police.

As darkness fell, a voice rang out: "She's found!"

In her book *Jane Goodall by Her Mother*, Vanne Goodall described a "dishevelled figure" finally returning home after Vanne had spent several frantic hours searching for her daughter.

When pressed on why she had hidden, Jane said: "I had to find out how hens lay eggs."

It was Vanne who delivered welcome news over lunch one spring day in 1956 at a restaurant near Bond Street in London. Twenty-two-year-old Jane had been living in a small, dark basement room in Kensington and Chelsea, working as a receptionist for Stanley Schofield Productions, which produced short advertisements and educational films. A letter had arrived for Jane, Vanne told her. Jane's friend Clo had invited her to her father's farm in Africa.

Having dreamed of visiting Africa all her life, Jane immediately resigned from her job and travelled to Bournemouth to stay in a small hut in the garden of her family's home. Vanne had relocated her family to her mother's home, "the Birches," soon after Jane's father, Mortimer, had shipped off to France in 1940—and stayed. (In 1950, Mortimer mailed Vanne a letter asking for a divorce.)

In Bournemouth, Jane found a job as a waitress at a local hotel, stashing her earnings under a corner of the living room carpet. By October, she had saved the 240 pounds required for a round-trip ticket to Kenya.

But that round-trip journey was not by air. The following March, Jane Goodall boarded the 576-foot, 17,000-ton "lavender-hulled, red-and-black-funnelled" passenger steamship, the *Kenya Castle*. She was embarking on a three-week, 14,500-kilometre trip to Mombasa, Kenya. While a journey on a steamer ship may seem uncomfortable—and for many of Goodall's fellow passengers who succumbed to seasickness, it was—she relished every minute of it. She loved watching the "dark inky blue" sea, breaking in "white and sky-blue foam" as the ship barrelled forward. She basked in the sunshine. She made friends on-board. There was dancing, deck tennis and swimming.

At Mombasa Harbour on the east coast of Africa, Goodall would say farewell to her shipmates and board the train to Nairobi to meet her friend Clo and truly begin her African adventure.

"I really do simply adore Kenya," she wrote in a letter home one week after her arrival. "It is so wild, uncultivated, primitive, mad, exciting, unpredictable."

A month into that adventure, on May 24, Goodall arranged to visit Louis Leakey at the Coryndon Museum in Nairobi, where he was curator. In another letter home, she wrote about how Leakey had spent the entire morning with her, detailing experiments on lungfish, showing her the museum's collection of snakes, and—importantly—describing his and his wife Mary's work in Olduvai Gorge excavating fossils.

Leakey was impressed with Goodall's interest in nature, and Goodall was enraptured with the charismatic fossil hunter. Leakey offered her a job as his assistant secretary—a replacement for young Rosalie Osborn, his former lover (though he left that part out). The position would start in September.

That summer, Goodall continued to visit the museum periodically. One day in June, Leakey proposed what he called a "glorious scheme." He and Mary were heading to Olduvai Gorge on an archaeological expedition. If they could work out the logistics of bringing another person, he said, how would Jane like to go?

Goodall could barely contain her excitement, which is evidenced in a letter to her family dated June 20: "If—and big IF—they can take enough water and food for one extra, they will take me!!"

The letter continued: "If I go it will be miles from anywhere in lion and rhino country, working very hard at digging up bones, very rough conditions—and absolute heaven."

Goodall's first foray into field research would begin on a Monday morning, July 15, 1957, when she was twenty-three years old.

"In those days," she wrote about Olduvai in *In the Shadow of Man*, "the area was completely secluded: the roads and tourist buses and light aircraft that pass there today were then undreamed of."

The excursion to Olduvai was an archaeological dig. Each morning, the team, including another young woman—Gillian Trace, a nineteen-year-old friend of Leakey's family and Goodall's new friend and confidant—would wake at dawn, eat breakfast and walk a mile to the dig site. They would dig, scrape and dust until noon, and then head back to camp where they would spend the hot part of the day under shade, sorting through and labelling specimens. They would return to the dig site around mid-afternoon, when it had cooled down, to continue their work.

Toward the end of the Olduvai expedition, after weeks of begging, Goodall and Trace finally got permission to carry their beds to the side of the gorge and spend their last few nights sleeping under the stars. Leakey had reluctantly given in so long as one of the young men, Hamish, carried a gun and accompanied them to protect them from the lions. Hamish and the two women carted a tarp and their mattresses up to the side of the gorge where they built a campfire and slept beneath the stars.

On one of those evenings, Leakey joined them, carrying a thermos of tea. He said goodnight, only to later return at 3:30 a.m., ostensibly to show Goodall the Pleiades and Orion constellations while the others slept. Goodall later described Leakey that night as a "dear midnight ghost."

It could have been that very night when Leakey told Goodall about his plans to sponsor the studies of the African great apes living freely in a remote forest—about the chimpanzees on the shores of Lake Tanganyika. Goodall later wrote, "I remember wondering what kind of scientist he would find for such a herculean task."

In September 1957, after returning from her excursion to Olduvai Gorge, Goodall began her job at the Coryndon Museum in Nairobi. There, Leakey spoke to her again about his desire to study great apes in the wild.

Eventually, Goodall could not contain herself. In her book, *Reason for Hope: A Spiritual Journey*, she recalled their conversation:

"Louis, I wish you wouldn't keep talking about it because that's just what I want to do," she confessed.

"Jane," he said. "I've been waiting for you to tell me that. Why on earth did you think I talked about those chimpanzees to you?"

Leakey had already decided that Goodall was just the person to study the chimpanzees. He needed a researcher with perseverance and a passion that ran deep enough that they would not quit. The person would be staying with the chimps for months, maybe even years, after all. He needed someone who wasn't afraid of being away from civilization for that long. Someone exactly like Jane Goodall.

She accepted Leakey's proposal "wholeheartedly and enthusiastically," as she later put it. So, Leakey began the challenging task of finding funding for the Chimpanzee Project. He wrote to several well-known anthropologists, including Sherwood Washburn, the pioneer of field primatology, and Solly Zuckerman, the British zoologist known for his work on primate behaviour, including his study of the London Zoo's Monkey Hill baboons. He also sought funding from the London Zoological Society.

Despite his efforts and enthusiasm, no funders emerged. A major concern, he was told, was that Goodall, the lead investigator on the project, was not only uncredentialled but (gasp!) a woman.

Like it or not, Jane Goodall had entered the academic world of the late 1950s and '60s—a world where again and again she would be dismissed as being "too pretty," "too blonde" and "too feminine" to be taken seriously as a scientist.

Frustrated by the scientific establishment's resistance to sending a young woman to study chimpanzees in their natural habitat, Leakey began to pursue unorthodox avenues of funding. He approached an American friend, Leighton Wilkie, who had made a fortune by inventing a metal-cutting band saw and distributing it through his company, DoAll. Wilkie had established a philanthropic organization called the Wilkie Brothers Foundation in 1951 and had previously supported Leakey's work.

In 1955, while touring southern Africa in a mobile home, Wilkie had attended the third Pan-African Congress on Prehistory, in Zambia. There, he saw Leakey, who was president of the Congress that year, give a memorable demonstration of how to skin and butcher a freshly killed animal using stone tools. Wilkie, who was passionate about the evolution of human technology, began sending roughly $1,000 each year in support of Leakey's work in Olduvai Gorge.

In 1959, when Leakey got notice of that year's grant, he wrote to Wilkie to thank him and ask for another grant to support the Chimpanzee Project. He mentioned Jane Goodall but, having been thwarted by so many others, he was careful to frame her qualifications differently. In his grant proposal, he wrote carefully that Goodall "has worked in Kenya with Dr. Leakey...and is at present doing further training in London. She has already shown considerable ability in getting into close contact with wild animals and living under very rough conditions in the wilds."

Wilkie responded enthusiastically, sending a cheque for $3,000 to cover the project's initial expenses. Wilkie even offered to provide a Jeep and a custom-built land yacht (an RV of sorts), suggesting it could be disguised as an elephant to avoid alarming the wild animals. The eccentric Wilkie assured Leakey that the disguise, which would incorporate a full-sized artificial elephant head, would be so convincing that it would "even fool elephants." In the end, Leakey gratefully accepted the cheque but politely declined the elephant yacht.

Soon after securing the money from Wilkie, in July 1959, Leakey made a huge find at Olduvai: the skull of "the oldest yet discovered maker of stone tools," *Paranthropus boisei*. The discovery shot Leakey to stardom—it made international news and was covered in a BBC documentary. After a lecture at the National Geographic Society in Washington, DC, Leakey secured a grant for $20,200, marking the beginning of the relationship between the Leakeys and National Geographic—one that would play a major role in Jane Goodall's story as well.

With the funding from Wilkie and National Geographic, the Chimpanzee Project was a go. But there was one more hurdle: the British district commissioner for the area in Tanganyika where Gombe Stream National Park was located would not allow a European woman to live alone in the area. An escort was required, he informed Leakey. Eventually, it was decided that Goodall's mother, Vanne, would accompany her to Gombe and help her set up camp to live among the chimpanzees for three months.

The camp was nestled on the shores of Lake Tanganyika in Gombe Stream National Park, a nineteen-kilometre journey by boat from the lake port of Kigoma in northwestern Tanzania. The lake's shoreline was peppered with small fishing villages of mud and grass huts, set against a backdrop of mountains and valleys. The site lay at a large rocky outcrop at the southern limits of the park.

In 1960, Gombe held a wealth of biodiversity—including a population of about 160 chimpanzees, as well as other primates like the dog-like olive baboons, the tree-dwelling red colobus monkeys and the wide-eyed, nocturnal bush babies. The park was also home to buffalo, bush pigs and hippos. Hyenas, leopards and mongooses. Birds, of course—in huge variety. Chameleons, frogs and tortoises. There were snakes, including the sixteen-foot-long python and several venomous adders, cobras and mambas. The forest was also filled with insects aplenty: scorpions, beetles, grasshoppers, wasps.

Goodall described Gombe in 1960 as "the Africa of my childhood's dreams."

But, as a primatologist, I am here to tell you that fieldwork often combines the magical with the maddening. Gombe is a long, narrow rectangle, bordered by the lakeshore to the west and the rift escarpment to the east. Water drains from the escarpment, forming about a dozen active streams that cut through the forest, creating many ravines. The park's high peaks and valleys are great for viewing the wildlife in the lush forest below but treacherous when slogging up and down to find the chimpanzees.

In Goodall's early days at Gombe, the chimps spent much of their time feeding on the round red-and-yellow berries at the tops of what her guide called msulula trees, and she could not hide her frustration. She knew the chimps were there and what they were doing, but she could see very little of it. As she wrote, she would only catch "an occasional glimpse of a black arm reaching out from the foliage and pulling bunches of fruit out of sight." In her journal, she described a depression that descended, writing: "How can I ever see any behaviour? All I see is chimpanzees stuffing themselves with various types of food."

The chimpanzees remained in the msulula trees for ten days, until the trees finished fruiting at the end of July. "Later I realized how lucky I had been during the fruiting of the msulula tree," Goodall wrote in *In the Shadow of Man*. "I probably learned more during those ten days than I did during the eight depressing weeks that followed."

During those weeks, Goodall and her two African assistants trekked through the reserve, up and down the valleys and through thick undergrowth in search of the chimpanzees. They were lucky if they spotted a glimpse of chimpanzees or even heard a sound. Even when they did come across chimpanzees, the primates would flee at the sight of the humans, or they were so far away that it was impossible to observe their behaviour.

In August, Goodall was still diligently searching the forest for chimps, even as she began to feel a little off. One day, she felt so unwell that she had to lie down in the forest. By the time she made it back to camp, she was registering a temperature of 101 degrees Fahrenheit. The next day, her temperature spiked to 104. Her mother, Vanne, had also become ill, with a temperature of 105. Despite pleas from their cook, Dominic, the two women refused to see a doctor because they did not feel well enough to make the three-hour boat ride to Kigoma. So, the cook was left to care for the ailing women for nearly two weeks, kindly bringing them tea and fussing over them. On one particularly difficult night, Dominic found Vanne delirious outside her tent, having wandered off.

Later, Goodall wrote that their illness was undoubtedly some sort of malaria, even though a doctor in Kigoma had told her there was no malaria in the area.

Malaria is a risk that often comes hand in hand with field studies. It's a disease caused by a parasite that spreads to humans through mosquito bites. Many tropical areas—where primates range—are malaria zones. In both Belize and Madagascar, for example, my colleagues and I took preventative drugs and tried to be mindful about wearing long clothing to help us avoid mosquito bites. Even still, on my first trip to Madagascar, my Malagasy field assistant, Andry, contracted malaria at our remote field site—a thirty-kilometre trek from the nearest village. I had to coordinate an emergency evacuation to bring a delirious Andry to safety. I pulled the plug on that first field expedition and returned to Canada earlier than I had anticipated. After I got home, I stopped taking my antimalarial medications, only to soon start experiencing fevers and chills. A blood test confirmed I had also contracted malaria.

Although I began treatment as soon as possible, the symptoms set in hard. They occurred in a cycle. It always started with the chills—I felt so cold that my teeth chattered uncontrollably. When that finally subsided, a fever ensued, making my head feel as though it was on fire. Hours later, when the fever finally broke, every joint in my body ached as though I'd just run a marathon. That cycle repeated several times until, finally, the malaria treatment did its job.

Malaria was rougher than any illness I had ever experienced, but, in a way, I'd been fortunate. I started experiencing the symptoms of malaria when I was at home in Toronto. I could lie in my own bed, and I had easy access to medical care. I can't imagine how uncomfortable and scary experiencing those symptoms while in Gombe must have been for Jane and Vanne. They didn't go to the doctor or receive treatment. They weren't even sure they had malaria. They toughed it out through the chills, the fever and the delirium, and by the time they recovered, two weeks later, it was the end of August.

Jane Goodall was frantic. In just a few months, her funding would run dry, and what did she have to show for it? A few observations of the chimpanzees feeding on the msulula trees? A glimpse of an arm?

Still weak, Goodall took to the forest once again. She wisely started by exploring the valleys near camp while she got her strength up. Her unrelenting determination paid off when, in those areas, she finally found many chimpanzees and was able to conduct fruitful observations of the primates engaged in a variety of behaviours—walking along paths, resting under trees and playing. In a letter home, Goodall wrote: "I've discovered more—since my fever, in about five days, than in all the dreary weeks before."

During this especially productive period, Goodall began to truly establish her observational methods. In the months leading up to her Gombe expedition, she had studied the writings of scientists who had published work on chimpanzees.

Henry Nissen, a Yale psychologist, was one of the few researchers, and probably the most notable before Goodall, to study chimpanzees in the wild. He worked in French Guinea (now Guinea) in West Africa in 1930. He spent nine weeks with the chimpanzees documenting their social organization, feeding and behaviour, while also evaluating the feasibility of studying wild chimpanzees and developing field research methodology, which he documented in his 1931 monograph *A Field Study of the Chimpanzee*. Oh, and while he was there, he would also "procure" a few chimpanzees for the Yale University research centre.

Nissen's approach was to conceal himself in a blind, like a hunter, in the hope he could observe the chimpanzees undetected. He soon discovered, however, that chimpanzees were sensitive to "artificial anomalies in the bush."

He cooked up another idea and hired forty African assistants to help. The plan was that when they came across a group of chimpanzees, they would surround the group and inhibit their movements for a day—enough time, surely, to find out basic information about the group's composition.

What followed was chaos. To contain the chimpanzees (who, I think it's safe to say, did not wish to be contained), Nissen fired his gun a few times and lit grass fires. His crew even tried to pull a baby chimp out of a tree. In the end, Nissen had to admit these methods weren't working. He resorted to "listening for the hoots and cries of chimps," and when he was able to get close enough, he continued alone, quietly. Then and only then was he able to make a few brief observations. The problem with this method, however, was that once the chimpanzees detected his presence, they saw him as a threat and fled.

When Goodall read Nissen's notes, she was shocked by his "dearth of observations." Perhaps it was from Nissen that she learned what *not* to do. Drawing instead on her experience with animals from her childhood, Goodall approached the chimpanzees quietly but did not hide like Nissen—she remained out in the open, only moving closer if the chimpanzees showed signs of being comfortable. If the chimps looked distressed by her presence, she would pretend to be just another primate in the forest—scratching herself, searching for insects on the ground and pretending to eat. She called it her "baboon act."

Although Goodall did not have formal scientific credentials at the time, she was amazingly thorough in the details she recorded about the chimpanzees. Where Nissen had described the chimpanzees in broad terms, Goodall studied them as individuals, noting physical characteristics that distinguished one from the other: the silvery hair on the "grizzled" chin of one individual; the frail female with thinning brown hair; the old, "belligerent" male whose head, neck and shoulders were nearly devoid of hair except for a small frill around his head "like a monk's tonsure." Like with David Greybeard, Goodall gave them names: Flo, Mr. McGregor. She sought to recognize individual group members and to observe and describe their interactions and behaviours.

Goodall later wrote: "Some scientists feel that animals should be labelled by numbers—that to name them is anthropomorphic—but I have always been interested in the differences between individuals, and a name is not only more individual than a number but also far easier to remember."

On the morning of October 30, 1960, at 7:40 a.m., Jane Goodall was sitting on her usual perch atop the Peak in Gombe, watching a cluster of three chimpanzees in the valley below through her binoculars. She could hear some "angry little screams," but she couldn't quite make out what was happening. Finally, she focused on one of the chimpanzees. As the sun lit up his face, she recognized the small white hairs on his chin—it was David. But what was that he was holding? Something...pink.

A new infant? Goodall wondered, jotting a note in her journal.

She looked up and noticed a fourth chimpanzee nearby, along with three baboons. There were more screams and then a loud crash. David, still clutching the pink object, chased after one of the largest baboons.

Goodall focused her binoculars on the ground below the tree, where two large, grey bush pigs were walking about. Twenty minutes later, she observed two of the chimpanzees sitting together in the tree. David now seemed to be eating the pink object.

Suddenly, it dawned on her. "Suspected meat," she wrote slowly and deliberately in her journal.

For the next three hours, Jane watched as the chimpanzees sat with the object, pulling pieces off with their teeth. The baboons continued to crowd around aggressively. Finally, David climbed down, followed by the other two chimpanzees. As they moved out onto a bare branch, Goodall could see clearly.

"The object was meat," she confirmed in her journal.

That evening, she reflected more on the incident in her journal. "It was rather like a detective book with not only the end chapter missing but the beginning as well. We have an unidentified victim, we do not know how he met his death, and we are not sure of the murderer. Most frustrating."

She would ultimately deduce that the victim was likely an infant bush pig who had met its demise at the hands of a chimpanzee. This was the first direct observation of carnivory—meat-eating—in wild chimpanzees.

During that first season in Gombe, Goodall only observed the chimpanzees eating meat a few times. Once she watched as they ate what she thought was a young bushbuck, and on another occasion, she was lucky enough to witness the hunt and kill.

Jane Goodall's observations were groundbreaking. The prevailing view at the time was that chimpanzees, like their gorilla cousins, were vegetarian primates. Hunting is considered one of the key behaviours that shaped human evolution, with humans once believed to be the only primates intelligent enough to hunt purposefully for meat. In Olduvai Gorge, Louis Leakey had been working to uncover stone tools that our human ancestors used for butchering meat and to discover who the toolmakers had been. With Goodall's observations, we learned that we could look to the chimpanzees to get a sense of how our earliest human ancestors might have behaved when it came to meat-eating. Did they hunt? Scavenge? Or both? And how did hunting affect their social relationships? The fossils couldn't tell that story, but Goodall's observations of chimpanzees in their natural habitat provided the insight that we humans, as a species, so desired.

In December 1961, Goodall was accepted into Cambridge University, where she would use her field notebooks as the basis for her PhD. Her supervisor was Robert Hinde, a British ethologist whom a former student described as "incredibly handsome" with "piercing blue eyes" and "silvery hair."

Goodall got along well with her advisor. Hinde, one of the rare male academics who was willing to mentor female students, found her to be "a very dedicated young woman," while she described him as "a dear." According to Dale Peterson's biography, during their private tutorials in Hinde's apartment, he would lie on his stomach by the fire while reviewing her work—something Goodall later admitted was "rather strange." Despite such oddities, the two insisted that their relationship remained professional, though rumours of an affair swirled among her classmates.

Goodall felt overwhelmed at Cambridge and yearned to go back to Gombe. She was tasked with taking her handwritten notes from her year and a half in the field and, somehow, translating them into scientific data. She was new to the academic world—she had not completed an undergraduate degree.

As Goodall worked, Hinde was quick to point out the flaws in her attempts at describing and quantifying the data. "We don't use this term in science," he might say, or, "You had better do more reading about this topic before you draw your conclusions."

Goodall often left Hinde's office in despair, returning to her room and throwing his marked-up pages into a corner. "How desperately I longed to give it all up and go back to the chimpanzees and the forests," she later wrote.

I can attest that, at some point, every graduate student on the planet will feel like they want to hurl their research into the corner of the room and escape to the forest. I remember completing drafts of my PhD thesis and triumphantly sending them to my supervisor. He would send them right back to me, marked up in red the whole way through. All I could think was, "The lemurs never sent me scores of edits to complete." But then, as all graduate students must do, I would take a breath, remind myself why I was doing this (for the lemurs) and address the comments one at a time, from easiest to hardest.

Jane Goodall, too, pulled herself up by her bootstraps and kept going. She created an index for her journals and worked on summarizing her observations, trying her best to quantify the data.

The next test of Goodall's mettle as a scientist came in the form of academic conferences.

She wrote home, "My future is so ridiculous. I just squat here, chimp-like, on my rocks, pulling out prickles and thorns, and laugh to think of this unknown 'Miss Goodall' who is said to be doing scientific research somewhere."

In April 1962, she hopped the train from Cambridge to London to attend her first symposium. It was a three-day affair entitled "The Primates," organized by primate taxonomist John Napier and sponsored by the Zoological Society of London. She gathered with the other scientists at a pre-symposium party in Napier's laboratory. It was a formal affair—men wore suits and ties, women were in heels and stockings.

Lemur researcher Alison Jolly was also in attendance. In an essay she would publish in Fedigan and Strum's *Primate Encounters*, Jolly recalled a series of photographs displayed on a poster board—chimpanzees using sticks and twigs inside termite nests—and the buzz among conferencegoers.

On April 12, Goodall took the stage alongside eleven other speakers, three of whom had completed long-term field research on primates—including Rosalie Osborn, who had gone on to study zoology at Newnham College. For the first time, Goodall publicly revealed her discoveries with the chimpanzees—their tool use and meat-eating.

Her results were met with skepticism. Zoologist Solly Zuckerman was chair of the symposium. Jolly described Zuckerman as having a "red face and white hair" and "always being centred in the chair in front of the room, doing the summing up."

On the day of Goodall's presentation, as Peterson recounts in his biography, Zuckerman's summary included some pointed remarks: "There are those who are here and who prefer anecdote" he said. He called out Goodall's presentation specifically, stating that her study wasn't representative of wild chimpanzee behaviour because the chimpanzees in her study were "living under very favourable conditions, plagued by few predators and enjoying abundant food."

As for meat-eating? He advised caution, suggesting it was premature to draw conclusions based on "a few contradictory and isolated observations." In Zuckerman's view, non-human primates did not eat meat.

Zuckerman believed non-human primate behaviour could be characterized by sex and violence, with males at the centre of it all. His conclusions, based on a three-month study of chacma baboons in South Africa and research on captive baboons at the London Zoo, had males maintaining harems, herding the females and fighting aggressively among each other. However, Goodall's research, and the work of several others in the 1960s, challenged Zuckerman's conclusions. Much to Zuckerman's dismay, scientists were learning that longer-term research on primates in natural settings yielded a better understanding of their behaviours and social lives.

I can imagine the pitch meeting.

A man in a suit stands at the front of a large boardroom table filled with National Geographic executives. He takes a deep breath. "A cover story and photo spread about Jane Goodall and her chimpanzees will be a hit with our readers," he says. "Picture this: blonde-haired Jane gazes out at the deep-green, mountainous forests. A close-up of her sitting next to the wild chimpanzees as they eat meat and use tools to fish for termites." A dramatic pause. "The piece would be penned by Jane, and the headline would be 'Miss Goodall and the Wild Chimpanzees.'"

But in real life, finding a suitable photographer for the job was not easy. After a few failed attempts, including photos taken by Goodall herself and later by her sister Judy, *National Geographic* magazine shelved the story. This decision was a blow. The publications's funding came with an expectation of a story in return, and when that did not pan out because of the lack of appropriate photos, future funding was put at risk.

Leakey, persistent and stubborn, continued to pursue funds through National Geographic. In 1961, he requested a grant of four hundred pounds (about $1,100) to support Goodall's first year at Cambridge, where she would write up the results of her field research. National Geographic declined at first but asked for more information about how that money would be spent. Leakey responded with a letter with nine points outlining the significance of Goodall's research and the amazing observations she had made of the chimpanzees—from tool use to meat-eating. The letter worked: National Geographic sent the cheque, and more than that, they wanted to bring back the magazine article.

But there was still the matter of the photographer.

That's when Leakey proposed an idea. He had recently met a young Dutchman living in Nairobi—a shy but talented filmmaker named Hugo van Lawick, who had impressed Leakey with his knowledge of animal behaviour.

Baron Hugo van Lawick, born in Indonesia in 1937 (then the Dutch East Indies), shared Goodall's love of wildlife. At fourteen, during a nature club trip to a national park in Holland, he discovered photography. A few of his friends had brought along rudimentary cameras and were snapping photos of the creatures they saw. Van Lawick realized that photography could bring him closer to nature. After a short stint in the Dutch army, he honed his skills by working as an assistant cameraman, in a film laboratory and as a stills photographer. In November 1959, he left for East Africa, where he found work as a cameraman for a Nairobi-based filmmaking couple, Armand and Michaela Denis.

Africa's wealth of wildlife, including wild dogs, hyenas and leopards, stole van Lawick's heart. In Africa, he could fulfill his dream of capturing wildlife on film.

It was during this time that van Lawick met the Denis's neighbours—the Leakey family. He became friends with Richard Leakey, Louis and Mary's son. Van Lawick happened to be visiting when a phone call came in from America: someone at National Geographic was requesting a background film for Leakey's next lecture. Van Lawick was just the man for the job. He made the film in a few months, impressing both Leakey and National Geographic.

Van Lawick used the funds from that gig to fly back to Holland, where he received National Geographic's next offer: for $100 a month, they would bring him to their headquarters for photographic training. Hugo accepted and was off to Washington, DC. After impressing the team there, he was assigned to work in Gombe.

As for the matter of the propriety of sending a male photographer to live alongside a woman on her own? Leakey solved that issue by convincing National Geographic to fund both van Lawick and Vanne Goodall, with the latter serving as chaperone.

Jane Goodall, meanwhile, was back in Gombe on July 8, 1962, after a brief stint at Cambridge, and she was elated to be there. Van Lawick arrived on August 15. Goodall's first impressions of the mild-mannered Hugo van Lawick, according to Peterson's biography, were mostly positive, though she didn't care for his heavy smoking. Van Lawick was twenty-five, slim with a muscular build and thick dark hair. Goodall wrote home: "We are a very happy family. Hugo is charming and we get on very well."

Vanne arrived in September, completing their family unit.

Goodall and van Lawick shared intimate experiences with nature and with the chimpanzees. They endured the rains and the challenges of fieldwork, finding joy and wonder in observing nature up close. Goodall had found a "kindred spirit" in the photographer. Against the backdrop of the forests and valleys, they would sit by the fire each night, discussing their shared passion:

"Mostly—chimp—chimp—and more chimp. Hugo loves them as much as I do."

When it was time for van Lawick to leave in November, Goodall knew she would miss him greatly. "I had found in Hugo a companion with whom I could share not only the joys and frustrations of my work but also my love of the chimpanzees, of the forest and the mountains, of life in the wilderness," she later wrote.

Hugo van Lawick departed having handed over a successful portfolio of photographs to National Geographic. It was time for Goodall to pen the story that would go with them.

In the spring of 1963, the pair returned to Gombe, their close friendship deepening into romance. Together, they worked to capture more photographs and film footage of the chimpanzees.

Meanwhile, *National Geographic* magazine published the article in August 1963—a thirty-seven-page feature titled "My Life Among Wild Chimpanzees." It captivated the magazine's three million subscribers with its story of a young, pretty woman living among the chimps in Africa. An amateur scientist, fearless in the face of hardships. And the photographs: images of Goodall up close to the chimpanzees, and of the chimpanzees carrying meat and fishing for termites. The article marked the beginning of Jane Goodall, the celebrity.

By December 1963, Jane and Hugo were officially in love. The two had talked about marriage and whether their feelings for each other were due to "being thrown together in the wilds, far from other European society." They wondered whether they would have fallen for each other had they met in London. They both believed their love was genuine but decided to test it by spending some time apart from the magic of Gombe.

Goodall returned to Cambridge for her third term. Van Lawick would join her there later, and together they would travel to the National Geographic Society in Washington to show their chimpanzee film. The couple did not need to wait until Washington to know that what they had was real. "As it turned out, we knew the very moment we were separated," Goodall later wrote.

Goodall left for home the week before Christmas, and on December 26, van Lawick sent a cable to her family home in Bournemouth. The message was simple: "WILL YOU MARRY ME STOP LOVE STOP HUGO."

Late one evening in 1966, after they'd returned to Gombe, Jane Goodall and Hugo van Lawick noticed a family of chimpanzees behaving strangely as they gathered around a low bush near the camp. They appeared distracted by something in the bush. Every so often, one would stand upright to look over the grasses, trying to get a better look at...whatever it was.

Goodall knew immediately that something was up. She and van Lawick rushed to the area and noticed the flies, which buzzed angrily as they grew closer. Goodall took a deep breath, bracing herself for what was surely a dead animal.

But when the poor creature came into view, she saw it wasn't dead. It was Mr. McGregor, one of the chimpanzees, feebly reaching for some small purple berries on the bush. The sight was horrifying: Mr. McGregor was grasping at the branches above his head and pulling himself along the ground, dragging his limp legs behind him.

"His legs..." van Lawick said.

It did not take Goodall long to grasp the grim reality.

"He was moving either by sitting upright and inching backwards using his arms as crutches, or by pulling forward on his tummy—when the vegetation was strong enough—or by rolling, or, somehow by using his arms to pull his body up and turning head over heels," Jane later wrote in a letter home. "He had lost bladder control, and all his legs etc. stank of wee. He was surrounded by clouds and clouds of flies."

Mr. McGregor's legs were paralyzed. He had contracted polio.

Polio, a disease caused by the poliovirus, spreads through contact with infected feces or droplets from sneezes or coughs. Once the poliovirus enters an organism, it can attack the nervous system. About one in two hundred cases of polio results in paralysis, most often of the legs, as with Mr. McGregor. Polio can be fatal if it paralyzes the muscles required for breathing.

The polio outbreak had started among the human populations of Kigoma, and since chimpanzees are so closely related to humans, they are also susceptible to the disease. Goodall traced the source to a village just sixteen kilometres south of the (somewhat controversial) feeding station she had built to offer bananas to the chimps to facilitate up-close observations. The chimpanzees were known to visit that village, and they almost certainly picked up the virus through discarded food scraps. The disease then spread north, reaching her study groups.

Mr. McGregor wasn't the only victim. Fifteen chimpanzees in the group had been affected. Some lost the use of a hand or an arm. When the couple realized what was happening, they worried for their own safety—they hadn't yet received their polio vaccines. Van Lawick arranged for a supply of oral vaccine to be delivered by plane, enough for themselves, the staff and even the chimps. Goodall laced bananas with the vaccine and developed a complex chart to keep track of the dosing regimen—each chimp needed three drops a month for three months.

Unfortunately, it was too late for Mr. McGregor. Over ten days, his condition worsened: his legs remained limp, he had not regained his bladder control and his rump was bleeding from dragging himself along the ground. Some of the other group members even began attacking him in his sorry state. On the tenth evening, Goodall and van Lawick discovered that Mr. McGregor had dislocated one of his arms—his only method of moving around. Though they had hoped for a miracle, they knew what had to be done.

Knowing Mr. McGregor wanted to make a nest to sleep in, Goodall brought him a large pile of vegetation. The next morning, she brought him two eggs—his favourite food. As he finished his treat, van Lawick stood behind him, gun in hand, ready to end Mr. McGregor's suffering.

Afterward, Goodall received a great deal of flak for the choices she made during the polio epidemic. Scientists are typically expected to remain objective—to observe and not interfere. The vaccine-laced bananas and Mr. McGregor's mercy killing were choices she made out of empathy for the chimps.

"It seems to me," she wrote in *The Chimpanzees of Gombe*, "that humans have already interfered to such a major extent, usually in a very *negative* way...with so many animals in so many places that a certain amount of *positive* interference is desirable."

The polio epidemic demonstrated how much Goodall cared for the chimpanzees she got to know at Gombe. But it wasn't until a conference in Chicago in 1986, "Understanding Chimpanzees," that she began to see the bigger picture. She realized her empathy needed to extend beyond just the Gombe chimpanzees.

The conference brought together people studying chimpanzees from across Africa, as well as those studying captive chimpanzees. As Goodall listened to the presentations, the picture became crystal clear: the chimpanzees were in serious trouble. Their populations were decreasing. Their habitats were being destroyed. And then there was the bushmeat trade—humans were hunting the chimpanzees for meat. Perhaps most troubling to Goodall was the live animal trade, where infant chimpanzees were captured—their mothers shot dead—for laboratory research or the entertainment industry.

Reflecting on that pivotal conference, Goodall later said: "I went as a scientist—I had my PhD by then—and left as an activist."

When Jane Goodall first visited Gombe in 1960, the human population of sub-Saharan Africa was 227 million. By 2050, it is expected to exceed two billion. Meanwhile, chimpanzee populations have continued to decrease. When Goodall began her research in Gombe, there were roughly 160 chimpanzees living in the protected park. Today, scientists count between eighty-nine and ninety-two—a significant decline. The International Union for Conservation of Nature now lists chimpanzees as "Endangered," with their numbers declining in the wild due to residential and commercial development, mining, agriculture, roads, hunting and diseases spread by humans to animals. Health monitoring in Gombe has revealed that infectious diseases, including respiratory disease, parasites and AIDS, are significant causes of chimpanzee death. These illnesses are likely transmitted between chimpanzees, humans, domestic pets and livestock.

The chimpanzees are also threatened by habitat loss. Satellite images from 1972 to 2003 show that 64 per cent of Gombe's forests—vital chimpanzee habitat—have been converted to farmland. Yet, communities need to live. Those surrounding Gombe are low-income, and many of the residents are refugees fleeing from conflict in neighbouring countries. A sustainable solution that involves local communities is essential.

Near the end of the 1986 conference, thirty chimpanzee experts—Jane Goodall among them—decided to form an organization to advocate for chimpanzee conservation. It was to be called the Committee for Conservation and Care of Chimpanzees—the CCCC. Goodall would back the organization financially through the Jane Goodall Institute—the charitable organization she founded in 1975—and she would be its public representative, leveraging her celebrity.

Goodall has not looked back since that conference. She has sought out partners and sponsors and spoken about chimpanzee conservation to anyone who would listen. She met with politicians, advocating for policy changes to reduce the capture of wild chimpanzees for research and entertainment. She also launched TACARE, a local conservation program in Tanzania, to find solutions that would benefit both the chimpanzee and human populations through better education, and improved health care and agricultural techniques.

Today, Goodall's conservation efforts have branched out beyond the chimpanzees. She is a global advocate for broader issues like climate change. Her Roots & Shoots program, which began in 1991 in Tanzania, is now active in more than sixty countries, encouraging children to develop projects to help protect the environment, such as planting trees, urban gardening and volunteering at animal shelters.

When I saw Jane Goodall at Meridian Hall in Toronto, she was eighty-nine years old, and her message of hope hadn't wavered. There is no question that her work studying chimpanzee behaviour in Gombe changed science, teaching us about our closest living relatives and ourselves. Yet, it is her tireless conservation efforts that will live on.

Jane Goodall's efforts marked the beginnings of a new kind of primatology, characterized by long-term research on individual behaviour and a commitment to working with local communities to find sustainable conservation solutions.

Her work has set the stage for many researchers who came after her. One of those was Louis Leakey's "gorilla girl," the lanky young woman with an olive complexion, infectious enthusiasm and, as Goodall carefully put it, "romantic notions" about the gorillas.

CHAPTER FOUR

Gorilla Girl

LIKE MANY, I WAS INTRODUCED to the story of Dian Fossey and the endangered mountain gorillas through the Hollywood movie *Gorillas in the Mist*, starring Sigourney Weaver as the dark-haired Fossey. The 1988 biopic was based on Fossey's book of the same name, as well as a 1986 article in *Life* magazine by journalist Harold Hayes. After I saw the film, I was inspired to learn more, searching for all the information I could find about this woman—including Canadian author Farley Mowat's retelling of her story through her diaries in *Woman in the Mists*. I was fascinated by this complex, passionate and troubled woman, who ultimately met a tragic end.

When I later learned about the predominance of women in primatology, Fossey's story stood out as an embodiment of several of the prevailing hypotheses for this trend. As one of the Trimates, Fossey was sponsored by Louis Leakey, which ties into the "goodwill of powerful men" hypothesis that I delved into by telling his story in chapter two. The media prominently featured Fossey during her life and after her death. Images of her with the gorillas were splashed across the covers of *National Geographic* magazine, and Fossey even appeared on *The Tonight Show* with Johnny Carson. She became known for her work with gorillas, and, like

Jane Goodall, she was a role model for other women interested in studying wild primates.

Fossey also felt a deep connection with the endangered mountain gorillas she studied, forging personal relationships with these gentle giants and viewing them as her friends. It's hard not to conclude that, to some extent, she was motivated by the "big brown eyes" of these charismatic gorillas.

Her story is complex and controversial, so it's no surprise that Hollywood got on board. Fossey's tale has it all: love, heartbreak, passion, fame and murder. To me, Dian Fossey's story illustrates that there may not be one single reason why females are drawn to the study of wild primates. Her path demonstrates that the forces driving women into this field are nuanced. Regardless of how she arrived at her calling, there is no question her studies of the elusive mountain gorillas in the Virunga Mountains shifted our understanding of gorilla behaviour and conservation.

The Karisoke Research Center was the scene of the crime. Karisoke is nestled in the heart of Rwanda's misty Virunga volcanic mountain range, along the borders of Rwanda, the Democratic Republic of Congo and Uganda. Just after celebrating Christmas at the research camp, sometime between midnight and five in the morning on December 27, 1985, fifty-three-year-old Dian Fossey was murdered in her cabin. By this time, Fossey had spent nearly twenty years at Karisoke, living among, studying and relentlessly working to save her "gorillas of the mountains."

Standing six-foot-one and lanky, Fossey often wore her long brown hair in a loose braid draped across her left shoulder. Her field uniform was very '70s: a button-up blue top, grey wool socks with a single red stripe along the top and brown leather boots. Fossey's years with the gorillas made her famous in America and England, where she was seen as a feminist icon and an unapologetic activist. She leveraged her fame to bring attention to the conservation plight of the gorillas she so loved.

When they found her that morning, Fossey lay sprawled on the floor, her head and one shoulder slumped over the bed mattress. Her pistol and a cartridge, which she kept for protection, lay beside her. Like something out of a horror movie, her eyes were wide open. In her right hand, she clutched a clump of hair—later identified in reports as Caucasian. Her skull had been split open. The authorities documented six blows to her head and face with a panga—a type of machete with an upturned point at the end of its long blade.

Wayne McGuire, one of Fossey's student assistants, was the last person on her team to see her alive. The blond, bearded, six-foot-tall PhD student from Oklahoma University had arrived at Karisoke in August of that year. He'd first met Fossey when she visited Oklahoma on a lecture tour. He'd been desperate to study gorillas—he wanted to show how male gorillas were loving and protective of their infants. Karisoke was one of the only places he could observe the gorillas up close. He, like so many others before him, wrote to the famous Dian Fossey in hopes of travelling to Karisoke to conduct his research.

McGuire was ecstatic when, after four years of letters, Fossey finally agreed. Fossey described that, upon his arrival, McGuire seemed "a nice enough young man," though she found him hopelessly disorganized and too naïve for life at a research camp—and she made it known, occasionally blowing up at him and writing to friends, complaining about his inexperience in the forest.

That morning, McGuire was still asleep when, at around six, the Karisoke staff and several park guards who had spent the night at camp celebrating Christmas rushed to his bedroom, shouting, "Dian kufa! Dian kufa!"

It took McGuire a moment to translate the Swahili. But when he recognized the word, his heart sank.

Kufa. Dead.

McGuire dressed hastily, and the men led him to Fossey's cabin. Lamps were smashed and furniture was toppled over. In his state of shock, McGuire couldn't stop staring at the still-standing Christmas tree with the neatly wrapped presents in place beneath it.

The men led McGuire into the bedroom. Books and clothing were strewn about the floor, and the bed mattress had been pushed off its frame. McGuire took a breath and stepped inside. When he saw Fossey, dressed in her long johns and slumped over the mattress, his first thought was that she'd had a heart attack. But when he approached to take her pulse, he saw the blood.

Dian Fossey had a lonely childhood. She was born on January 16, 1932, in San Francisco, California. Her father, George Fossey, was the son of an English immigrant. A lover of the outdoors, he was miserable in his job as an insurance agent. George was also a drinker, which led to divorce when Dian was a child. When Dian turned six, her mother, Kitty, married Richard Price, a building contractor. After the divorce, Dian gradually lost touch with her birth father. Her stepfather, who never officially adopted her, was distant and strict. Dian wasn't allowed to eat dinner with her parents until she was ten, instead having her supper in the kitchen with the housekeeper.

As an adult, Dian Fossey refused to say much about her childhood. She often referred to Kitty as "the mother." Kitty, a petite fashion model, treated the six-foot-one Dian as an oddity, even taking her to the doctor to get her checked out for her height.

Not surprisingly, Fossey grew up with a skewed view of her appearance. She felt awkward and gangly, even though to outside observers, she was a dark beauty with delicate features.

When she finished high school, Fossey enrolled in California's Marin Junior College, taking a business course. Richard and Kitty, now well-to-do thanks to Richard's thriving business, provided some financial assistance. Still, young Dian asserted her independence by supporting herself through various jobs. She found work at a dude ranch in Montana for a summer when she was twenty-one, thanks to her love of horses—she had been on the riding team in high school.

Rebelling against her stepfather's desire that she study business, Fossey left business school and enrolled as a pre-veterinary medical student at the University of California, Davis. Her connection with animals had only grown stronger, but she struggled with the required chemistry and physics courses (I hear ya, Dian!), so she transferred to and ultimately graduated from San José State College with a degree in occupational therapy, setting her sights on working with young tuberculosis patients.

Soon after graduation, she landed a job at Kosair Children's Hospital in Louisville, Kentucky—about as far away from California and her parents as she could get.

At the hospital, Fossey met Mary White Henry, the secretary to the chief administrator, who quickly became a close friend and introduced her to Louisville society. In 1960, Henry was planning an African safari and invited her new friend to join her. Fossey was forced to turn down the offer because she did not have enough money to pay her way. Still, that invitation awoke something inside her.

Determined to take a safari of her own one day, Fossey began saving every penny. She pleaded with her mother and stepfather to guarantee a bank loan so she could raise the necessary $5,000. They initially agreed but soon backed out, viewing the trip as a dangerous and rash venture.

As Fossey's struggles demonstrate, it's not always easy for primatologists to cut their teeth. There's an unwritten expectation that before you commence your studies, you must get hands-on experience, whether through volunteering as a research assistant or enrolling in a field school. Since primates live primarily in the tropics, depending on where you call home, studying them in their natural setting usually involves travel. Flights cost money, and field schools require tuition. How can someone earn a living while spending one to three months in the field as a volunteer?

My own first foray into field studies of primates was at a field school in Belize. I was privileged because I had savings I could pull from to cover the cost, which was a few thousand dollars. I was living at home with my supportive parents and could put money into a savings account by holding down part-time jobs as a cinnamon bun baker and shoe store attendant.

Not everyone is so lucky. Some, like Dian Fossey, must make major sacrifices to get what they want. And sure, that builds character, but it's also a barrier.

To raise enough funds for her trip, Fossey, much to her mother's chagrin, mortgaged her income from the hospital for three years to a loan company at a crushing 24 per cent interest. On September 26, at the age of 31, Dian Fossey set out for Africa.

Fossey's first trip to Africa was a safari. She hired a guide, a handsome British hunter named John Alexander. Fossey referred to him as "Great White," viewing him as a caricature of a big-game hunter of European descent, trophy-hunting his way through southern Africa. On their first morning, he was late, "cranky" and "hateful," according to Fossey.

"I feel as though a huge tsetse fly were hovering over my head all the time I'm with him," she later wrote in her diary.

Despite the tensions between them, the guide got the job done. He brought her to Nairobi and then south to Tanzania's Serengeti Plain, where Fossey photographed the animals she had dreamed of seeing—giraffes, elephants, buffalo. Next, the two reluctant travel companions headed to Kenya to visit the Ngorongoro Crater. There, a rhino charged at their Land Rover, an event that excited

Fossey, but her guide wouldn't keep the vehicle in one place long enough for her to get a photo.

After the crater, Great White took her to Olduvai Gorge. According to Fossey, a stop at Olduvai was her idea, but Alexander contends he had been the one to suggest it, as he did for all his clients.

Regardless of how it came to be, Olduvai changed everything, according to Fossey. There, she chanced to meet the enigmatic Louis Leakey.

In *Gorillas in the Mist*, Dian Fossey wrote about her visit to Olduvai, saying, "Dr. Leakey spoke to me enthusiastically about Jane Goodall's excellent work with the chimpanzees at the Gombe Stream Research Center in Tanzania" and noting that he "stressed the importance of long-range field studies with the great apes." Fossey recalled that Leakey spent time with her and encouraged her to visit the gorillas in Congo.

This encounter might be exaggerated. In an article she later published about her safari in the *Louisville Courier Journal*, Fossey described seeing Leakey—and there is photographic evidence to prove it—but she wrote that he had no time for her as he was suffering a "bout of emphysema."

She also wrote about her trip to Olduvai to see the fossils, when she lost her footing and cracked an ankle. This much is true—in journalist Harold Hayes's biography of Fossey, Mary Leakey recalled the fall and nursing Fossey's ankle back at camp. However, she does not remember any discussion of gorillas.

Hayes also detailed that, according to Alexander, the topic of gorillas came up on the next stint of their journey, during a visit to the Serengeti Plain, where he introduced Fossey to a Belgian biologist named Jacques Verschuren.

Verschuren, dressed in khaki shorts and knee-high socks, told Fossey, "Gorillas are the most impressive of all primates—of all three of the great ape species. The problem is that these amazing creatures are nearing extinction."

He went on to describe a study by his friend George Schaller, which had taken place in the Virunga volcanoes.

Schaller was a German-born American biologist who, along with his wife, Kay, had travelled to central Africa in the late 1950s to study the mountain gorillas of the Virunga volcanoes for twenty months. During that time, he made huge progress toward our understanding of the gorillas. He managed to habituate them to his presence and record observations of their social structure and diet.

Fossey knew she had to visit the Virungas. But her guide was reluctant. Alexander was likely aware of the problems that can arise when interacting with the Congolese military, such as the risk of these men "appropriating" your vehicle.

Fossey, however, was like a dog with a bone.

Alexander might have changed tack to one of dollars and cents, warning Fossey that she would need to fork over the funds to insure the Land Rover and equipment. She would also have to pay for a visa. And then there was the matter of gifts for the mountain guides required to trek to the Virunga forests.

Fossey was incensed. How many times did she have to tell this man that she had exhausted her funds? Still, she offered up a blank cheque—anything to get to the gorillas.

As Fossey made her way to the Kabara meadow in Virunga National Park in the Democratic Republic of Congo, bouncing along in Great White's Land Rover, she had visions of George Schaller's gorillas dancing through her head.

On October 15, 1963, she arrived at the Traveler's Rest Hotel near the Uganda-Congo-Rwanda border. Alexander would have selected this hotel because it was within hiking distance of the mountain gorillas living on the western slopes of the Virunga volcano chain. The proprietor, a German man named Walter

Baumgartel, was known for being an expert on the local gorillas. Tourists would stop at his hotel to hear news of the elusive creatures. When Fossey arrived, Baumgartel had news to share, indeed: the famed wildlife photographers Joan and Alan Root were currently filming the gorillas on Mount Mikeno for a photographic documentary. The Roots, both twenty-six at the time, had been working in the Congo section of the Virungas for weeks.

Fossey and her sullen guide made their way to Mount Mikeno. To reach the site, they climbed from a small village of thatched huts, hiring eleven porters and two guides. The journey to the camp took six and a half hours, climbing to an altitude of nearly 3,500 metres. Fossey later recalled, "My rib cage was bursting, my legs were creaking and in agony, and my ankle felt as though a crocodile had his jaws around it."

After setting up camp and spending a day unsuccessfully trying to find gorillas, Fossey felt her luck change when, like a dream, Joan and Alan Root emerged from their nearby "rickety" wooden cabin with a tin roof. Fossey described Alan Root as gentle and soft-spoken. He was blond, wore studious, grey plastic-rimmed glasses, and had a stooped posture that Fossey speculated resulted from years of photography. He was born in London but relocated with his family to Kenya when he was a child. His wife, Joan, was born in Nairobi, the daughter of a British banker who had become a coffee planter in Africa. Fossey described Joan Root as made in Alan's image—she, too, wore glasses, and she kept her blonde hair out of her face by shoving it under a baseball cap.

The filmmakers, as Fossey put it, took pity on her and invited her to join them to find the gorillas. Fossey was in awe of Alan and Joan, who knew their way around the terrain. They led her straight up the mountain, where they came across a recently abandoned sleeping site that had belonged to thirteen gorillas.

"Sound preceded sight," Fossey later wrote. "Odour preceded sound in the form of an overwhelming musky-barnyard, humanlike scent. The air was suddenly rent by a high-pitched series of screams followed by the rhythmic rondo of sharp *pok-pok* chest beats from a great silverback male."

The gorilla was hidden behind a thick wall of vegetation. Now hip-deep in a "wet bed of stinging nettles," Fossey took her cues from the Roots. She stood perfectly still until the sounds of the screams and chest beats dissipated.

Alan Root motioned for her to move forward, and Fossey followed as quietly as she could manage until they could peek through the vegetation at the group of "furry-headed primates." It was a group of six adult gorillas, and, for Fossey, it was love at first sight. She wrote that she was "struck by the physical magnificence of the huge jet-black bodies blended against the green palette wash of the thick forest foliage."

As Alan set up his camera and began to film, the sounds caught the gorillas' attention, and they climbed into the trees to get a better look at the strange human creatures. Fossey couldn't take her eyes off the gorillas, noting their every move—the yawns, the branch-breaking, the chest beating. She wrote that she was drawn to the individuality of the gorillas, and the "shyness of their behaviour."

Dian Fossey left Mount Mikeno the next day, but after that encounter with the gorillas, she knew she would find a way to return and "learn more about the gorillas of the misted mountains."

Three years later, in December 1966, after her encounter with Louis Leakey in Kentucky had set the stage for her long-term field study with the gorillas, Fossey returned to Africa. She was headed back to Kabara in the Virungas. At the outset of her trip, it was Joan and Alan Root who once again took her under their wing. By chance, Fossey ran into Joan at the London airport when Joan was paged by the front desk for a call from Alan. Fossey later wrote in her diary that she "flew across the lobby" to greet her friend. When she mentioned she was headed to study the gorillas at Kabara, she could hear Alan's "squawks of incredulity" through the phone. "It was only later that I was to realize how very fortunate this unexpected meeting was for me," she reflected.

Upon arriving in Africa, Joan Root helped Fossey shop for food and camp supplies, sharing her knowledge of equipment like stoves, tents, lights and bedding. Meanwhile, unbeknownst to Fossey, Alan Root had confronted Leakey about his plans to send her to study the gorillas of Kabara. Alan thought the idea was "sheer madness" and made his feelings known to Leakey. He couldn't believe that Leakey was about to send this inexperienced young woman "some seven hundred miles across Africa to the Congo" to carry out the research alone.

Fossey, meanwhile, spent a few days learning how to drive the Land Rover (which she nicknamed "Lily") that Leakey had purchased for her. She was raring to go.

After a two-day sojourn to Gombe to learn about camp organization and data collection from Jane Goodall, Fossey returned to Nairobi. Two days before she was scheduled to embark on her journey to the gorillas, Alan reached out with an offer: he would accompany her to Kabara to make sure she got there and assist with securing the necessary permissions to set up the research camp. In retrospect, Fossey wrote, "It is difficult to see how I could have begun the project at that time without his assistance."

A few days later, Fossey and Alan Root reached the Traveler's Rest Hotel. But they were met with warnings from Walter Baumgartel: the Kivu province was in revolt against the Congolese government. Baumgartel implored Root to persuade Fossey to work with the gorillas on Mount Muhabura instead and wait until things in Congo calmed down.

Root knew how strong-willed Dian Fossey could be. He could not convince her to change her plans but hoped fate would intervene, and the border would be closed.

But the border was open, and Fossey and Root crossed into Congo, in no small part thanks to Alan Root's experience dealing with officials. They arrived at Virunga National Park headquarters, arranged for two camp workers and two armed park guides, hired some porters and set out on the journey up the mountain.

As they climbed, Fossey observed Root instructing the porters to move quietly and keep an eye out for evidence of gorillas. When they arrived at the camp, Root could only stay for two days, so they worked quickly, setting up and looking for gorillas. Even in that short time, Root taught Fossey all he could about how to track gorillas.

On one memorable occasion, they found fresh gorilla tracks. Thrilled, Fossey bolted ahead, eager to follow the apes through the dense foliage, certain she would soon come across the group responsible for the tracks. About five minutes passed before she realized Root had not followed her. She retraced her steps and found him patiently sitting where they had first come across the tracks.

"Dian," he said, "if you are ever going to contact gorillas, you must follow their tracks to where they are going rather than backtrack trails to where they've been."

Fossey later wrote that she never forgot that first lesson in gorilla tracking.

On the eve of Fossey's thirty-fifth birthday, it was time for Alan Root to head home. He did a final check of the camp—inspecting the latrine pit and the rain barrels where they would collect their drinking water—and wished Fossey good luck.

Imposter syndrome hit Dian Fossey immediately, and hard. She wrote of feeling panicked and described clinging to a tent pole, "simply to avoid running after him."

Fossey was alone at camp for four days with just a few other people, all of them Africans who spoke no English. The camp consisted of a seven-by-ten-foot tent that served as her bedroom, office, bath and drying area for her clothes. She had covered a few wooden crates with cloth and piled them in various configurations to function as desks, chairs, cupboards and file cabinets. On the walls, she hung pictures, skins, tusks and horns, and she even made curtains out of some colourful material. The kitchen was in a small wooden building that also housed her local team members. There, Fossey prepared her cuisine, which mainly consisted of hot dogs, Spam, powdered milk and corned beef. Fresh food was only available for a few weeks after Fossey's monthly supply run to a small town at the base of Mount Mikeno.

Just a few moments after Alan Root's departure, one of the men approached Fossey and asked, "*Unapenda maji moto?*"

Drawing a blank on the Swahili she had studied over the past year, Fossey burst into tears and retreated into her tent. Unsure of the meaning of his words and feeling paranoid, she imagined he was threatening her. After an hour of feeling sorry for herself, Fossey began to wonder: how could she be certain he was threatening her? What had those words meant? She worked up the courage to approach him again and asked him to slowly repeat his previous statement.

In her calmer state of mind, Fossey understood: "Do you want hot water?" The man wasn't threatening her but trying to help, to make her more comfortable.

Over the next four days, Fossey was laser-focused on her mission—fieldwork, searching for gorillas. On her first day out, after a ten-minute walk from camp, she spotted a single male gorilla sprawled across a horizontal tree trunk overlooking a small lake, basking in the sun. With her heart in her throat, Fossey reached for her binoculars, but as soon as the gorilla heard the rustling of the binocular case, he bolted and disappeared into the forest. Despite clambering through the forest for the rest of the day, Fossey couldn't find him again.

On her second day, Fossey was joined by a Congolese park guide who was there to help temporarily until her permanent guide and tracker, Sanwekwe, arrived. Fossey had met Sanwekwe in 1963 during her first visit to Kabara. He had been tracking gorillas since he was a boy and had worked for George Schaller, who had observed gorillas in the wild, and Carl Akeley, a naturalist interested in collecting specimens for the American Museum of Natural History. The temporary guide, however, did not appear to have the same experience as Sanwekwe. Fossey's second day in the field was spent wandering aimlessly, finding no signs of gorillas.

On the third day, the aimless wandering appeared to perhaps be a solid strategy.

"Shh, shh," said the tracker, pointing up ahead.

Fossey saw it too—a figure that looked like a gorilla sunbathing a few hundred feet away, across a deep ravine. Her heart in her throat once again, Fossey pulled out her binoculars, notebook, pen and stopwatch. She searched for a better vantage point, finally settling down to watch, content, for about an hour while her guide "quietly snored" behind her.

After an hour of watching the creature sit there and do nothing, Fossey was getting restless. Sure, observing gorillas requires a great deal of patience—she had been ready for this reality—but this was taking the cake. This large individual had been sitting there, inactive, for so long that Fossey's first data sheet was nearly blank.

She told her guide to stay put while she tried to get a better view.

As Fossey got closer to the animal, she suddenly could see clearly that it wasn't a gorilla at all, but a giant forest hog. When the hog spotted her, it slowly rose and slipped away into the forest. A few days later, Fossey came across the creature again, though this time it was just its carcass; it had somehow died, likely of natural causes, she suspected.

Finally, after the fourth day, Sanwekwe arrived at camp. Fossey respected this man immensely, describing him as having "a marvellous sense of humour in addition to being an untiring tracker and a man who cared deeply for the gorillas and other animals of the forest." She knew that having Sanwekwe around would not only make her work with the gorillas easier, it would also quell her loneliness.

Day after day, Fossey and Sanwekwe went out into the cold, misty rainforest, hiking through the rain and along the rugged terrain. With Sanwekwe's help, she found three groups of gorillas within a five-square-kilometre area. She began to observe and learn about the gorillas' social structure.

Back at camp, Fossey typed up detailed notes at her makeshift desk, writing about her encounters with the gorillas. Through her observations, she learned that the gorillas lived in groups ranging from as few as two to as many as twenty individuals. Usually, a group included one large silverback male—silverbacks can weigh up to nearly two hundred kilograms, so we're talking *large*—who was the leader of the group. There would often be one young male—a blackback—and three or four adult females, each about half the size of the silverback. Then there were the young ones—the infants and juvenile gorillas. Once they grew to maturity, these individuals would leave their natal groups, a pattern of behaviour that likely evolved to reduce inbreeding.

For Fossey, those early days with the gorillas must have been both exhilarating and frustrating. She was making observations, yes, but finding it challenging to get up close because the gorillas would flee when they saw her and Sanwekwe. But she persisted.

Though it was tempting to hide behind a tree or a rock so the gorillas wouldn't run away, Fossey opted to remain out in the open as much as possible. Her goal was to get the gorillas used to seeing her, to habituate them to her presence so she could eventually move closer without disturbing them. She even began to imitate their behaviour—scratching and feeding when they did and copying their vocalizations, which she thought indicated contentment: *Naoooom. Naoooom.*

Fossey also mimicked their characteristic style of locomotion. Getting on all fours, she would bear-crawl with her weight on her knuckles. She would sit and groom herself while she nibbled on a stalk of celery. Like an actor studying for a new role, she immersed herself in the world of the gorillas. Fossey became a gorilla.

At the same time, Fossey was learning how to track the gorillas, tutored by Sanwekwe. She learned to recognize broken branches, gorilla knuckle prints in the ground and, of course, dung along the paths. She also got to know the gorillas' smell—a botanical odour reminiscent of a barnyard.

As time went on, the gorillas permitted Fossey to stick around more and more, and she began to identify individuals within the group. She examined the gorillas' noses carefully—a practice she shared with George Schaller, who knows that no two gorillas have the same nostril shape or ridges on the bridge of their noses. It was a perfect trick to tell them apart. Fossey sketched the gorillas in her notebook and gave them names. The first was an older female whom Fossey described as having no nose—she became "No-nose." Then there were Ferdinand, Dora, Hugger, Scapegoat, Popcorn and others. As Fossey grew familiar with the groups, the names she chose reflected each gorilla's personality as much as their physical appearance.

At night, after a satisfying day spent with the gorillas, Fossey would curl up in her cot and listen to the sounds of the forest. In a letter home, she described "the trumpeting of elephants ringing up the gorge between the mountains, the snorting of the buffalo, the chest beating and hooting of lone gorillas, the barks of the duiker, the soft, moaning cry of the tree hyrax" and "the weird cries, hoots, shrieks and laments of the nocturnal birds."

The first few months in Kabara were magical.

Then, on July 9, 1967, at 3:30 p.m., it all came crashing down. Fossey and Sanwekwe had just finished an especially rewarding day with the gorillas, but their hearts must have sunk when they approached their camp and saw what was happening. A group of armed soldiers and porters were waiting for them.

The soldiers informed them that a rebellion was happening in Kivu province in Zaire. They had been instructed by the director of Virunga National Park to escort Fossey off the mountain, and they had a letter to prove it.

Just two days before, the eastern region of Congo had come under siege. European mercenaries serving the rebel leader Moïse Tshombe had taken the cities of Kisangani and Bukavu, and antiwhite sentiment had become widespread. Flights, mail and telephone services had been suspended. The threat of violence loomed.

The director's advice was sound, but Fossey took it as an affront. She, of course, had been living in the bush, falling asleep to the sounds of elephants and owls, and so had not been exposed to the violence that was unfolding. She didn't want to leave her gorillas—not after all the progress she had made—but she didn't have much choice. The next morning, Fossey watched helplessly as the men disassembled her camp. She followed the soldiers and porters down the mountain, considering herself a "refugee" since she couldn't leave Congo until the borders reopened.

The soldiers dropped her off at Rumangabo, where the park headquarters and a military post were located. From her bedroom there, Fossey could see the slopes of Mount Mikeno, where she knew the gorillas were ranging. She had no idea if she would ever climb those slopes again.

By the end of the first week, Fossey began to ask more questions—Why was she being held here? Could she go back to her camp? Overhearing conversations, she learned that a military general would soon be arriving at the army camp, and Fossey had been "earmarked" for him.

Fossey didn't intend to wait around to find out what that meant. She began to plot her escape.

She told the guards she needed to transfer her Land Rover's registration from Kenyan to Zaïroise. But, she said, the $400 in cash she needed for the fee was in Kisoro, Uganda. If the guards could take her there, she could pick up the money and register the vehicle. Fossey knew exactly what she was doing—that much cash was impossible to resist. Then there was the vehicle itself. The soldiers agreed to bring her to Uganda.

Fossey did not rest that night. She loaded her Land Rover with her data, cameras and even the chickens she had acquired. She had given up a small .32 automatic pistol to one of the park guards when they arrived at Rumangabo, but he now brought it back to her, advising her to keep it within reach on the drive, especially when they crossed the Zaire-Uganda border. Fossey shoved the pistol into a half-empty box of tissues tucked away in the open glove compartment.

The next morning, the crew embarked on their journey. At the border, they were met by drunken soldiers and customs officials. Fossey kept her cool as the men snatched the authorization papers and argued among themselves. Ultimately, they concluded that Fossey was a *bumbavu*—an idiot—and harmless. They opened the barricade for Fossey and her "escorts" to pass.

Fossey must have felt overwhelming relief when she was back in familiar territory—just a few minutes away from her friend Walter Baumgartel's hotel, the Traveler's Rest. She screeched into the driveway, bolted out of the vehicle and ran to the hotel's farthest room. She hid under the bedsheets as Baumgartel called the Ugandan military to arrest the Zaïroise soldiers.

That was Fossey's version of the events, at least.

However, according to Fossey's biographer, Farley Mowat, this version of events "was coloured by the writer in her." As for the general? Mowat suggests he might have been imagined by Fossey to "add zest to the story."

Mowat points to two sworn affidavits written by Fossey shortly after the events. According to those accounts, the story begins on June 1, when Fossey was visiting Kisoro on one of her supply runs. There, she was informed by Congolese customs officials that her permit for Lily was due to expire in a week. If she didn't renew it, she would be giving up a $300 bond. But Fossey argued that she had another month, and the officials took her word for it, on the understanding that she would return the next month to pay the fee and fill in the paperwork. But she didn't return, and the "understanding" was soon forgotten. Fossey was in a pickle and eventually drove to the main customs office in Goma to complain. She was told to return to discuss the issue with the chief of customs, who was set to return on July 10.

Fossey returned to camp but was escorted down on July 9 due to safety concerns.

The next day, Fossey asked to go sort out the vehicle problem. She hopped into Lily, headed to the border with a park guide as driver and the bilingual secretary to the park director, who had been told to help her sort things out. When they arrived at the border, the customs officer was drunk. He threatened to seize and impound unregistered Lily. Fossey wasn't having any of it. She jumped into Lily, grabbed the key and sat defiantly behind the steering wheel. The scene escalated, with yelling, cussing and threats to take Fossey to prison. Finally, when the head customs officer produced a document from the capital ordering the military to seize all improperly registered vehicles, Fossey was forced to back down.

Fossey's driver then asked if the officer would take $300 in payment to not seize the vehicle. The catch was that Fossey needed to cross the border to Kisoro to get the money. At first, this sent the man into another rage, but he eventually agreed, on the condition that Fossey leave her passport with him and that one of the Congolese guards accompany them.

Here, the two tales overlap: at the Traveler's Rest, Baumgartel is our hero. With the aid of a captain in the Uganda Rifles, he sent the Congolese guard away and lent Fossey the money she needed to pay for the registration. The next morning, Fossey, with her driver and the bilingual secretary in tow, returned to the border, paid the debt and got her passport back.

Artistic licence aside, there was an undeniable reality to Fossey's situation. Officials warned her that if she attempted to return to Zaire, she would likely be shot on sight. In fact, while Fossey was paying off the registration at the border, Baumgartel and some of his guests had watched, mouths agape, as a light aircraft was nearly shot down by soldiers from both sides of the border before landing at an inactive airstrip near the hotel.

Leakey, who had received a cable from Fossey about her situation when she arrived at the Traveler's Rest, had chartered a flight to bring her back to Nairobi. But Fossey was determined to stay in Kabara. She reasoned with the park director that she had never received an official military order forbidding her to stay. The director agreed to let her go back, and she returned to the park headquarters and arranged to bring her equipment back up to Kabara. But just as she was about to head off, a telegram arrived from the military camp: under no circumstances should Fossey be allowed back up that mountain.

A more-than-frustrated Fossey returned to Goma to appeal but was informed it would be two to four months, or even more, before she could go back. Still unwilling to accept her fate, she stayed at the park headquarters and sulked for a few more days. Now, she really did feel trapped, like a prisoner. Finally, on July 26,

Dian Fossey accepted her reality. She packed up her equipment, loaded up Lily and hit the road toward Kisoro.

Once again, she was stopped at the border. She offered a bribe to get through but didn't have the cash with her. Once again, she was told she would need to take one of the guards across with her and return with the promised money.

Here again, the two versions of this story overlap. Upon arrival at the hotel, a sweaty Fossey bolted out of the vehicle and ran past Baumgartel. Baumgartel confronted the Congolese soldier, who was under orders to bring Fossey back with him, along with the money she had promised. Baumgartel stood firm.

"Miss Fossey is not your prisoner," he said, according to Mowat. "She is going to stay here. If she wants to return, I shall tie her to that tree out there."

The next, day, the American ambassador arrived to take Fossey to the embassy in Kigali and then to Nairobi, where Leakey was waiting.

At the embassy, Fossey was asked to prepare an affidavit about her treatment by the Congolese. When asked whether she had been "ill-treated or physically abused," Fossey replied, "I was cussed out in French and Congolese. And a soldier tried to pull me out of my car but didn't make it. No, I was not abused."

Mowat points out that there is a "widely circulated" version of Fossey's story in which she was raped by the Congolese soldiers—some accounts even describe it as a gang attack. Yet, Mowat noted that the record of events Fossey wrote just a few days after the incident "makes no reference to rape, attempted rape, or indeed to assault of any kind." What's more, "Dian herself consistently and vehemently denied the story." Mowat dismissed the rape narrative as a "racist and salacious" myth.

But, just like the sequence of events itself, the truth is nearly impossible to decipher. The website Encyclopedia.com published claims that Fossey confided in her close acquaintances that she had been raped. This source attributes Houghton Mifflin editor Anita McClellan as saying that Fossey kept her mouth shut because she worried that if anyone knew what she had truly experienced they would have sent her home. In her 2006 biography *Gorilla Dreams: The Legacy of Dian Fossey*, Georgianne Nienaber wrote about the event, insisting that Fossey used language characteristic of post-traumatic stress disorder and had told friends and colleagues that the Congolese militia had caged her, urinated on her and, yes, raped her.

This version of events is also found in the pages of Dale Peterson's biography of Jane Goodall, in which he wrote that Goodall had heard about Fosssey being "taken down to park headquarters at Rumangabo, imprisoned, and 'earmarked' as she later phrased it, for the personal attentions of an important military general. She was put on display in a cage, urinated and spat upon, and probably raped."

In a 2010 article published in *Biography*, Gillian Whitlock considers Fossey's story in the context of "feminist engagements with the 'distant suffering' of victims of rape warfare" and the "ongoing presence of mourning and violence in central Africa." She writes that the "possibility that Fossey herself was a victim of rape warfare is a reminder that in 1967, as in 2009, women are subjected to violent assault, that militia who act with impunity have now traumatized generations of women in the Kivu region."

We may never know the full truth of what took place. What is clear is that whatever happened was not about to deter Fossey from her mission with the gorillas. After meeting with the embassy, she flew back to Nairobi, where she was met at the airport by a welcome and smiling face—Louis Leakey.

The two discussed her situation. Should she work on the lowland gorillas in West Africa? Or perhaps study the orangutans in Asia? Leakey needed someone to go to Indonesia.

But Fossey was set on going back to the Virungas—back to her gorillas. When they called the local American Embassy, however, they were told it would be impossible for her to go back to Rwanda; she would be "immediately extradited to Zaire as an escaped prisoner."

Leakey asked Fossey to leave the room while he and the embassy representatives engaged in a heated debate for more than an hour, their animated voices echoing down the hallway. Fossey wrote that, when Leakey finally emerged, he had "a sparkling twinkle in his eyes" that told her everything she needed to know.

Within a few weeks, Fossey was back on the Rwandan side of the Virunga volcanoes, searching for and setting up a new campsite from which to study her beloved gorillas.

When Dian Fossey met one five-year-old gorilla in September 1967, it was love at first sight. She described the young male, whom she named Digit because of his twisted middle finger, as "a bright-eyed, inquisitive ball of fluff."

Fossey's research on gorillas in their natural habitat had been rough going, embroiled in the complex politics that characterized eastern Africa at the time. But with the help of Louis Leakey, she had regrouped and rebuilt her camp on the Rwandan side of the mountains. She called her camp Karisoke after the two volcanic peaks nearby—Mount Karisimbi and Mount Bisoke.

"Right in the heart of central Africa, so high up that you shiver more than you sweat, are great, old volcanoes towering up almost fifteen thousand feet, and nearly covered with rich, green rain forest—the Virungas," Fossey wrote. She set up her camp ten thousand feet up the chain of extinct volcanoes.

Not long after she arrived, Fossey discovered that the area was frequented by local herders and poachers. The herders drove their animals through the meadow, and the poachers hunted, using bows and arrows and setting snare traps.

On her first day in Karisoke, Fossey met two poachers who offered to show her the location of a gorilla family just forty-five minutes from camp. Fossey was torn—on one hand, she was desperate to see the gorillas, but on the other, her instincts and love of animals told her to drive the poachers away. In the end, her desire to see gorillas won the day, and she followed the men, but she warned them that from now on, there would be no more cattle herding or poaching in "her" part of the park. These were the park rules, and Fossey intended to enforce them to their full extent.

Rosamond Carr, a fifty-three-year-old American expatriate who lived near the Virungas and had become a close friend and confidant to Fossey, implored her not to take such a hard line with these men. Carr understood the complexities surrounding the poaching—the local people were impoverished, with few options for making a living. Many lived in squalor with minimal prospects.

Fossey argued that the poachers' snares could harm the gorillas, and some even intentionally killed gorillas, making grisly souvenirs out of their body parts—creating ashtrays from their hands and mounting their heads to sell as trophies. The herders, according to Fossey, were only marginally better—they kept more cattle than they needed, devastating the habitat and crushing plants that the gorillas depended on for food.

In 1959, George Schaller estimated that the entire Virunga mountain gorilla population—confined to about 450 square kilometres in three parks along the borders of Rwanda, Uganda and the Democratic Republic of Congo—amounted to just 450 individuals. By 1978, based on Fossey's census of the gorilla population, the population had plummeted to 260.

Now contrast those numbers to the human population. The Virunga Mountains are located near areas where rural human populations are some of the densest in the world. Fossey wrote that Rwanda is "one-eighth the size of Kenya and smaller than the state of Maryland" but contained "4.7 million people, a population expected to double by the end of the century." And indeed, it did: by 2019, Rwanda's population was estimated at 12.63 million.

The high human densities are the biggest threat to the mountain gorillas due to habitat destruction and poaching. As Fossey noted, Rwanda was one of the poorest countries in the world, and people relied on the land for survival. Agricultural practices like subsistence farming and cattle grazing force the gorillas farther and farther up into the mountains. Soon, they will run out of places to retreat, which is why gorillas are now listed as "Critically Endangered" by the International Union for Conservation of Nature.

Fossey made it her mission—often resorting to extreme measures, including doling out physical punishments to poachers—to save the "furry-headed primates" with "bright eyes" and "huge jet-black bodies." For Fossey, the plight of the gorillas was deeply personal—the gorillas were more than study subjects to her. They were her friends.

Fossey was taken with Digit and the other members of his group right away. The group quickly accepted her presence, and they soon became a favourite for her to spend time with. Digit showed a strong affinity for humans, especially Fossey, which she attributed to the group dynamics—Digit was too old to play with the younger members, yet too young to associate with the older females. Over the years, Fossey observed that "Digit really looked forward to the daily contacts with Karisoke's observers as a source of entertainment." She and Digit would often sit together on the periphery of the group, grooming each other. Digit was always the first to approach visiting humans and would "invite" Fossey to play with him by "flopping over onto his back, waving stumpy legs in the air."

Despite her attempts to remain scientifically objective, Fossey became emotionally attached to Digit. During her lectures in the United States, she would refer to him as "my friend, Digit."

From the start, Fossey had mixed feelings about habituating gorillas to humans. She knew poaching was a major threat to the survival of her Karisoke gorillas, and it was where she focused her conservation efforts. She hired African guides—some of them even former poachers—to help her track the gorillas, but she restricted habituation to white people only.

"Gorillas have known Africans only as poachers in the past," she wrote. "The second that it takes a gorilla to determine if an African is friend or foe is the second that might cost the animal its life from a spear, arrow or bullet."

When it came to bushmeat, Fossey knew the poachers set snares for antelope, hyrax and other game. Even though these snares weren't meant for gorillas, the animals would sometimes get caught in the wire nooses and, although they could usually struggle free, the snares would often leave the gorillas injured for life, sometimes resulting in death.

Poachers also directly targeted the gorillas. For example, they deliberately captured infant gorillas—killing the rest of the family in the process—for the international pet trade. The demand for baby gorillas was driven by private foreign zoos, and an infant could earn a whopping 86,000 pounds on the black market. Unfortunately, there was also a demand from Western tourists for gorilla body parts as trophies.

On February 24, 1969, Fossey received an urgent message from her doctor friend: a young gorilla had been captured by poachers six weeks earlier and was now confined to a small wire cage in the office of the national park's Rwandese conservator. Fossey immediately rushed down the mountain, hopped in Lily the Land Rover and drove to the "rambling old barrack buildings" that made up the park offices.

It didn't take her long to locate the young gorilla. When she arrived, she spotted a crowd of people, many of them children, gathered in the garage behind the buildings. They were laughing and pointing at a "coffin-like" wooden box with a bolted door that had been shoved between a sparkling new Land Rover and a stack of wood. Fossey noticed a wire cage on the ground nearby.

She knew immediately that there was some poor creature in the box, though she didn't want to believe it. She pushed through the mob of children and released the door of the wooden box. The captive, a three-year-old male gorilla, hurled itself toward her, shrieking in fear. This scene further delighted the crowd, and Fossey quickly shut the door and arranged to have the box brought into the conservator's room. There, she opened the door again—once more, the baby gorilla hurled itself forward, this time managing to bite the conservator's leg. The frightened gorilla ran to the windows, where the crowds had now gathered, and began banging on the glass with such force that Fossey was afraid the windows would shatter. Eventually, she filled an ashtray with water and lured the poor creature back into the box.

When things calmed down, Fossey, still incensed, grilled the conservator: "What's the meaning of this?"

The conservator, doing his best to remain calm, explained he had recently met some Germans who wanted a mountain gorilla for the Cologne Zoo. In return for his trouble, they had gifted him with a brand-new Land Rover and promised a large sum of money for conservation work in the park and a free flight to Cologne. The conservator had hired a poacher to capture the infant gorilla, and Fossey learned later that in their effort to capture this one infant, ten group members had been killed.

Unfortunately, this scenario was par for the course when great apes were captured. Poachers would approach a group of gorillas and kill any of the adults who tried to protect the infant they were attempting to steal. The poachers would then sell the meat in the bushmeat trade, profiting even further.

Although Fossey was seeing the tail end of capture for zoos—which began to die down in the 1970s—the illegal capture and trade of great apes, including gorillas, for pets continued to be widespread. Between 2005 and 2011, more than 22,000 wild great apes died because of the illegal pet trade.

Fossey told the conservator she would be taking the baby gorilla back with her.

It was a miracle that the infant was still alive within the box—even the conservator was worried he wouldn't survive. The baby had been tied onto bamboo poles by his arms and legs, kept for two weeks in a tiny wire cage, and then transferred to the wooden box where he was fed corn, bananas, bread and soup. By the time Fossey arrived, the gorilla was suffering greatly from malnourishment, dehydration and infected wounds from the wires.

In truth, the conservator was probably relieved that Fossey had shown up—it was obvious the gorilla would most certainly die en route to Germany in its current condition.

"Once he is healthy, you will bring him back, and I will send him to Germany," the conservator said. Fossey didn't bother arguing.

She sent word to her staff in Karisoke to convert the storeroom of her cabin into a gorilla nursery. They nailed wire mesh over the windows—Fossey didn't want another scene like the one in the conservator's office—and installed a wire door between her room and the storeroom. They covered the floor with mounds of vegetation for nesting and food.

Meanwhile, Fossey knew the gorilla urgently needed liquids, vitamins and glucose. Before she could go back to camp, she would have to go to town to get supplies. She loaded the wooden box and its inhabitant into her Land Rover and made her way to the home of a European couple that lived close to the park boundary. There, she managed to transfer the gorilla into a child's playpen and nail it shut.

"The stressful transfer from one container to the other was accompanied by the infant's bellows and combined rage and fear," Fossey later wrote.

Fossey fed the infant bits of vine and thistle and spent a fitful night next to the pen. She hashed out a plan to release the gorilla back into the wild after nursing it back to health, and she knew just the group to accommodate the young gorilla. She also came up with a name: Coco, after an old female in that group who had recently died of natural causes.

The next day, Fossey coordinated the long trip back to camp with the gorilla. She hired eight porters, who took turns carrying the playpen. When they arrived and Fossey checked out her newly converted storeroom, she was pleased—it was a "facsimile of a gorilla habitat."

All of Fossey's attention was now focused on young Coco and returning him to health. During the first week, she monitored his feeding habits and gave him milk laced with vitamins. There was one rough patch on the third day when Coco stopped eating and his stool became bloody. Fossey started him on antibiotics, but his health continued to decline. She worried he wouldn't make it and brought him into her bed, assuming she would wake up to find him dead in her arms. She was thrilled when Coco not only made it through the night but also appeared improved in the morning.

Then, on March 4—just a week into Coco's rehabilitation—a group of porters arrived at Fossey's camp carrying what looked like an "oversized beer barrel suspended between long poles."

The head porter gave Fossey a note from a friend.

"Dian," it read. "They've captured another gorilla. They want you to take care of it, but I didn't know how to send it up to you, so I improvised this thing. Hope all is going well with the first. Doubt this one will survive either."

Fossey was in shock—another gorilla? Had the conservator arranged for this captive as a backup for the Cologne Zoo?

If it was possible, this young female gorilla—whom Fossey estimated to be about four and a half years old—was more skittish than Coco had been. Fossey opened the barrel in Coco's room and observed quietly from her own room until, eventually, the two infants reached out to each other. The new gorilla was emaciated and had devastating wounds on her head, wrists and ankles, likely from being bound by wire. Fossey named this gorilla Pucker, for her morose, pursed-lip expression.

It took weeks, but Fossey somehow nursed the two baby gorillas back to health. She began bringing them on small excursions into the forest to get them used to being in their natural habitat.

With the gorillas now healthy, Fossey began to worry about their fate. She wrote letters to the mayor of Cologne and the Cologne Zoo, imploring them not to import these gorillas.

It wasn't long before the conservator arrived at camp. He told Fossey that the gorillas were expected in Kigali on April 4 and were scheduled to depart for Germany the next day. The conservator even had the audacity to ask her to handle the exportation details.

Fossey tried to buy some time, telling the conservator that the gorillas weren't well enough to travel. She was hoping that if she had a few more weeks, she'd be able to pressure the Rwandan authorities to consider an alternative.

Unfortunately for her, just at that moment, the two gorillas appeared, deep in play, chasing and wrestling each other. They were clearly healthy and happy.

The conservator, claiming he was being pressured by the Cologne Zoo, threatened Fossey: if she didn't agree to release these two gorillas, they would capture two more.

Fearing the additional bloodshed that would certainly result from another capture, Fossey folded. She cabled the Cologne Zoo officials: she would release the gorillas once they were well enough for the journey.

A few weeks later, Fossey lovingly built travel crates for the infants. On May 3, the two baby gorillas were sent by jetliner to Cologne, where they arrived safely.

The day they left, Fossey took to the forest. "There is no way to describe the pain of their loss," she reflected in her memoir.

In 1978, nine years after their arrival at the Cologne Zoo, Coco and Pucker died suddenly—both from congenital immune system defects—within a month of each other.

Ten years into her study of the Karisoke gorillas, tensions between Fossey and the local poachers had escalated. Fossey's hard-headedness in the beginning quickly transitioned into full-on warrior mode.

She referred to her approach as "active conservation," and boy, was it active. The feminist scholar Donna Haraway has described Fossey's tactics, perhaps more aptly, as "anarchist direct action." Fossey funded a team of anti-poaching patrollers who set out daily, cutting traps and releasing animals from snares.

Fossey would also capture and interrogate poachers. She kept a collection of Halloween masks she would use for a "black magic" routine. She knew the locals wore amulets as protection from evil, and took advantage of those cultural beliefs. She wanted to build an image of herself as a witch to scare off the poachers.

Her tactics soon escalated beyond theatrics.

In the spring of 1977, park guards brought her a poacher, and Fossey happily paid them $120 for their efforts. The guards told her they would turn the man over to park officials. But just as the men departed, one of her African staff turned to her and asked, "Why did you let them leave?" He filled her in on their scheme: the guards had met the poacher at a village bar and cooked up a plan to get paid.

Enraged, Fossey drove to the village to find the poacher and turn him in. By the time she arrived at his home, he had disappeared, leaving five wives and several children behind. Fossey searched the hut for his gun, and when she couldn't find it, she tore matting from the walls, then dragged the matting outside and set the pile on fire. Next, she turned her attention to his wives, demanding they turn over his weapon and even grabbing one of the children—a four-year-old boy. Fossey threatened to harm the child if the wives didn't obey. Terrified, the women fled, leaving the boy with Fossey.

According to one of Fossey's students, the even-keeled Ian Redmond, the boy stayed with Fossey's team for several days, living in Redmond's cabin, happily "eating and playing with toys he was given, becoming completely at home."

Ultimately, the poacher obtained a legal judgment against Fossey, and she was forced to release the boy and pay a $600 fine.

The tensions between Fossey and the local people escalated even further on January 1, 1978, when her head tracker, Nemeye, returned to camp with news that he had not been able to locate Digit's group. By this time, Digit had developed into a large silverback, but he never lost his gentle, trusting nature. Nemeye had tracked the group and found that their trail crossed with those of buffalo, elephants, poachers and dogs. Most concerning: he had found "a great deal of blood along the trails."

The next day, Nemeye and Ian Redmond headed out in search of the group. A few hours into their search, they came across a patch of flattened vegetation covered in liquid gorilla dung—there was no doubt that the group had been there, and the diarrhea indicated that they had fled in fright. Redmond backtracked to see if he could determine what had scared the group. A few metres in, he nearly tripped over the crushed body of a dog.

Then he spotted something else. A large, black mound with flies buzzing around it.

As his eyes focused, his heart sank. It was the giant corpse of a gorilla. The large male's stomach and chest were gashed with spear wounds, and his head and arms were chopped off.

Redmond ran back to camp, where he found an unsuspecting Fossey, who had been enjoying the warmth of the day.

"Dian, it's Digit," Redmond said, breathing heavily. "He's been murdered."

From that moment on, Fossey wrote, she lived "within an insulated part" of herself. She described Digit as having been killed "in service," a hero trying to protect the rest of his group from the poachers—fending them off so his family could flee. She painted Digit as a father figure, a protector—unlike any father she had ever known. Fossey saw to it that Digit's body was buried in front of her cabin.

Out of the tragedy, Fossey launched the Digit Fund. She described it as offering "personal incentive on a one-to-one basis with individual Africans, not only to take pride in their park but also to assume personally some of the responsibility toward the protection of their heritage." She planned to use the fund to expand the anti-poacher foot patrols. Fossey felt strongly that there was a need for further enforcement of anti-poaching laws and other long-term conservation efforts. With only about two hundred mountain gorillas left in the wild at that time, she knew the issue was not just important, it was urgent. As she put it, "It only takes one trap, one bullet to kill a gorilla."

An iconic photograph of Dian Fossey, taken by English wildlife photographer and filmmaker Robert Campbell, tells the story of her relationship with the gorillas. Campbell had been sent by National Geographic to get photos and film footage of Fossey and the gorillas. He had been working with Richard Leakey at Koobi Fora, a set of paleoanthropological sites in northern Kenya. Campbell, whom friends knew as Bob, was the son of a British soldier and lived in Nairobi. He was a quiet, unassuming man, but he had a great deal of credibility, having tracked and filmed animals in their natural habitats for fourteen years.

The famous photograph was taken in early January 1970. Fossey and Campbell had set out that morning to find one of the groups of gorillas. Fossey was leaving for England the next day to work on her PhD and was looking for a day to remember. They found the group feeding in a shallow ravine and hunkered down on a fallen tree to watch. It wasn't long before one of the juveniles in the group, whom Fossey had named Peanuts, headed toward the two human observers.

As Fossey described it, Peanuts was "wearing his 'I want to be entertained' expression." She left her perch on the tree trunk and pretended to eat some vegetation while Peanuts watched intently. She lay back in the foliage and extended her hand, palm up. Peanuts looked at her hand and extended his own to touch his fingers against it—just for an instant—before scurrying off to rejoin his group, beating his chest in excitement. Campbell managed to capture that moment, and the photograph of Fossey holding a juvenile gorilla's hand made its way into *National Geographic* magazine across a two-page spread.

When he'd first arrived at Karisoke in 1968, Bob Campbell was almost forty years old. He covered his bald spot with a beret. Partway through giving Campbell a tour of camp, Fossey received a telegram from her stepmother, Kathryn: Fossey's father, George, had committed suicide.

Upon learning this devastating news, Fossey turned to Campbell for comfort, and he listened with great sympathy. "Bob is so kind," she wrote in her diary. "He listens but doesn't speak about such things in an embarrassing way."

Campbell held down the fort at Karisoke while Fossey went to America for her father's funeral. When she returned, she was impressed to find everything running smoothly. Campbell shrugged off the praise. For him, this kind of work was second nature. He was only doing his job.

Campbell was scheduled to leave camp after Fossey returned, but the two kept in touch through letters.

In February 1969, Fossey received a letter from Campbell saying that National Geographic would fund him to return to Karisoke for at least a year to continue photographing her and the gorillas. As it turned out, he arrived back in Karisoke just in time to help Fossey prepare to send her beloved orphaned gorillas, Coco and Pucker, to Germany—and, of course, he made sure to take some photographs.

A pattern was emerging: Campbell was there for Fossey during her times of need. He was sharing in the magic of the gorillas too. He and Fossey would spend hours in the forest with the gorillas, her scribbling research notes while he snapped photographs.

Still, the two did not develop romantic feelings for one another. Fossey had a tough and abrasive demeanour and, according to journalist Harold Hayes, Campbell wasn't her type anyway. Hayes interviewed Campbell and learned that he also wasn't attracted to Fossey—and why. For one thing, she wasn't easy to work with, and he constantly felt as though he was being scrutinized. Although he acknowledged that Fossey "could transform herself into a startlingly attractive woman" when she was off the mountains, he also said that sometimes it was difficult to make her look good in photos, and sometimes she simply "looked terrible."

Yikes.

Fossey's role, it appeared, wasn't just to study the gorillas but, as a poster child for National Geographic, to also look good while she was at it.

As someone who has lived and worked in remote areas of Madagascar and Belize, conducting scientific fieldwork through rain, heat and bugs, I can definitively say that looking good in the field was low on my list of priorities. I was more concerned with keeping my feet dry to avoid contracting "jungle rot," a tropical skin ulcer caused by infections from microorganisms. (And yes, it looks as bad as it sounds.) If you are a woman—or any person—considering entering the field of primatology, rather than spending hours in front of a mirror, I suggest spending that time with primates instead. I promise it is much more rewarding, and the primates could care less whether the human observer standing under their sleeping tree is fashionable.

Fossey, I like to think, didn't give a second thought to her looks either. After all, she was too busy solving problems.

During this time, a new student assistant from San Diego, Michael Burkhart, arrived at camp. Burkhart, bearded and burly like a lumberjack, had arrived during a period of pure chaos: Fossey's dog Cindy had been kidnapped—something that had happened in the past due to her ongoing battle with the poachers—and some of her slide transparencies from Congo had been lost in the mail. Her cabin had also recently been broken into; all her money was stolen along with the jewellery her recently deceased father had left her.

"Somebody stole my jewellery. Get out of my way," Fossey said when Burkhart arrived—at least that's his account of the events.

After he had been just a few days in Karisoke, Fossey sent Burkhart to the other side of the mountain—on his own—to count gorillas for her census. Soon after, she got word from her porters about "the young man's activities, many of which were not related to census work." To Leakey, she wrote that he "spent all his time sleeping, tinkering with his camera and radio, and taking trips."

To journalist Harold Hayes, Burkhart later admitted that he didn't agree with the methods being used for the census. He couldn't fathom why Fossey would count the gorilla feces, and he believed the work could be done faster by tracking the gorillas with the poachers' dogs and following them by motorcycle. He planted a garden where he grew "killer black Congo marijuana" and complained he wasn't getting enough food.

The situation came to a head when, according to Burkhart, he decided to hike to Karisoke to hash it out with Fossey. He told Hayes she was "drunk and belligerent," and their argument escalated. In his own interview with Hayes, Bob Campbell defended Fossey. According to Campbell, Fossey wasn't drinking in those days, and she was certainly never drunk. He told Hayes that Fossey called Burkhart back to camp, and asked Campbell to tell him he was fired. "With me there, he just had to back down because he wasn't prepared to go at the two of us," Campbell said.

Back in Nairobi, Burkhart gave Leakey his version of the events. "Dian is having a mental breakdown," he said. "She's ruining the gorilla study." He went on to pitch Leakey his ideas about getting more publicity for the gorilla study and finding ways to get medicine to the local residents to help ease the harms of poverty and overcrowding.

Loyal to Fossey, Leakey brushed Burkhart off, and officially removed him from the project. Burkhart headed to Israel, where, Hayes wrote, he "spent some time in a kibbutz, trying to calm his rattled nerves."

Bob Campbell's help with the Burkhart situation shifted their relationship. Fossey was falling for him, but it wasn't simple—Campbell had a wife, Heather, back in Nairobi.

Fossey and Campbell didn't speak of Campbell's wife or his life in Nairobi, though Fossey may have wondered about it. She began dyeing her hair—she was thirty-eight and had started to get a few greys. She cooked him elaborate meals on special occasions like his birthday. She even took on small domestic projects, such as sewing curtains for his cabin.

One night, Fossey was lying in bed, feeling especially lonely. She walked out of her hut and over to Campbell's tent. She woke him up and made advances. Campbell resisted.

Fossey returned to her hut in a "huff," according to Campbell. More likely, she was humiliated by the rejection. The next morning, she glossed over the incident, claiming she had only visited his tent to thank him for his help.

Over the next three years, Campbell frequently came up and down the mountain to and from Karisoke. Fossey missed him greatly when he was away.

As Campbell remembers: "We had some pleasant, wide-ranging talks, as I recall—until, on one occasion Dian again decided to make love to me, and I did not resist."

As the romance progressed, they spoke about Campbell ending his ten-year marriage. Each time Campbell went down the mountain, he promised Fossey he would break things off with his wife. Yet every time he returned, the task remained unaccomplished. His wife had no idea he was seeing Fossey romantically. Still, the affair continued.

"She and I retained our independence, kept to our separate establishments, cooked and ate on our own. For me it was not an affair of the heart," said Campbell. "I did not fall in love with her."

In late November 1971, Fossey got pregnant. It was Campbell's. "You can't be a 'cover girl' for *National Geographic* magazine and be pregnant," Fossey would later say.

She didn't tell Campbell about the pregnancy. Instead, she sought an abortion from a doctor across the border in Congo.

The procedure did not go smoothly: "I swallowed my tongue during surgery and was turning purple before it came up," Fossey later wrote of the ordeal. She spent several days recovering at Rosamond Carr's home before heading back to camp, despite her friend's protests.

When Fossey reached the base of the mountain, she began to hemorrhage. Campbell later found her lying in bed. By then she had confessed what had happened, but she didn't let on how bad things were. She sent a note to the hospital requesting pills. When her porter returned with the medication, he also passed along a note from the doctor imploring Fossey to come down for proper treatment. Fossey ignored it, insisting she needed to stay at camp and that the pills would work.

The pills didn't work.

On the fourth day, Campbell left for Nairobi but was deeply concerned about Fossey. He spoke with her doctor, who confirmed just how bad Fossey's condition was. Campbell immediately sent ten porters up to bring Fossey down. They carried her down the mountain to the hospital, where her doctor performed emergency surgery. Once Campbell received reassurance that Fossey would be okay, he headed to Nairobi for a break from the gorilla project.

In January 1972, after being away for forty-two days (Fossey kept track, according to Farley Mowat), Campbell arrived once more at Karisoke. Though their romance continued, something felt off to Fossey. While running errands in town, she received a letter from a friend who, knowing nothing of her romance, mentioned that Bob Campbell would "soon be leaving Karisoke." When Fossey confronted him, Campbell confirmed it. Still, neither could let go of their affair—at least not while they were still up near the magical Virunga volcanoes. Their relationship continued until late March, when Campbell left for two weeks to go back to Nairobi, leaving Fossey with declarations of love.

He returned three days later than he had promised.

Then, on May 29, 1972, Campbell finally left Karisoke for good, marking the end of their love affair.

Fossey wrote: "'I love you, Dian—I just don't know how to say it.' Bob told me this today while he was crying, crying, crying. I told him I wanted him to be happy and he hid his head and cried and cried."

Just two weeks before her death, Fossey trekked down the mountain in her worn brown leather boots to Rwanda's capital city to renew her visa. It was a process that had become a point of immense frustration. Without her visa, she couldn't continue her work with the mountain gorillas, and she had to renew it every two months; she would slog down the mountain to Kigali and spend days waiting in the office of tourism to get the letter she needed.

This time, however, fate was on her side. After a day of dealing with rigid officials unwilling to help her with her permits, she stopped at the hotel bar for a drink. There, she met the editor of a local paper who had written about her work in Karisoke. He recommended that she leverage any connections she had to get a meeting with someone who had political authority. Following his advice, Fossey visited the secretary general in charge of immigration and explained her logistical nightmare in obtaining the necessary permits and visas.

"Why did you not come and tell me all of this before, Dian?" he asked. "You are one of our cherished guests and can stay in Rwanda as long as you wish." He helped her with a special visa authorizing her to stay in Rwanda for two years. As he handed it to her, he laughed and said, "The next one will be for ten years if you want it!"

Fossey was over the moon as she headed back up the mountain, a huge weight lifted off her shoulders.

Two weeks later, she was dead.

Dian Fossey's murder remains unsolved. Fossey would be the first to admit she had a lot of enemies—it's why she owned guns. Locals had nicknamed her *Nyiramachabelli*, meaning "the woman who lives alone in the forest." Since the day she arrived at Karisoke, she had been at war with the poachers and cattle herders. She did not get along with Rwandan government officials. And there was nothing she wouldn't do for her gorillas, including resorting to violence and kidnapping.

Before she was murdered, Fossey's cabin had been locked, so it's believed that her killer had come in through the wall, ripping off a section of corrugated metal from the southeast corner of her bedroom. The hole was in a spot that wasn't blocked by a bed or other furniture, which could indicate that the person who made it knew the layout of her bedroom.

Another hypothesis has the killer gaining entry to Fossey's cabin because she had let them in—perhaps it was someone she knew. The metal siding could have been removed following the murder to make it look as though entry had been forced.

The cabin was ransacked, but nothing was taken—it wasn't a robbery. The killer left behind Fossey's money, jewellery and thousands of dollars in camera equipment.

The use of a panga as a murder weapon gave weight to the idea that Fossey had been killed by poachers. Many who knew her and her interactions with the local poachers believed this to be the case. Kelly Stewart, a former student, has said of Fossey, "She viewed herself as this warrior fighting an enemy who was out to get her. It was a perfect ending."

A diplomatic Jane Goodall recorded a message for Fossey's memorial at National Geographic, stating: "It's probably true that Dian chose wrongly when she decided to take the law into her own hands, to try to fight the poachers by herself."

Rwandan police searched Fossey's house for clues but did not collect forensic evidence—no fingerprints, no blood samples. Although the camp was filled with trackers, no one thought to follow the footprints leading to Fossey's cabin. Where had they come from?

A French doctor was called up the mountain for the coroner's report, but he decided there was no need for an autopsy. The cause of death was obvious: a machete to the face. Others have since pointed out that it would have been useful to know whether there was alcohol, drugs or poison in her blood.

At least the police examined the hair Fossey was clutching. They determined it belonged to a white person, but it wasn't analyzed for DNA. It could have been Fossey's own hair or that of her attacker.

Fossey's assistant, Wayne McGuire, stayed at Karisoke for six months following her murder, hoping—perhaps somewhat foolishly—to complete his research despite a murderer being on the loose. Unfortunately for McGuire, the Rwandan authorities did not wish to accept the idea that poachers had killed Fossey out of revenge. They believed it was an inside job, carried out by someone who was familiar with Karisoke. During their investigation, they arrested the entire Karisoke staff, as well as one individual, Emmanuel Rwelekana, who had been fired several months earlier. Most of the staff were cleared, but not Rwelekana. The police charged Rwelekana and McGuire with Dian Fossey's murder. Rwelekana was later found dead in prison, reportedly having hanged himself.

This left McGuire accused of murdering Fossey so he could get a leg up in the cutthroat world of academia by stealing her precious papers and data. Knowing what I know about academia, this theory does not ring true. So what if McGuire did get his hands on Fossey's data? How could he possibly expect to murder her in such a brutal fashion and then turn around and publish data about the gorillas that was obviously not his own? There's no way anyone familiar with the academic world could expect such a convoluted scheme to work.

McGuire, having caught wind of the authorities' theory, fled to the United States just weeks before the charges were laid. In December 1986, he was tried in absentia, convicted of Dian Fossey's murder, and sentenced to death by firing squad if he ever returned to Rwanda.

Today, most believe that Fossey's murder was an act of revenge. In 2001, a new suspect with a strong motive emerged: Protais Zigiranyirazo, known as "Monsieur Z," was the governor of Ruhengeri province in Rwanda when Fossey was working there. This man is alleged to have played a role in planning the 1994 Rwandan genocide, which resulted in the deaths of 800,000 Tutsis and moderate

Hutus. He was also allegedly involved in illegal trading of endangered species and was rumoured to have operated a network of poachers. There is evidence that Fossey was threatening to expose him. With her visa renewed and a promise to be able to continue to renew it without further hassle, Fossey was not going anywhere, which meant that, eventually, she might indeed expose Monsieur Z and his ring of poachers. In 2008, the International Criminal Tribunal for Rwanda found Zigiranyirazo guilty of genocide and extermination as a crime against humanity, and he was sentenced to twenty years in prison. However, in 2017, the Appeals Chamber reversed this conviction and set Zigiranyirazo free. He was never tried for Fossey's murder.

Dian Fossey left behind a dark and complex legacy as a primatologist. While she is celebrated for her pioneering research on mountain gorillas and her tireless efforts to save these primates from extinction, many of her conservation tactics are now viewed as questionable or even downright inhumane to the people who were affected by her actions. What she called "active conservation" could effectively amount to psychological torture and destruction.

We have learned a lot since Dian Fossey's time. Most primatologists now believe that working with local communities—engaging and empowering them to care for and protect the animals in their own countries—is much more effective in the long term. This approach, known as community conservation, seeks to benefit both humans and wildlife. It is now being proposed for the conservation of the Virunga mountain gorillas.

Ecotourism is one element of this strategy, and it has had a positive impact on the mountain gorillas. The idea is that these ventures, which involve guides bringing small groups of tourists to view the mountain gorillas, will benefit the local economy as those visitors spend their dollars. Aside from the economic benefits, ecotourism also raises public awareness about the wildlife.

However, even this method of conservation is not without complications. In some cases, those tourist dollars seem to only benefit local government and private businesses, leaving the residents feeling left behind. Some communities in Virunga National Park, for example, don't see themselves as benefiting from tourism, so there is no incentive for them to support these efforts.

Then there are the health concerns. Because humans and gorillas are so closely related, contact between the two species can lead to the spread of disease, including parasites, respiratory disease and Ebola. In fact, for a time, respiratory disease was the second most common cause of death among the mountain gorillas of the Virungas. For that reason, precautions must be taken. Many gorilla tourism sites require a seven-metre distance between humans and gorillas, limit the time spent with the gorillas to one hour each day, cap group sizes and ensure that people with visible symptoms of illness do not view the gorillas.

Fossey chose to focus on the downsides of tourism. She believed tourists would cause trouble by bringing disease and that the money used to bring in tourists could be better spent on enhancing patrols in the Virungas. In Fossey's mind, there was no time to wait for the long-term benefits of ecotourism to kick in. She wrote that it was necessary instead to focus on "the immediate perils existing within the park." She went on to say that "educating the local populace to respect gorillas and working to attract tourism do not help the 242 remaining gorillas of the Virungas survive for future generations of tourists to enjoy." She categorized ecotourism as "theoretical conservation" and argued that there was simply no time for it in the case of the gorillas and that their immediate needs required her active approach.

On one hand, Fossey is held up as a conservation warrior—a fierce advocate for a primate species on the brink of extinction. On the other hand, her conservation tactics have been called into question, and rightly so. From the moment she stepped into the

Virungas, she declared war on local poachers and cattle herders. Dian Fossey had a reputation for being a difficult woman to work with, caring more for her gorillas than any primate of the human variety. Yet, she did make a positive impact. Over eighteen years, she habituated and studied these highly endangered and elusive mountain gorillas. She brought their plight to the public's attention through National Geographic, making people care about these gentle giants.

Reflecting on Dian Fossey's life and tragic death, fellow primatologist Biruté Galdikas said, "I knew Dian would be killed, I knew this was her destiny. I saw her in New York City in 1983. She said she would be returning to Rwanda and told me not to expect her back. What killed Dian was Africa."

CHAPTER FIVE

The Ape Lady of Borneo

IT'S THE KIND OF IMAGE THAT STICKS WITH YOU. A young woman with auburn hair, wearing a brown shirt and blue jeans, walks through a field of grasses. Her face is solemn, her eyes fixed on the ground in front of her. In her left arm, she cradles a red-haired infant against her hip. But the infant is not of the human variety—it's an orangutan, a great ape and a close relative of humans. Walking alongside her on the right is another orangutan, a juvenile, resembling a human toddler.

This image, which appeared on the cover of *National Geographic* in 1975, tells a story of determination and resolve.

At first glance, the photograph is deceiving—it almost looks as though the juvenile orangutan is holding the woman's hand, standing on two legs with its lanky right arm held high in the air. But on closer inspection, the young ape is slightly ahead of the woman. If not for the striking red hair covering the apes' bodies and the distinctive black face of the juvenile, the photo could be mistaken for a mother walking with her two children.

It was 1971, and the woman in the photograph—Biruté Galdikas—was twenty-five years old. Alongside her then-husband, Rod Brindamour—the photographer behind the now-famous magazine cover image—Galdikas was living in Kalimantan in Borneo, the third largest island in the world. The young couple had journeyed to the extreme southwest of the Pacific Ocean on a mission to study the large-bodied, shaggy, red-haired great apes—the charismatic orangutans.

Here again, we have an example of the National Geographic effect. In Birutė Galdikas, we find yet another woman, sponsored by Louis Leakey, whose journey with the apes was splashed across magazine covers. There's no doubt Galdikas would go on to serve as a role model to other young women, just as Goodall and Fossey had served as role models for her.

Galdikas had also stumbled upon studying apes as a student in one of anthropology's parent disciplines—psychology. Her journey provides evidence for yet another of Linda Fedigan's hypotheses for the predominance of women in the field of primatology. Fedigan describes anthropology as the "intellectual offspring" of psychology—where there are also many female scientists—so perhaps Galdikas landed in primatology simply because the odds were in her favour.

In interviews, however, Galdikas cites a different motivation. She'd always had a desire for adventure and travel. She recalls drawing inspiration from the man with the yellow hat of *Curious George* fame. When she met Louis Leakey and a door opened for her, she seized the opportunity with both hands. She was passionate about conservation from the start, looking for ways to contribute to protecting the red-haired orangutan.

Orangutans are the largest primate in Asia, found on the islands of Sumatra, Borneo and Java. These solitary animals can live up to fifty or sixty years. Researchers recognize two different species—*Pongo pygmaeus* found in Borneo and *Pongo abelii* in Sumatra. Sadly, orangutans are threatened with extinction. The Bornean orangutan, which Galdikas studied, is listed as "Critically Endangered" by the International Union for Conservation of Nature. This species is primarily under threat due to habitat loss—between 2000 and 2010, the average rate of deforestation in Borneo was a colossal 3,234 square kilometres per year, with just 22 per cent of the Bornean orangutan's habitat falling within protected areas. And, in fact, much of their range lies within commercial forest reserves that are exploited for timber, agriculture and other land uses.

One major threat to orangutan habitat is palm oil production. Check the ingredient list of almost any product you can find at the grocery store—chips, chocolate, peanut butter, shampoo, toothpaste, makeup—and there it is in neat block letters: PALM OIL. Palm oil is a type of vegetable oil that is derived from the fruit of African oil palm trees. These trees can grow up to twenty metres tall, with a single trunk that terminates in a crown of fronds.

The tree's black, one-inch oval fruits are what people are after—inside lies a single oily seed, known as the kernel, which is refined into vegetable oil and used to create those grocery store products. Palm oil trees are cultivated in massive plantations that only grow these trees—the very definition of monoculture. Tropical forests in Asia, Africa and Latin America have been cleared to make way for palm oil plantations, which is highly problematic for biodiversity and human communities that rely on forests for survival. Between 2000 and 2010, around 5 per cent of the orangutan's range was converted for palm oil production.

Beyond habitat loss, orangutans are also threatened by illegal hunting and the pet trade. Local hunters kill orangutans for meat, a practice the large, slow-breeding ape populations cannot withstand. Poaching for the illegal pet trade is also a concern, with an estimated five hundred infant orangutans dying each year as a result. Orangutans are one of the most trafficked primates in the world. The UN Environment Programme estimates that six thousand great apes are captured or killed each year for the pet trade, and up to 70 per cent of these are orangutans.

Not long after arriving in Borneo in 1971, Galdikas learned about the captive orangutan infants in Kumai, a port in Central Kalimantan province in Indonesia. Keeping orangutans as pets was common, often considered a status symbol for the upper-middle class and even government officials, despite it being illegal even back then. The infants were kept in small wooden crates that frequently exuded the smell of urine.

A week into their trip, Galdikas and Brindamour visited the Forestry Department in Kumai, which she later wrote about in her book *Reflections of Eden*.

The head of the Forestry Department, an English-speaking man named Mr. Aep (honorifics like "Mr." are used prevalently in Indonesia as a show of respect), served the two researchers tea. "I have been told to be of assistance to you," he said with a flourish. "That your every wish is my command."

Galdikas and Brindamour exchanged glances, and Galdikas raised her eyebrows before turning back to Mr. Aep: "Why don't you confiscate the orangutan infant and give him to us to release in the reserve?"

The orangutan Galdikas was referring to was a tiny male she and Brindamour had discovered was being kept in one of those small wooden crates in a local residence. The baby orangutan was one of several captives they had heard about in Kumai.

Mr. Aep hesitated, but Galdikas and Brindamour would not relent. Eventually, he agreed to visit the house where the orangutan was being kept. A man answered the door and let them in.

Galdikas's worst fears were realized. In a dark corner of the home sat the small wooden crate. Inside, wrapped in urine-soaked rags, was the tiny orange infant.

"It can't be more than a year old," Galdikas whispered to her husband.

"You must tell this man that it is illegal to keep this orangutan as a pet," Brindamour told Mr. Aep with confidence. "We must confiscate it."

After some spirited back and forth, the man agreed to give up his pet, provided he was reimbursed for the milk and bananas he had fed the infant. Brindamour was livid at such a request.

Galdikas, hesitating slightly, pulled Brindamour aside. She reasoned that a small payment allowing the man to save face could make all the difference in getting the infant back to the forest where it belonged. They agreed upon two thousand rupiah—about five US dollars at the time.

Galdikas reached into the crate and grasped the infant, who clung to the wooden bars. Calmly, she pried his fingers and toes loose, one by one, then held him against her body. The infant clung to her, and Galdikas was startled by the strength of his grasp.

"At that moment, I felt no maternal affection for the smelly but firm-bodied bundle in my arms," Galdikas later wrote. "Yet I felt exhilarated. We had saved the infant from almost certain premature death in captivity."

Galdikas and Brindamour named the orangutan infant Sugito, in honour of Mr. Soegito, an Indonesian forestry officer who had helped them navigate the politics of setting up their research camp in Tanjung Puting National Park.

When they set out on their grand adventure, the couple didn't believe a family was in their future. But much to their surprise, their shared hut in the wild forests of Indonesia was soon filled with "furry orange children." Sugito was their first, and, as Galdikas discovered, raising an infant orangutan was no small task. She did her best to raise him as an orangutan, to prepare him to eventually return to the wild. But Sugito was demanding—constantly squealing, squirming, biting and urinating.

Their family quickly grew. Much to the surprise and delight of local officials, Galdikas and Brindamour gave names to the apes brought to them for care and release—a concept the locals in Indonesia found hilarious. There was Sinaga, Akmad and Sobiarso. Some were infants, others older. Real family dynamics emerged—sibling rivalries, co-sleeping. It wasn't unusual to spot young Galdikas trekking deep into the forest to study wild orangutans with an orphan orangutan strapped to her back.

Biruté Galdikas was born in 1946 in Wiesbaden, Germany, to Lithuanian parents. Growing up, she often heard stories of the hills, swamps and woods of their home country.

At the beginning of World War II, Nazi Germany and the Soviet Union divided Europe, including Lithuania and the other Baltic states. On June 15, 1940, Lithuania was occupied by the Soviet army.

Galdikas's parents were two of the lucky ones. Her mother, Filomena, and her family were especially lucky because they were able to flee legally by train—Galdikas's aunt had just married a member of the Baltic German nobility. Galdikas's father, Antanas, fled Lithuania on his own, leaving behind relatives who did not see the need to leave their homes. Antanas could see that the Soviet army was there for good.

After Germany surrendered to the Allies on May 8, 1945, foreign refugees were sent to camps by the Allied forces. Galdikas's parents met at a dance at one such camp near Standal, Norway. Filomena and her family, now with Antanas in tow, left the refugee camp and travelled west, heading for the American-occupied sector of Germany. They briefly paused their journey in the small town of Oebisfelde, where Filomena and Antanas married in June 1945.

The family was moving west on foot, dragging carts filled with their belongings behind them. From time to time, they would get lucky and hitch a ride to the next village with local German farmers in horse-drawn wagons. Eventually, they reached their destination.

A year later, Biruté Galdikas was born.

Her family did not wish to remain in Germany. They dreamed of the United States. Her grandfather had snuck across the border into Germany to avoid being conscripted by the Russian army and sailed to America. On a return visit to Lithuania, he met Galdikas's grandmother, and the two became engaged. Maria was whisked away to America in 1914, and their first daughter, Bronice, was born in Brooklyn, New York. After World War I ended, the family returned to Lithuania to continue their peaceful life on the farm.

The emigration process split up the family. Biruté's aunt Bronice was able to quickly relocate to the US, having been born there. Her grandmother and another aunt headed to Australia, finding the US emigration process too long and drawn out. Biruté's father headed to Canada for work in the gold and copper mines in Quebec, and her mother followed with two-year-old Biruté a few months later. From Quebec, the family moved to Toronto, where Biruté's brother and sister were born.

Young Biruté's first language was Lithuanian. As she put it in *Reflections of Eden*, this language "was already old when Sanskrit and classical Greek were living tongues." When she began kindergarten in Toronto, she couldn't understand a word her teacher or classmates said.

Still, the family found connections to the Baltic community in vibrant Toronto. Biruté went to Lithuanian elementary school every Saturday morning until grade nine. She credits her Lithuanian upbringing and the turmoil faced by her family with fostering a focus on education. Starting when she was young, her parents instilled in her that education "came before all else" and that getting an education was the "only way that we children could get ahead."

No surprise, then, that when Biruté learned that a PhD was the highest degree possible, that became her goal.

Besides education, the Galdikas family valued nature. They would spend their weekends outside, picnicking in parks, hiking and camping.

Galdikas recalls a trip to the public library, where she checked out the book *Curious George*. She was enthralled, but it wasn't just the unruly, orphaned monkey, George, that roped her into the series. She was also intrigued by the strange, tall man with the large, yellow hat—the jungle explorer who rescued George. That book stirred something inside young Biruté and, at six years old, she decided she would become an explorer, just like the man in the yellow hat.

Biruté finished high school in Eliot Lake, in northern Ontario, after the family relocated for her father's work in the uranium mines.

Despite setting up a life in Canada, Biruté's parents held on to dreams of moving to the United States—specifically to California, where Biruté's aunt and uncle had emigrated. They figured they would make more money in California and began looking into how they could relocate. Since they had a relative who was an American citizen—Biruté's aunt, Bronice—they would move to the front of the line for visa applicants.

While they waited for their visas, Biruté's family moved to Vancouver on the west coast of Canada, reasoning that it was the closest Canadian city to California. In 1963, at age seventeen, Biruté enrolled at the University of British Columbia. Just a year later, she joined her family in Los Angeles, where they lived in a "white bungalow surrounded by avocado trees." She attended the University of California, Los Angeles—a decision that ultimately led her to the enigmatic Louis Leakey.

A few weeks after arriving at "Camp Leakey" (which Galdikas had named after her mentor and sponsor) in central Borneo, Galdikas learned about yet another young orangutan—a female this time—that had been captured by loggers and was being kept in a cage at their camp. As she thought about the orangutan's capture, Galdikas quickly filled in the blanks of what must have happened. She knew that the only way to get hold of a wild infant orangutan was to kill its mother. When the hunters approached, this infant would have rushed to her mother, clinging to her body tightly. The mother might have tried to flee, but she was now also carting an infant, meaning she would move a lot slower than she normally could. Out of fear, the mother likely vocalized and dropped a few branches in a futile attempt to scare off the attackers. This meant the hunters would have a clearer view of where she was in the canopy. It probably only took a few bullets to bring her down. The infant wouldn't have fled—she would have stuck close to her dead or dying mother as her attackers pried her loose so they could process the carcass for consumption.

The goal would be to sell the infant abroad, probably to a zoo, the entertainment industry or as a pet. The infant would be stashed in a crate, handed off to a sea captain who would take a cut of the profits, and stowed below deck without food and water until the ship exited Indonesian waters. Galdikas knew that out of every five infant orangutans smuggled out of the country, at least three died in transport.

Galdikas and Brindamour agreed that they needed to act. That day, while Galdikas continued her research in the forest, Brindamour headed out to confiscate the orangutan. He wasn't alone: he led a team consisting of an assistant, Mr. Hamzah, and a young Forestry Department official.

Mr. Hamzah carried the young female orangutan home to Camp Leakey in his arms. Galdikas named her Akmad, after Sjamsiah Akmad, an official from the Indonesian Institute of

Sciences who had been especially kind to her. Akmad the orangutan was about six years old, and Galdikas likened her to "a lady from Paris." She writes: "Her long face was serene, the fluid brown of her eyes veiled by thick lashes."

Akmad became Galdikas's first adopted orangutan "daughter," and the two were inseparable.

That first night, Galdikas lured Akmad into the jackfruit trees in front of their hut. The young orangutan climbed into the trees, made her nest and promptly fell asleep. The next morning, while Galdikas was preparing breakfast, Akmad daintily climbed down to be with her. Galdikas was surprised at how willingly Akmad took to life at Camp Leakey.

To Galdikas, it seemed Akmad had one ambition: "To be my foster child." There was rarely a moment when Akmad was not by her side. Each day, when Galdikas returned from the forest, Akmad would be there waiting to share a meal.

Then, a few months after Akmad's arrival, Galdikas decided to relocate her living quarters. They were too far away from the forest, and she was getting exhausted. The plan was to bring Akmad along, but on moving day, she was nowhere to be found. After waiting as long as possible, Galdikas and Brindamour reluctantly went on without her.

As the days and weeks passed, Galdikas was overcome with worry and guilt. Then, one morning—six months after the move—Galdikas spotted a flash of red outside the hut.

She looked a little different—skinnier—but it was her. Akmad.

Galdikas rushed to the kitchen and mixed some milk powder with water. Hands shaking a little from the shock and excitement, she handed the cup to Akmad, who hungrily slurped up the milk. When the cup was empty, she extended it to Galdikas for a refill—three times. When she finally finished, she gingerly placed the cup on the table in typical Akmad fashion.

Galdikas beamed. Sure, Akmad had returned, and she was happy to see her, but more than that, it proved that an orangutan, once domesticated—ripped from the forest—could go back to its home in the wild and survive. The many illegally captured orangutans in Indonesia could be saved. It was the start of something big.

Although they were both Canadians, Biruté Galdikas met Rod Brindamour in Los Angeles. It was 1966, and Galdikas was a senior undergraduate student at UCLA. The couple's "meet cute" took place when Galdikas was driving home one day in her family's green Studebaker. She passed a young man wearing a black leather jacket. The two made eye contact, and he smiled at her. Distracted, Galdikas swerved onto the sidewalk, nearly running him over.

"You trying to kill us?" her younger brother exclaimed, appearing out of nowhere. He'd been standing next to the handsome stranger. The two boys had met through a mutual friend and were searching for a store on Sunset Boulevard. Galdikas later described her relationship with Brindamour as "instant and mutual love and respect."

Aside from sharing a home country (and perhaps a love of maple syrup), Galdikas and Brindamour shared a passion for science and nature. Rod Brindamour was outdoorsy, having spent a few summers working for logging companies in British Columbia. When they met, Brindamour was seventeen and still in high school, but he had ambitions to go to college and travel. Nineteen-year-old Galdikas already knew she wanted to go to Borneo and Sumatra to study orangutans. She had established a working relationship with Louis Leakey and was in the beginning stages of finding a research site and securing funding. Could she be ready to leave for the field that September? Leakey wanted to know.

Although the wheels were very much in motion, getting to Borneo took longer than Galdikas had expected. September came and went, and she continued her graduate studies. In 1970, she and Brindamour got engaged. When Leakey learned the news, he was over the moon. The marriage solved two challenges: Galdikas would have an escort, so she wouldn't be travelling alone as a woman, and Brindamour could double as the project photographer.

More waiting ensued. Galdikas and Brindamour got married, first in Mexico and then, unsure of the ceremony's validity, again in Los Angeles. At that point, they were living long-distance—Galdikas was going to grad school in Los Angeles, and Brindamour was still in Canada, graduating high school and starting college. They would commute from Vancouver to Los Angeles to see each other—a roughly twenty-hour drive.

Despite their best efforts, progress on the Borneo project was painfully slow. Galdikas and Brindamour were prepared to leave with nothing but their savings, but a pragmatic Leakey insisted they drum up at least $5,000 in addition to their plane tickets. The holding period proved to be a challenge for both Galdikas and Brindamour. As Galdikas recalled in *Reflections of Eden*, it was "emotionally bruising." Frustrations mounted around not knowing when—or if—their trip to Borneo and the orangutans would ever happen. The couple couldn't make any other plans in case they were suddenly told it was time to leave.

Finally, after two and a half years of waiting, two grants came through—one from the Wilkie Brothers Foundation and another from the Jane and Justin Dart Foundation—thanks to Leakey's efforts. In 1971, Galdikas and Brindamour were finally on their way.

Borneo or bust.

Accompanied by an Indonesian forestry official and a camp cook, Galdikas and Brindamour boarded a forestry boat and travelled up the black-water Sekonyer River, along which the Indigenous

Dayak people, primarily hunters and farmers, lived. Ten hours later, the group arrived at Camp Leakey, which consisted of an abandoned thatched-roof hut that had once been home to forest rangers.

Before Galdikas, only a small number of scientists had ventured into the wild to study orangutans. John MacKinnon, for example, had spent twelve hundred hours observing orangutans in the province of Sabah, in northern Borneo. He noted that orangutans were solitary, ate durian fruits, spent their time in trees and built sleeping nests. When Galdikas arrived at Camp Leakey, there was still much to learn about these elusive apes, particularly their social behaviours. How did they mate? How did mothers care for their young? There was also more to learn about their diet and reproductive cycles.

The forested area surrounding Camp Leakey was a tropical peat swamp—a unique ecosystem where fallen leaves and vegetation can't decompose because the soils below are waterlogged. As a result, the vegetation accumulates and, like a giant sponge, holds the moisture. Eventually, peat swamps form a dome that rises above the surrounding flood levels. Peat swamp forests are home to amazing creatures, including the endangered Sumatran tiger, several endangered gibbon species and, of course, the Sumatran and Bornean orangutan.

Conducting research in the peat swamp forest was no walk in the park. Every day, Galdikas would bravely wade through the "acidic, tea-coloured swamp water" up to her armpits, hoping to find a wild orangutan in the canopy above. The forest was cold, too, with the thick canopy above blocking the sun, and the water numbed her fingers and toes.

I know the feeling. Three and a half years before I worked in Monkey River, Belize, Hurricane Iris—a Category 4 hurricane with winds up to 230 kilometres per hour—had demolished the area, stripping every leaf off the trees. The undergrowth of the forest grew back thick with new trees and tangled vines. We hired guides to clear our trails, which amounted to tunnels through the dense undergrowth, and we carried machetes with bright orange plastic handles to cut through the tangles and maintain the paths as best we could. It was shocking how quickly the forest would grow back, especially after a heavy rain. Sometimes the rain and winds would knock down trees, blocking our trail system. We would spend hours cutting new paths. During the wet season, the forest would flood, and to reach the monkeys, I had to wade through hip-deep water. Some days, I stood in that water for eight to ten hours collecting behavioural samples. Coping with the hardships of the forest was a reminder that nature can be harsh and unforgiving.

When Galdikas began her work in Borneo, she imagined "a jungle alive with colourful blossoms, gigantic butterflies, raucous birds, pythons coiled on every branch, teeming wildlife, and enormous trees that seemed to buttress the sky." Instead, Tanjung Puting presented "flat" and "featureless" terrain with swampy forests. Even the nearby tropical heath forest did not live up to Galdikas's vision—it was "drab" and "monochrome," with an understory of tangled vines.

Still, there was something about Tanjung Puting. Galdikas wrote, "The forests in Tanjung Puting are beautiful like one or two women I have known: initially, they seem plain, but then they turn their heads, the light hits their face at a certain angle, and suddenly they are transformed."

At Camp Leakey, Galdikas and Brindamour lived a simple life. Their meals, cooked over an open fire, mainly comprised rice, tinned sardines and bananas. The couple split up the work: every day, armed with a thermos of cold coffee, her notebook, binoculars and machete, Galdikas would trek through the forests in search of orangutans. Brindamour, meanwhile, would grab his machete and head out to cut trails through the tangled undergrowth. Both were braving extremely harsh conditions, including risks from venomous caterpillars, long-snouted crocodiles, fire ants and cobras. Channelling a grit that could only be fuelled by pure passion, the two persisted each day, often not returning until dark.

Wading through swampy waters wreaked havoc on their shoes and clothes. At one point, Brindamour had to affix rattan to the soles of his shoes. When they stripped off their clothes at the end of the day, they would find leeches "bloated with their blood."

To glimpse a wild orangutan meant wading through blackened swamp water for hours, leaving Galdikas chilled to the bone and her hands and toes shrivelled like prunes. But this was her dream. Two days after she arrived, she was treated to seeing her first orangutan. After that, however, the great apes proved elusive. Two months in, she had spotted many night nests in the trees, but no orangutans.

Galdikas wondered how a "large, lumbering, two- to three-hundred-pound male orangutan covered with bright red hair" could disappear among the dark leaves of the forest. She discovered that, despite their imposing size, orangutans move in silence, sometimes thirty metres up in the dense forest canopy. The hulking apes are slow and solitary. Even when Galdikas did spot an individual, it didn't mean she would soon come upon others. She also learned that their red hair would not be the beacon in the forest she'd hoped for. In fact, when orangutans are in the shade, their hair can "melt into the dark shadows of the canopy."

Jane Goodall, who had her own struggles with finding and following the chimpanzees in Gombe, once weighed in on the difficulties of studying wild orangutans: "The orangutan is the hardest of the three great apes to study. It takes Biruté a year to gather information and to see behaviours I might see in one lucky day."

Even when Galdikas managed to catch a glimpse of an orangutan, it was fleeting—they would bolt at the sight of her.

During the rainy season, it was nearly impossible to keep up with the large arboreal apes from the swampy ground as they moved swiftly through the forest.

Galdikas learned to rely on her other senses. She listened for the sound of the animals crashing through the leaves, for the breaking of branches. If the orangutans were on the move, she could find them. In my own studies in Belize of the black howler monkeys, whose black fur blended into the thick tree canopies, I implemented Galdikas's techniques. I walked quietly—heel-toe, heel-toe—so I could hear leaves crashing from above. I listened for the sound of discarded fruits—the remnants of a meal—showering down like rain. Often, I would find the howler monkeys by smell. Since they are primarily leaf-eaters, their feces have a pungent, botanical odour. By the end of my project, I could tell the difference between the smell of fresh poop and day-old poop. I grew to love the smell of fresh poop (there's a sentence I never thought I would write) because it meant the monkeys were nearby.

It was by using her senses that Galdikas found Beth on Christmas Eve.

She and Brindamour had set out on a trek through the forest, leaving camp before dawn. As Galdikas jotted down the date and time in her notebook, she heard it: *snap!* She spun around in time to see the leaves above her shaking. Her eyes focused on a female orangutan amid the foliage.

Galdikas did a double take. Wrapped around the orangutan's neck "like a scarf" was an infant, staring blankly at Galdikas with "big round eyes."

Galdikas could not believe her luck. She had come across these orangutans on dry ground, making it possible to follow them when they inevitably took off.

Galdikas and Brindamour followed the thirty-five-kilogram Beth and her infant, whom they named Bert, for the entire day.

Unlike Jane Goodall and Dian Fossey, who received their scientific training through field experience and later returned to school for their PhDs, Galdikas arrived in Borneo with formal scientific training under her belt. She understood modern data collection and statistical analysis. Where Goodall and Fossey took narrative field notes, Galdikas methodically recorded behaviours on a check sheet, focusing on one individual at a time. She also collected and catalogued hundreds of plants and insects to get a complete picture of the orangutan diet.

As Galdikas watched, Beth constructed a day nest, intricately "twisting branches into a circular platform and covering it with a cushion of leafy twigs." She took note of what Beth ate—bark and fruits—and painstakingly described each piece of fruit and how Beth prepared the food. When she could, Galdikas collected remnants of Beth's meals that dropped down from above. She wrote down everything the female orangutan did—where she travelled and how she interacted with the infant. In that one day, Galdikas managed to fill thirty pages of her notebook.

Eventually, Beth built her night nest atop a tree and settled in.

Galdikas and Brindamour had completed their first full-day follow of wild orangutans!

"I had proved to myself that it was possible to follow wild orangutans for days at a time," Galdikas later wrote. "I was overjoyed."

"Aren't you afraid?" one of the forestry officials asked Biruté Galdikas.

"Afraid?" she replied.

"Of being raped." He paused, then clarified, "By the orangutans."

The official explained that many women had been raped by orangutans. According to him, the powerful male apes would grab a woman, lift her into the canopy and have his way.

Galdikas choked back a laugh, not wanting to insult her acquaintance. His description sounded like something out of a movie like *King Kong*! Surely, this was just some old piece of folklore.

She learned later that there was indeed local folklore behind the man's story. As the Dayak legend goes, the male orangutan's long call is a cry out to his human lover, a woman stolen from a riverboat who had escaped from the orangutan's night nest.

Later, Galdikas and Brindamour had a good laugh over this man's words. Orangutans raping women. Ridiculous.

Or so they thought.

Out in the wild, Galdikas was beginning to understand the intricacies of the orangutan mating system. She described two mating tactics: consortship and forced copulation. With consortship, the male makes his long call through the forest. A receptive female responds, and the two find one another. The pair might move through the forest together for two to ten days, going about their day-to-day activities. When the female is no longer interested, she departs.

Then there are the forced copulations. These encounters most often involve the subadult males attacking the females. The females struggle, grunting in distress while trying to bite the male and flee. Galdikas even gave the female vocalization—only heard in this context—a name: the "rape grunt."

Galdikas has reasoned that the young males might force copulation because in the wild it takes them up to twenty years to mature. Until the male matures, females are uninterested in copulating with them. Yet, the young males are capable of and interested in sexual activity, so they use force.

As Galdikas learned more about mating in the wild orangutans, her family of captive orangutans was growing, and she began to observe sexual behaviours among them.

When Sugito, her first captive orangutan rescue, arrived at the camp, Brindamour took the orphan orangutan to a small jackfruit tree just outside their hut for climbing practice. Sugito would enthusiastically climb, but if Brindamour moved away, he would quickly descend, squealing—terrified he might lose his person. Brindamour would stand beneath the small tree, not moving a muscle, while Sugito played in the low branches.

On the third day, Brindamour went out to the usual spot but returned to the hut after just ten minutes. He looked flustered.

When Galdikas asked what happened, Brindamour sighed and reluctantly described Sugito playing in the tree as usual, dangling by his long orangutan arms, until… "Look, he uh…he tried to put his penis in my ear. Then he…he…grabbed my hand and tried to use it to masturbate."

Galdikas couldn't disguise her amusement.

To Brindamour, the incident was anything but funny. Sugito had lost all innocence.

By the mid-'70s, Galdikas and Brindamour had accumulated quite a family of ex-captive orangutans. Their first wild-born sub adult male was Gundul, who, unlike little Sugito, was a hulking adolescent ape when he arrived.

One day, sixty visitors were coming into camp to hear a talk from Galdikas, and Gundul was not pleased. "His hair was erect, tripling his size. His eyes blazed," Galdikas later wrote. He went down to the dock and pulled a large log, "at least twenty inches in diameter and perhaps ten feet long," out of the water. He "heaved the log up and down, shaking it and bouncing it like a basketball."

The boat of visitors turned around and didn't return.

Gundul even intimidated Galdikas, who was normally quite confident around her ape family. She knew she was no match for his size and energy.

Soon after Gundul's arrival, Galdikas and her team installed a new feeding platform a short distance from the camp to encourage the ex-captives to be more independent and venture away from camp more often. The team brought food to the platform across the river in a dugout canoe.

In her memoir, Galdikas recounted a memorable day when her Indonesian cook and a North American visitor accompanied her to the platform to restock the food.

Gundul arrived.

Galdikas recalled that he "ate a little but seemed distracted." She didn't think much of it until, all at once, Gundul grabbed the cook by the legs and wrestled her down to the platform. The cook screamed and cried as the large ape bit her and pulled at her clothing.

Galdikas lunged at Gundul, trying to shove her fist down his throat to break him out of his rage. She yelled to the visitor to take the dugout and get help.

As she tried to fend off Gundul, she noticed he wasn't fighting back. He wasn't out for blood: his interests lay elsewhere.

The cook went limp in Galdikas's arms, softly mumbling that it was "all right."

"He raped the cook," Galdikas writes, simply, in *Reflections of Eden*, recalling how the ape's "eyes rolled upward."

The "forced copulation," as Galdikas has referred to it, ended as quickly as it began, with Gundul releasing the cook and moving into the trees, going about his business as though nothing had happened.

Galdikas could hardly believe what she had witnessed.

The cook was rattled but relieved it was over and that she had survived.

Back at camp, Galdikas was shocked to find that the Indonesian people didn't seem overly shaken by what had happened. The cook's husband said, "It was just an ape. Why should my wife or I be concerned? It wasn't a man."

Reflecting on the incident, Galdikas remembered the forestry official's warning that orangutans are known to rape women—and how she'd laughed it off. Now, she felt a bit foolish. But she also reasoned that this rape had likely occurred because Gundul was

ABOVE: In 1972, Linda Fedigan travelled to La Moca Ranch near Laredo, Texas, to study the Arashiyama West Japanese macaques. In this photo, taken that same year, she pauses by two of the macaques while collecting data. LINDA FEDIGAN

BELOW: Linda Fedigan observes macaques on the roadside on Yakushima island, Japan, 1989. LINDA FEDIGAN

Linda Fedigan makes a return visit to the Arashiyama West Japanese macaques in 1998.
JOHN ADDICOTT

In the name of a 1994 population census on the primates, Linda Fedigan scales a rock face to access remote areas of Santa Rosa National Park, Costa Rica, where she set up her long-term field research site.
JOHN ADDICOTT

ABOVE: An infant capuchin monkey rides on the back of her juvenile female sibling in Santa Rosa National Park. JOHN ADDICOTT

LEFT: Linda Fedigan observes a capuchin monkey high in the canopy of Santa Rosa National Park in 2007. JOHN ADDICOTT

ABOVE: Louis Leakey poses with his wife, Mary, in 1962. Louis is holding the fragment of an early human jawbone.
SMITHSONIAN INSTITUTION ARCHIVES / WIKIMEDIA COMMONS

BELOW: Olduvai Gorge, in the Serengeti Plain of Tanzania, is where Louis and Mary Leakey first uncovered evidence of early humans, including many fossils and stone tools.
NOEL FEANS / WIKIMEDIA COMMONS

ABOVE: Louis Leakey and Mary Leakey stand by the layers of sediment where *Zinjanthropus* was found in this circa 1959 photo taken in Olduvai Gorge. KEYSTONE PICTURES USA / ZUMAPRESS, ALAMY

BELOW: Louis and Mary Leakey dig at a site in Olduvai Gorge in 1961. SMITHSONIAN INSTITUTION ARCHIVES / WIKIMEDIA COMMONS

Jane Goodall poses with a chimpanzee at Gombe Stream National Park in Tanzania in 1965. EVERETT COLLECTION INC./ALAMY

An adult female chimpanzee is photographed with an infant in Gombe Stream National Park, where Jane Goodall conducted her research. IKIWANER/ WIKIMEDIA COMMONS

ABOVE: In 2018, Jane Goodall received an honorary degree, a doctor of science, honoris causa, from Simon Fraser University in British Columbia. SIMON FRASER UNIVERSITY / WIKIMEDIA COMMONS

BELOW: Primatologist Dian Fossey studied the mountain gorillas in the Virunga Mountains between 1966 and 1985. ALAMY

ABOVE: Dian Fossey referred to the Virunga Mountain gorillas as her "friends." She was especially fond of a male gorilla whom she named Digit, and who was killed by poachers in 1978. ALAMY

BELOW: Dian Fossey's old research centre in Volcanoes National Park, Rwanda, is now her gravesite. On December 27, 1985, fifty-three-year-old Fossey was found murdered in her cabin. ARIADNE VAN ZANDBERGEN / ALAMY

Dian Fossey's efforts with the gorillas and her tragic story were Hollywoodized in 1988 with the film *Gorillas in the Mist*. In this undated photo, she poses in Rwanda with a young mountain gorilla. LIAM WHITE / ALAMY

Birutė Galdikas was featured on the October 1975 cover of *National Geographic* magazine. BOOKSR / ALAMY

Starting from her first trip to Borneo in 1971, Birutė Galdikas worked to rescue and rehabilitate orangutans that had been held captive in the pet trade. Here, she visits with an orangutan in Tanjung Puting National Park, Indonesia.
A & J VISAGE / ALAMY

Birutė Galdikas poses with an orangutan at Tanjung Puting Orangutan Rehabilitation Centre in Indonesia, circa 2005.
SUZANNE PLUNKETT / ALAMY

ABOVE: Jeanne Altmann spent years studying the baboons in the Maasai-Amboseli Game Reserve (now Amboseli National Park) in southern Kenya. This photograph captures her in the fall of 1991. ROBERT DREA / UNIVERSITY OF CHICAGO LIBRARY, SPECIAL COLLECTIONS RESEARCH CENTER

BELOW: A yellow baboon takes a seat in Amboseli National Park. PAUL MANNIX / WIKIMEDIA COMMONS

ABOVE: Mount Kilimanjaro is a striking sight from Amboseli National Park. SERGEY PESTEREV / WIKIMEDIA COMMONS

BELOW: In this photo taken by her husband, Dan, Sarah Hrdy observes the langurs at Mount Abu in Rajasthan, India. Her research there spanned 1971 to 1979. DAN HRDY

Sarah Hrdy visits the langurs in Ranthambore National Park, northeast of Mount Abu, circa 1972. DAN HRDY

ABOVE: Sarah Hrdy observed several instances of kidnapping among the langurs, including this juvenile female at Mount Abu photographed taking an unwilling infant from a young adult mother. SARAH HRDY

BELOW: Today, Sarah and Dan Hrdy reside in California, where they operate Citrona Farms. The couple grows walnuts and restores the habitat by planting native grasses, hedgerows, shrubs and trees. DAN HRDY

LEFT: Alison Jolly, known as the Mother of Lemurs, conducted the first long-term field study of ring-tailed lemurs in Madagascar in 1962. NATURE PICTURE LIBRARY / ALAMY

MIDDLE: Alison Jolly's research demonstrated that ring-tailed lemurs are female-dominant. When Dreamworks executives visited Madagascar to research the 2005 animated film *Madagascar*, Jolly pointed out that they had it wrong with King Julien—he should have been a queen. TRAVIS STEFFENS

BOTTOM: Alison Jolly conducted her research at Berenty Reserve in eastern Madagascar. MAKY (ALEX DUNKEL) / WIKIMEDIA COMMONS

Author Keriann McGoogan undertook a fourteen-month study in Ankarafantsika National Park, in northwest Madagascar. In this 2008 photo, she is seen observing a group of Coquerel's sifakas in the park. TRAVIS STEFFENS

The Jane Goodall Institute, a conservation organization dedicated to combatting biodiversity loss and climate change, now has offices around the world, and organized an event in Kitchener, Ontario, to mark Goodall's ninetieth birthday in 2024. The author—unable to resist the photo op—poses with a poster at the event. TRAVIS STEFFENS

an ex-captive, raised by humans. It was no surprise that he had developed a sexual interest in humans. As she had seen in the wild, his behaviour was not unusual for orangutans—it was only the species he'd gotten wrong.

In the second month of her study, Galdikas woke up sick.

"It's finally happened," she said, staring up at the ceiling. Earlier, her friend Barbara Harrisson, a conservationist, had warned her of "mysterious fevers," and here one was.

Turning to her husband, she reluctantly said, "I'm going to stay back." She felt a pang. What was it? Dejection? This was the first day she hadn't gone into the forest since she'd arrived. Still, she knew it was the right call.

Brindamour and Mr. Hamzah headed out to cut trails while a feverish Galdikas lay alone in camp on a reed mat, going in and out of a restless sleep.

BANG WHAP! BANG WHAP! BANG WHAP!

Galdikas was jolted out of her resting state. Dozens of times, the sound emanated from just north of camp. She sat up, puzzled and unsure of what the noise was.

That evening, Galdikas described the strange noises to Brindamour, saying they were like thunder or cannons going off.

Brindamour squinted knowingly. "Someone's cutting down trees," he told her.

Galdikas didn't want to believe it, but Brindamour would know—he had worked for logging companies in British Columbia as a teenager.

Galdikas was in disbelief. The Forestry Department had assured them that no logging would happen there. They had come to an informal agreement.

But the fact was, when Galdikas arrived at Camp Leakey within the borders of Tanjung Puting, it was not a nature reserve. It was a *game* reserve—and there's a difference. Although killing animals was illegal, there were no restrictions on how people could use the land. The reserve also went by another name, Kotawaringin-Sampit Reserve, but Galdikas decided that name was "unwieldy." Tanjung Puting was better. It was the name of a peninsula in the Java Sea.

In *Reflections of Eden*, Galdikas recalled how, when she arrived, "Borneo's forests already were being cut down for logs, boards and plywood." Just outside Tanjung Puting Reserve, she witnessed trees being cut by handloggers and small local companies. Slash-and-burn agriculture, also known as swidden or shifting agriculture, was common. This method involves cutting and burning forests to clear the way for crops. Burning brings forth a nutrient-rich layer of ash that helps fertilize crops, but the trouble is that it is not sustainable in the long term. The land can only remain fertile for a few years before the nutrients disappear. Farmers then abandon the fallow land and move on to the next plot, clearing even more forest in the process. With only game reserve–level protection, slash-and-burn agriculture was legal within the borders of Tanjung Puting Reserve.

Galdikas couldn't understand how a reserve could protect animals without also protecting their habitat. So she set to work, using her influence and good standing with the local government.

Her approach to problem-solving was pragmatic. She was mindful to observe local etiquette and worked hard to build relationships. She quickly realized that a direct approach—like what Dian Fossey was using in Rwanda—would not fly in Indonesia. This was a culture that valued a softer touch.

Galdikas took the time to befriend the local government officials and ask them questions about themselves. She learned about their families and discussed the local news. With time, she grew familiar with the officials and she could comfortably bring up the issue that had been weighing on her.

She told them that, just outside of Camp Leakey, villagers were cutting down trees, trapping animals and fishing the river.

Then, to solidify her cause, she declared, "Tanjung Puting is a nature reserve."

Galdikas committed to this lie. In every report she wrote to the government, she referred to Tanjung Puting as a *nature* reserve. She said it out loud in conversation. Eventually, the officials also began referring to Tanjung Puting as a nature reserve.

In the field, Galdikas continued her orangutan research. At camp, she threw herself into the rehabilitation of the ex-captives. Meanwhile, Brindamour became a vigilante, going on daily patrols to evict the loggers.

"Local people assumed we had the right to evict them from the reserve," Galdikas wrote in her memoir.

In 1977, the village of Tanjung Harapan was evicted from the area.

"When I look back at how we did it, it's incredible to me that we persuaded them to move the village, when in reality the village had every right to be there."

Like in *I Dream of Jeannie*, Galdikas had folded her arms, nodded her head and conjured up a nature reserve out of nothing.

Then she came up against Kayu Mas.

In 1973, two years into her study, Galdikas was following an adolescent female and a subadult male, thrashing through the wet forest. She came across a set of trees that had been slashed, marked with bright red numbers. The paint was fresh.

Her heart sank. Brindamour had told her about "timber cruising"—companies would work their way through the forest, collecting information on the "inventory" to determine how much money they could make by logging an area.

Galdikas followed the cruise line, her heart beating fast. Fresh footprints dotted the earth beneath her feet. She turned the corner and saw them: a line of men. One wore a bright yellow hard hat and thick-soled logging boots. While the other men jumped at the sight of Galdikas, this man didn't flinch.

Galdikas asked the men why they were there, even though she already knew. They told her they worked for Kayu Mas in East Borneo. Galdikas nodded. Kayu Mas was a major logging company.

As confidently as she could, she said, "This is a nature reserve. No logging is permitted here."

The man stared back at her.

The crew continued their work the next day. Kayu Mas had rights to the entire northern part of the reserve, including Galdikas's study area.

Desperate, Galdikas wrote letters to Mr. Walman Sinaga, the head of the PPA (Indonesia's nature conservation and wildlife management agency), pleading for help. She had a special relationship with Mr. Sinaga; she and Brindamour had visited his home, and he had taken a shine to the Canadians. Yet, he wasn't responding to Galdikas's letters, and she began to fret. Was he truly not in her court?

Several months went by, and Galdikas and Brindamour travelled to Jakarta to visit their friend.

Once there, Mr. Sinaga told the couple the problem was solved. He had spoken directly with the owner of Kayu Mas. The company was already logging a portion of another game reserve in East Borneo and had been permitted to build a large road. In exchange for those concessions, Mr. Sinaga demanded that the company leave Tanjung Puting alone. The owner agreed. As long as Galdikas was studying the orangutans in Tanjung Puting, Kayu Mas and the concession holders agreed not to log.

There it was: an unofficial guarantee. Galdikas's efforts were beginning to pay off in other ways as well. The couple had also befriended a man named Mr. Binti, an assistant to the Dayak governor of Central Kalimantan province. Over the years, Mr. Binti had visited Camp Leakey several times, and on one of those visits, Galdikas filled him in on the situation with Kayu Mas.

Mr. Binti agreed to speak with the governor, and the Forestry Department eventually agreed to move the reserve boundary northward, well beyond Camp Leakey. Finally, the protection Galdikas had conjured up was real and in writing.

Deep in the forests of Borneo, Galdikas and Brindamour were in isolation together, spending twenty-four hours a day, seven days a week with only each other and their orangutans. Galdikas noted that her husband, a typical male primate, "did not play a constant role in the daily care and nurturing of the orphaned orangutans." While he made himself useful, he was happy to sit back while Galdikas did the heavy lifting.

Despite this, their rehabilitation efforts continued to grow, as did their research on the wild orangutan groups. But one day, a family group they were following came down with a mysterious illness, losing hair from their heads and shoulders. It was mange, a contagious skin disease caused by microscopic mites. Animals with severe mange are lethargic and unable to eat, leading to poor nutrition, or worse: starvation. Hearing and sight can also be compromised due to scabbing around the ears and eyes.

When it came to what to do about the mange in the orangutan group, Galdikas hesitated. On one hand, she desperately wanted to help the orangutans who couldn't help themselves. But another part of her brain reminded her of her scientific training.

She knew she should do nothing. She reminded her husband that they were there as scientists, first and foremost. It was their job to remain objective observers and nothing more.

As the days passed, the group's condition worsened. Galdikas and Brindamour stood watch as, one by one, orangutans they had grown to love either disappeared or died.

Brindamour fell into a deep depression.

Galdikas later reflected that this experience was a turning point for Brindamour. He lost interest in following the orangutans.

Rod Brindamour had once been Galdikas's champion, as excited as she was to learn all there was to know about these amazing creatures of the forest. Now he was checked out and even questioning the importance of the work. Galdikas believed the shift in Brindamour was related to the loss of that orangutan group. Instead of taking the time to mourn, he turned his attention to the loggers, taking unnecessary risks to protect the forest.

"Our idyllic Garden of Eden existence had been shattered," Galdikas wrote.

In 1975, four years after they had first arrived in Indonesia, Galdikas and Brindamour travelled back to North America together for the first time. Although Galdikas had briefly returned before, this was Brindamour's first trip home in years, on a one-month exit visa. They spent a few days at the National Geographic offices in Washington while Galdikas wrote her article for the magazine. National Geographic also paid Brindamour for his photographs. When he did the math on his portion of the payment, he joked, "I've been working for about ten cents an hour all these years."

He mentioned the low payment a few times, supposedly in jest, but Galdikas could practically see the chip forming on his shoulder.

The couple next headed to Los Angeles to visit family and friends. During their visit, Galdikas's mother had a premonition. Galdikas mentioned that Jane Goodall and Hugo van Lawick—the chimpanzee power couple—had divorced. Goodall had remarried, Galdikas said.

"Crazy," her mother said, shaking her head. "The whole world is crazy."

It's easy to imagine Galdikas and Brindamour sitting on the living room sofa, exchanging a glance or a raised eyebrow. Perhaps catching their exchange, Galdikas's mother turned her attention to Brindamour and said, "Don't you dare get a divorce." Then again: "Don't you dare get a divorce."

The couple's next stop was the doctor, following a recommendation from a friend and colleague that they make sure everything was fine before heading back to the wilds. After they each received a thorough poking and prodding, the doctor called with an update: Galdikas was fine, but Brindamour had an infection that required further testing. The couple were due to leave for the airport in an hour.

Brindamour protested. He felt fine, he told the doctor. Their visas would expire in just two days, and one of those days was already accounted for with the international travel. They had to get on that plane.

The second Brindamour placed the phone on the receiver, Galdikas announced that she intended to board the plane with or without him.

Brindamour was quiet. He'd been under the impression there would be a discussion, that they would decide as a team. Perhaps sensing that she may have been too blunt, Galdikas suggested Brindamour see a doctor in Jakarta—the location of the best hospital in Indonesia. Brindamour hesitated but ultimately agreed, much to his Los Angeles doctor's dismay.

In Jakarta, an American doctor examined Brindamour, prescribed medication and ordered follow-up tests. On re-examination, Brindamour's infection was gone.

Galdikas was vindicated, but Brindamour grew sullen.

The subject of children—of the human variety—also loomed over the couple. In Indonesia, where having children is highly valued, they often faced questions: "Married for eight years and no children? I am so very sorry," people would say.

Galdikas and Brindamour were of the firm belief that the world was overpopulated. If they were to have children, they decided, it would be through adoption. It was the only moral choice.

Then one day, Mr. Binti, Galdikas's most trusted Indonesian mentor, visited their camp. A short, round man with lustrous black hair, Mr. Binti "had a bit of shaman in him." He pulled Galdikas aside and told her it was time to have children. He knew how busy she was, he said, but he and his wife would be happy to help raise the baby.

Two months later, Galdikas was pregnant.

Despite appeals from family, friends and professors in North America to return home for the birth, Galdikas remained in Indonesia with Brindamour. Her parents sent telegrams, begging her to come back, but she would not.

As her belly grew, Galdikas continued to wade through the swampy forests in search of wild orangutans. She had never been pregnant before, and she felt as though she was losing control of her own body. Brindamour, the only person she had to confide in, was less than sympathetic. He viewed the pregnancy as his wife's cross to bear and was uninterested in the details. The two didn't even discuss how this baby would inevitably change their lives.

Just a few weeks before Galdikas was due, the couple flew to Jakarta. They stayed in a comfortable hotel until it was time to go to the hospital. Brindamour wasn't allowed in the delivery room, and Galdikas urged him to leave and get some rest rather than stay in the sweltering, mosquito-filled waiting room.

Much to Galdikas's surprise, the Indonesian doctors practised natural childbirth, even in the hospital, which meant no painkillers. That night, as she gave birth to her first child, "the word 'pain' took on new meaning," Galdikas recalled.

The baby was born in the wee hours of the morning, but no one bothered to phone Rod Brindamour. He arrived at seven the next morning and learned he had a son. They named the child Binti, meaning "small bird that flies very high" in the Dayak language, in honour of their friend and mentor.

A friend in Jakarta insisted that the couple stay in her home after the birth, but Brindamour grew restless and yearned to return to camp. Galdikas felt that Binti was still too small to travel and decided to stay, observing the Indonesian custom of not letting a baby touch the ground for forty days. During this time, she realized she would need help with the infant if she were to resume work. She borrowed a seventeen-year-old nanny, Yuni, from her friend for a few months. Galdikas would see to it that Yuni learned English in exchange for childcare.

Back at camp, the two women worked in tandem to care for Binti. It was a well-orchestrated dance—mealtime, playtime, bath time. Both Galdikas and Brindamour carried Binti on their backs in baby carriers, the child peering curiously over their shoulder as they trudged through the forest. Galdikas tasked Brindamour with teaching Yuni English, and the pair began spending hours together in the house where Yuni was staying.

On the surface, it seemed like the couple had this whole raising-a-child business down to an art (they were doing it while living in the forest, for crying out loud!), but in reality, they were coming apart at the seams. Galdikas and Brindamour were arguing more than ever. Their fights centred on childcare and were becoming more frequent and intense. Galdikas felt that having Binti was "a natural expression of being a woman," while Brindamour grew consumed by the idea of being a provider for his child—if he could not support his child, he viewed himself as a failure.

Meanwhile, Brindamour and Yuni were growing closer. Yuni admired her teacher, and as Galdikas later wrote in *Reflections of Eden*, she represented "an escape from feelings of self-doubt" for Brindamour. He and Yuni would sit together during meals and take walks in their spare time.

The morning before Yuni was set to return to Jakarta, she and Brindamour went ahead to the dining hall, leaving Galdikas with Binti, waiting for Yuni to return. Usually, Yuni would take about fifteen minutes for her meal before coming back so Galdikas could head to the forest. But this time, half an hour went by, then another.

When Yuni finally returned, Galdikas tore a strip off her. The argument escalated, and Galdikas accused Yuni of trying to steal her husband. A stunned Yuni became hysterical and fainted.

Brindamour, concerned by the commotion, came to see what had happened. When Galdikas relayed the chain of events, he reassured her: "I could never give this up, living in the forest, with the orangutans... You don't have to worry."

Yuni left camp the next day, leaving Galdikas and Brindamour alone once again in their Garden of Eden.

In the years that followed, the couple made a few short trips back to Los Angeles. Galdikas wrote and defended her PhD thesis while Brindamour helped with the computer side of things. He also spent time alone at the camp in Indonesia.

As the months passed and they spent more time physically apart, the emotional distance between them grew as well. While in LA, Galdikas prioritized working on her PhD and didn't bother to write to Brindamour. When she returned to Indonesia, she sought out Yuni to bring her back to camp to care for Binti. But when she arrived at the home where Yuni was staying, she noticed a letter. It was from her husband.

In *Reflections of Eden*, Galdikas describes feeling touched at the sight of the letter, assuming that Brindamour had written to her despite her radio silence while the couple were apart. When she picked up the letter, though, she felt "a chill" when she saw it was addressed to Yuni.

When Galdikas finally arrived at camp to greet Brindamour after months apart, they didn't embrace but instead shook hands.

Then one night, while lying in bed, Galdikas worked up the courage to ask her husband the question she had been avoiding. His answer was no surprise, but Galdikas still could not believe it. Brindamour intended to marry Yuni after she finished high school and planned to bring her back with him to North America. He wanted a divorce.

Devastated, Galdikas escaped back into the field. Back to her orangutans.

Dr. Biruté Galdikas is a triple threat in the world of primatology.

Threat one: Scientific discovery. Galdikas's research on wild orangutans provided insights into their behaviour and social interactions. She found that orangutans eat fruit and, through her many years of study, has catalogued more than four hundred different kinds of food consumed by the red apes. She also documented orangutans' long birth intervals and showed that orangutan mothers can care for their young for as much as seven years. In 1977, she was the first to observe and record the entire birth process in the wild.

Threat two: Rehabilitation. For more than fifty years in Borneo, Galdikas tirelessly balanced her fieldwork with her rehabilitation efforts. She and Brindamour set up the first rehabilitation and release program in Kalimantan in response to the pet trade, a growing threat to orangutans.

Galdikas has likened herself to a "working mother," as the orphaned orangutans required hands-on care. Some of the apes could be left to their own devices, but many were infants and very dependent on their human caregivers. Brindamour and Galdikas took turns going into the forest, sometimes bringing camp assistants as "babysitters" to stay with the ex-captives.

On more than one occasion, Galdikas strapped an infant orangutan to her back and trekked into the forest. Her ultimate desire was to release the orphans back into the wild, and she did all she could to prepare them for that future. She took the orphans on long walks through the forest, even climbing into the trees with them. Other times, she would just watch them play from below, beaming as the apes enjoyed their true home and gained important skills like nest-building and navigating the treetops. Today, Galdikas continues her work through Orangutan Foundation International, a nonprofit dedicated to the conservation of wild orangutans and their habitat. She still spends much of her time in Borneo at the rescue centre in Camp Leakey.

Threat three: Habitat conservation. Galdikas is the reason Tanjung Puting is a nature reserve. She knew that to release captive orangutans into the wild, it was critical to conserve the surrounding habitat. Through Orangutan Foundation International, she has raised millions to purchase and preserve forest land where both wild and ex-captive orangutans can thrive.

For more than five decades, Biruté Galdikas has studied the orangutans and contributed to their conservation and rehabilitation. She has worked tirelessly to advise Indonesia's Ministry of Forestry on conservation issues, and she has published multitudes of academic articles and books. As a university professor at both the Universitas Nasional in Jakarta and Simon Fraser University in British Columbia, she inspires the next generation of scientists. Galdikas's research and conservation efforts with the orangutans demonstrate how we cannot study the primates in isolation: understanding the interactions between humans, non-human primates and the environment is critical.

"Extinction happens in front of our eyes, and we don't actually see it," she said in a 2014 talk at the University of British Columbia. "We watch it, eyes wide open, and don't actually understand it. This is the situation facing all the great apes of today."

CHAPTER SIX

The Mathematician and the Monkeys

A LOUD THUD ECHOED through the Madagascar forest. It sounded like someone had dropped a heavy sack of potatoes from above. I gasped and brought my hand to my mouth. The prancing, snowy-white lemur infant, who just moments ago had been deep in play, had slipped from a branch and fallen six metres to the ground. Instinctively, I lurched forward, but then abruptly stopped as I watched what happened next.

One by one, the entire group of tree-dwelling primates—seven adult sifaka lemurs in all—descended from the trees and surrounded the fallen infant. I craned my neck to see, but my view of the baby was obstructed by the group.

I checked my digital Ironman watch—I was in the middle of a ten-minute behavioural sample of a female lemur with a crooked tail. I had been well trained in behavioural sampling methods. I kept a close eye on the female and my watch. Every time she changed her behaviour, I wrote down what I observed. In the comments section of my data collection sheet, I wrote:

> *Baby fell to ground whole group descends and surrounds it*
> *Sitting on the ground w/ baby*

For an entire minute, the group remained in place, encircling the infant on the sandy forest floor. Eventually, one of the lemurs—the baby's mother, I presumed—grabbed hold of the infant and moved back into the tree. I breathed a sigh of relief as the infant recommenced jumping and playing like a toddler at a playground. The remainder of the group, including the female I was watching, resumed feeding on flower buds as though nothing out of the ordinary had happened.

My watch chirped. I had hit the ten-minute mark, meaning my sample was complete. As always, in big block letters at the bottom of the page, I wrote *END* and moved the completed data sheet to the back of my clipboard.

I sat down on my portable camp chair—a lifesaver for lemur watching—and thought about what I had just witnessed. Had the lemurs all gathered on the ground to help the infant? Were they surrounding the baby in a circle to protect it from potential predators? I knew raptors and snakes would both snatch infants if given the opportunity.

As these questions and possible answers swirled through my mind, I thought about one of my primatology idols, Jeanne Altmann. A rock star among primatologists, Altmann published a seminal paper in the 1970s, still cited today, which detailed the very methods I was using to record lemur behaviour. I had studied her methods during my primatology undergrad, practised data collection on the monkeys at my local zoo, and now here I was, applying them to my PhD research on the behaviour and ecology of the wild lemurs in Madagascar.

Altmann also brought new insights to our understanding of the social dynamics within primate groups. Alongside her husband, Stuart, she conducted a long-term study of wild baboons in Kenya. While previous primate studies—especially those of baboons—had focused on male behaviours and interactions, Altmann flipped the script. She focused on baboon *females* and was especially interested in documenting the relationships between mothers and infants.

Jeanne Altmann's story supports the "it's the appeal of the primates themselves" hypothesis for why women are drawn to primatology. As a mother, she made no secret of her interest in the important role females play within primate societies.

I wondered what Altmann would have thought about what I had just witnessed with the lemurs. I had no doubt she would have something to say about it, and I only hoped I could do her proud.

I looked up at the sifaka infant, still jumping from branch to branch. Smiling, I grabbed my clipboard. It was time for the next sample.

In 1963, a mother, father and their toddler left wintry Edmonton in north-central Alberta, bound for East Africa. Their destination: Nairobi National Park on the outskirts of Kenya's capital city. The plan was that, over the next fifteen months, the parents would study baboon behaviour in a natural setting.

The baboons of Nairobi National Park had already been studied by anthropologist and evolutionary biologist Irven DeVore. When Jeanne and Stuart Altmann arrived, DeVore, known to friends as "Irv," was in the park running a census of the baboon population, and he spent time with the young couple, showing them the ropes.

After a few weeks of getting the lay of the land, Jeanne and Stuart reflected on the suitability of Nairobi National Park for their field study. The park offered several advantages, including a previously studied and habituated baboon population and proximity to a major city where they could easily obtain supplies. However, a major disadvantage was that the site was overrun with tourists, which influenced the baboons' behaviour and compromised the integrity of their research. Even DeVore told the couple that the tourist problem—people hand-feeding the baboons—had worsened since he began his study in 1959. Feeding the baboons can influence their behaviour, changing their natural home range and creating conflict within the group and with humans. Not only that, tourist provisioning can be detrimental to the primates' health. For example, a study of Barbary macaques in Morocco found that feeding by tourists led to elevated stress levels and more instances of alopecia, or hair loss.

If Jeanne and Stuart Altmann wanted to understand the natural behaviour of the baboons—unaffected by human interference—they knew they needed a new location for their study.

The young couple purchased a Land Rover and equipped it with a custom rooftop platform—perfect for primate viewing. They set out on a two-month road trip through Kenya and Tanzania, searching for the best tropical research site to study baboons in their natural habitat.

Jeanne was just twenty-three years old, Stuart was twenty-six, and their toddler, Michael, was about to turn two.

It was Stuart's research that had brought the young family to Africa; he was a faculty member in zoology at the University of Alberta. Jeanne, however, was never meant to study primates on this adventure. She was as green as one could get when it came to field research. Writing in 2009, she joked that her camping experience had been "limited to a very happy summer week spent in Girl Scout camp in the mountains of Virginia."

I can relate to Jeanne Altmann on that front. I grew up in suburban Calgary, Alberta. Although I had some camping experience—my parents owned a tent trailer, and we would take good advantage of the Rocky Mountains near our home—I had never camped in the backcountry under rough conditions. I never had to filter my drinking water or make a fire. That all came later, on my path to the primates. I eased myself into it, first living in a cabin in the forests of Belize, then in a tent in remote Madagascar. When I worked as a field assistant for my partner Travis's PhD project, we lived so remotely that we had no water source. Travis arranged a water delivery service where locals would fill red and green plastic jerry cans with water and load them onto a wooden cart pulled by zebu (Malagasy cattle). Suffice it to say, I have a newfound appreciation for easy access to clean running water—I'm grateful each time I turn on the kitchen faucet.

Despite her lack of camping experience, Jeanne Altmann was game for her epic African adventure. The original plan was for Stuart and a PhD student to spend their days observing the baboons, while Jeanne stayed at camp caring for young Michael. Then, when Stuart and the student returned to camp, Stuart would take over parenting duties, and Jeanne, a skilled mathematician, would tabulate and analyze the data on the spot.

However, the PhD student dropped out at the last minute, ostensibly because he felt baboons had already been well studied. As Jeanne Altmann put it later, "This was the explorer's era in tropical field research" and "many scientists wanted 'their own species.'" That student's decision set her on a new trajectory—she would now join Stuart in the field observations rather than stay at camp.

But first, there was the matter of finding the right field site.

Jeanne Altmann recalled, "We bought a long-wheelbase Land Rover and outfitted it simply to store all we would need while being able to use it for a toddler's playroom and adults' rooftop observation site during the day, sleeping quarters at night."

After celebrating Michael's second birthday, the family piled into the Land Rover and hit the road. They visited six different national parks and reserves, but it was their first stop at the Maasai-Amboseli Game Reserve (now Amboseli National Park) in southern Kenya that stuck with them.

The Maasai-Amboseli reserve is located just north and west of Mount Kilimanjaro, with the great mountain, "Kili," visible behind the acacia tree woodlands, open grasslands, swamps and marshes. The runoff from the snow atop Kilimanjaro flows under the savanna, creating hollows in the ground that become pools, lakes and swamps. These pools are notorious for attracting malaria-carrying mosquitoes, leading locals to refer to the tall acacia trees near the waters as "fever trees." When the Altmanns visited, Amboseli was a game reserve, historically home to the Maasai people and their cattle herds.

The allure of Maasai-Amboseli for the Altmanns was the abundant wildlife, including a population of thousands of yellow baboons, named for their yellowish-brown fur. Male yellow baboons typically weigh around twenty-five kilograms, while females weigh about eleven. Like all baboon species, they have a large, dog-like muzzle. The males also have long, sharp and intimidating canine teeth, which they use for feeding on meat and during aggressive interactions with other baboons.

The baboons of Amboseli were ideal for a primate behaviour study because, unlike the baboons the Altmanns encountered in Nairobi National Park, they did not flee from or show any special interest in humans. It was as close as one could get to naturalistic observations.

Unable to find anything that came close to the perfection of Maasai-Amboseli during their two-month reconnaissance trip, the Altmanns returned to that idyllic site. That year, they spent thirteen months in near isolation, studying the baboons and documenting the social system, movement and feeding behaviours of this fascinating primate species.

Each day, the couple rose at dawn, drove to the area where the baboons slept and watched them from the roof of their Land Rover. In total, they collected nearly fifteen hundred hours of behavioural observations on the baboons of Maasai-Amboseli.

Field research for this young family was a juggling act, combining the care of a two-year-old with days in the field observing monkeys. The couple had hoped to hire local staff to assist with childcare, but they couldn't find anyone to do the work—it turned out that none of the locals wished to live in a tent in an area where lions, elephants, buffalo and leopards roamed. Go figure. And so, as Jeanne put it, "this was a year of maximum multi-tasking as childcare and camp living activities were juggled along with searching for and observing baboons."

As Jeanne Altmann embarked on this unexpected journey with her husband, balancing the demands of family and fieldwork, she had no idea where it would lead. She didn't know that the Amboseli baboon project would run for decades, that she would complete the first detailed study of mother-infant behaviour in a wild mammal, or that, in the 1970s, she would publish the seminal guide to primate observation, still referenced in primate behavioural studies today.

Jeanne Altmann's childhood was the antithesis of what one might expect of a future field primatologist. It was nothing like the nature-loving Jane Goodall's upbringing. There were no backyard worms, no chickens and no stuffed chimpanzee. The "big brown eye" hypothesis doesn't apply here.

Altmann was born in New York City in 1940 but was raised in Maryland in a series of apartments. Her parents, who she describes as "true New Yorkers," weren't exactly nature enthusiasts: her mother was "allergic to virtually all mammals," and her father was "overprotective." Nature, for young Jeanne, was made up of "scattered patches of grass lawn and occasional playgrounds populated with swings and slides and climbing bars."

Her parents valued education, and even though we are talking about the 1950s, they expected their daughter to go to college. But, she wrote, their expectations around education for a girl still fit within the "nineteenth-century model" that prioritized becoming a wife and mother. If something were to happen to your husband? Well, at least you had a skill to fall back on.

An elementary math teacher set young Jeanne on the first bend in her journey toward the primates. This teacher had taught mathematics at army bases, travelling around the world in the process. When Jeanne learned of this possibility—combining math with travel—she was thrilled. Perhaps it was her city upbringing that left her yearning to see what the world had to offer—what lay beyond the walls of the apartment. She could easily imagine a career where she could travel and enjoy what she loved: math and science.

It was ideal: she would become a mathematics teacher and see the world.

Jeanne's family, however, wasn't as thrilled by this revelation.

Like many in those years—it was 1957—her father viewed teaching as a lower calling. Jeanne's grandmother "reluctantly" gave in to her request for a slide rule—a mechanical device that enables mathematical calculations—as a high school graduation present. However, she made sure the slide rule was small enough to fit in Jeanne's purse, so the device could be discreetly tucked away from prying, judgmental eyes. A woman in mathematics? Shocking.

Despite the mixed message the tiny slide rule represented (fine, do math, but for God's sake, don't let anyone see!), for Jeanne, it symbolized a world of possibility.

Soon after Jeanne's graduation, her father was transferred to Los Angeles, and the family relocated. Her family could only afford university if Jeanne lived at home, so she enrolled in the mathematics department at the University of California, Los Angeles.

Jeanne enjoyed her classes at UCLA but quickly became disillusioned by the math department's attitude toward women. She was among just three female undergraduate students, and none of them were assigned advisors. The explanation? It would be a "waste of time."

"A baby before a BA?" Jeanne Altmann's mother exclaimed when she learned the earth-shattering news that her twenty-year-old daughter was pregnant. She'd only just recovered from the fact that her daughter had gotten married at eighteen.

Jeanne's whirlwind romance had kicked off the summer after her first year as a mathematics major at UCLA. She was working a summer job at the National Institutes of Health in Bethesda, Maryland, when she met a "tall, handsome and captivating biologist" named Stuart. He had a head of thick, dark hair and sported a bushy beard.

Stuart Altmann was born in St. Louis, Missouri, but grew up in Los Angeles. Like Jeanne, he attended UCLA, where he completed his bachelor's and master's degrees in biology. His focus was the mobbing behaviour of birds. After UCLA, Stuart was drafted into the army and served as a research scientist at Walter Reed Army Medical Center, where he worked on parasites. Stuart had a passion for wildlife and adventure, and, following his service, he hitched a ride to Panama to study the howler monkeys on Barro Colorado Island. He then attended Harvard University, where he had the distinction of being the first PhD student of famed biologist E.O. Wilson. Under Wilson's guidance, Stuart developed a research program focused on non-human primate sociality. His PhD research on rhesus macaques took place on Cayo Santiago Island in Puerto Rico, and was sponsored by the National Institutes of Health.

It was at the National Institutes of Health in Maryland where Stuart met Jeanne in the summer of 1958. Their first date—true to Stuart's brand and perhaps a glimpse into the couple's future—was at a zoo. "I went to the zoo with a zoologist," Jeanne wrote in a letter home.

Jeanne and Stuart became a couple and began navigating a long-distance relationship between Los Angeles and Maryland. They married just one year later, in 1959.

"We might not have much money, but I can assure you that I will show Jeanne the world," Stuart Altmann told Jeanne's parents when he broached the topic of marriage. Her parents may not have felt entirely comforted by that, but they liked Stuart and so were supportive of their daughter's decision despite her young age.

Jeanne Altmann decided she was done with UCLA—let's face it, it hadn't been the warmest of environments—and moved to Boston to be with her new husband. Never one to sit idle, she enrolled as a part-time undergraduate student at MIT while Stuart finished his final year at Harvard. In her spare time, she did some computer programming for anthropologist Beatrice Whiting and helped Stuart analyze his PhD data. Jeanne became an unofficial member of Harvard's anthropology circles.

Following the year in Boston, Stuart Altmann landed a faculty position in the Zoology Department at the University of Alberta in Edmonton. The couple relocated north, and Jeanne transferred to the U of A, where she enrolled in the mathematics program.

Jeanne had just been invited to join U of A's honours mathematics program when she learned she was expecting. Unfortunately, she couldn't join the program part-time, so she had to turn down the offer. Instead, while raising Michael, Jeanne finished her degree by going to school part-time in the evening.

Jeanne wrote, "I cannot imagine, either emotionally or intellectually, having missed the intimate and intense involvement in raising my children, at once the most challenging and fulfilling experience of my life."

Still, she sought out further intellectual opportunities whenever she could. She had a passion for pure math, and whenever possible, she would immerse herself in the world of numbers and equations, losing "all sense of time and place" for "hours or even days."

This state of mind, Jeanne Altmann admits, was not compatible with mothering—a role that required much of her attention.

As the primary caregiver, she reflected: "My parenting experience was probably a significant fork in the road that eventually led me to focus on behaviour rather than mathematics."

"0700 hours, adult female in seated posture is feeding on grass plant."

Jeanne Altmann spoke softly into the handheld tape recorder while her husband snapped a photograph. The female baboon was stuffing her face with grass, her cheek pouches getting larger by the second. Cheek pouches, a characteristic trait of Old World monkeys like the yellow baboons, are like grocery bags for the mouth. They extend down both sides of a baboon's mouth between the jaw and the cheek and are a handy adaptation for storing food.

Jeanne and Stuart spent hours watching the baboons of Amboseli. They kept detailed records of where the monkeys slept, their sleeping postures, where they moved, what they ate and how they interacted. Their goal was to "understand how the animals cope with the problems that they face in their natural habitat."

During that first field season in Amboseli, which lasted just over a year, Jeanne and Stuart Altmann usually made their observations of the yellow baboons from a respectful distance. Unlike Jane Goodall, Dian Fossey and even the more scientifically minded Biruté Galdikas—who each had practically become members of the groups of primates they studied—Jeanne and Stuart kept their distance and were careful to maintain a "neutral relationship with the baboons."

The couple most frequently made their observations while perched atop the observation platform of their Land Rover station wagon, accessed through a hatch in the roof. The two observers would climb up, set up their canvas folding chairs and take in the bird's-eye view of the vast, short-grass savanna, where the large, land-dwelling baboons roamed among myriad other wildlife.

"We tried not to move our field vehicle directly toward the group, and if we could anticipate their line of progression, we tried never to stop in their pathway," the Altmanns wrote in *Baboon Ecology*, the publication born from their first season in the field. "We never fed anything to any of them."

Eventually—only after the baboons became accustomed to the Land Rover—Jeanne and Stuart began making observations at a closer range.

Their data collection methods were rigorous and structured. They traced an aerial photograph of the area, which showed the major features and even individual trees that peppered the landscape. Then, they split that larger map into smaller sections that fit onto standard sheets of letter-sized paper and made multiple copies that they would mark up with information showing the baboons' movement patterns.

The couple collected the behavioural data, noting the time to the nearest minute. They used a tape recorder rather than handwritten notes so they could "keep the animals under continuous observation," without having to look down at a pesky notebook all the time.

In *Baboon Ecology*, Jeanne and Stuart Altmann provide detailed descriptions of their observation methods alongside neatly labelled tables, charts, figures and photographs documenting the baboon population dynamics, group structures, group movements, diet and interactions with other animals in the landscape.

Alongside the rigorous science, there are glimpses of a lighter side. The monograph is peppered with line drawings, including one of their trusty Land Rover and, of course, several baboons. Even the names they gave the monkeys—"Humprump" and "Even Steven"—hint at their sense of humour.

It's easy to forget that it wasn't just Jeanne and Stuart who spent all those months in Amboseli with the baboons—Michael was there too. Imagine raising a toddler going through his terrible twos while conducting research among the monkeys on the African savanna. Although perhaps a two-year-old might be able to relate to monkey groups better than most.

So, over those thirteen months, Jeanne Altmann had to wear multiple hats: field assistant, wife and mother. Although their Land Rover had been kitted out with a double mattress in the back, the couple opted to set up a tent when they arrived in Amboseli. This freed up the back of the vehicle, where they set up a playroom for young Michael.

A year of balancing the sciences with raising a young child would be a blur for anyone, but for Jeanne, it was compounded with other challenges. Her memories of the baboons are hazy, as she recalled, because "the year was also one in which we had more life-threatening medical crises than we were to have in total since then."

During that first field season, Stuart came down with pleurisy—inflammation of the lungs—and later developed appendicitis, requiring an emergency appendectomy. But these rather dramatic events would be the least of their health concerns for that year. What really broke the Altmanns was when young Michael contracted a virus that left him paralyzed from the neck down. The family rushed to Nairobi, where they placed an iron lung—a ventilator that simulates breathing by enclosing an individual's body and varying the air pressure—near Michael. It took two full months for Michael to recover enough for Jeanne to take him back to the US and the National Institutes of Health Clinical Center.

Reflecting on the ordeal, Jeanne wrote, "Anyone who has experienced the thrill of a child's first steps can perhaps imagine the even greater thrill of a child's first steps after a life-threatening paralysis."

It was an unceremonious end to an otherwise successful field season.

Jeanne and Stuart Altmann stepped out of their vehicle and surveyed the Amboseli landscape in 1969. It had been five years since their first visit. Stuart had received a research grant from the National Science Foundation, enabling them to go back for a few months.

But things in Amboseli weren't as they had left them.

Five years earlier, the Maasai-Amboseli Game Reserve had been a thriving grassland habitat, peppered with yellow-trunked, open-crowned fever tree woodlands. The reserve was home not only to thousands of baboons but also to many other animals, including ungulates, carnivores and several bird species.

But now, the scene before the two researchers was nearly unrecognizable. The fever trees, so loved by the baboons, were gone. The landscape was barren and stark.

Jeanne soon learned that the decline of the fever tree woodlands was the result of several factors. Although time had passed, and the landscape would have changed due to a natural aging process, that was only a small part of it. The more impactful cause, Jeanne and Stuart Altmann would learn, was that Amboseli had experienced a severe drought followed by several years of heavy rains. This unusual weather pattern had caused the water table to rise, drowning the fever tree roots and killing them. The rising water table had also brought a salt layer to the soil's surface, which can also kill the tree's roots.

As Jeanne would also find out, human actions had compounded these environmental changes. Amboseli had initially appealed to the Altmanns because it was largely untouched, though the baboons did have some contact with humans. The area was also home to the Indigenous Maasai pastoralists, a nomadic people who range along the Great Rift Valley in Kenya and Tanzania. A central part of their culture is a reliance on cattle for food, clothing and shelter.

After Kenya gained independence from Great Britain in 1963, the government implemented new development plans, including group ranches intended to "modernize" the Maasai. They also set up barriers in Amboseli to restrict the grazing patterns of the Maasai herds, and these changes affected the way the community engaged with the wildlife.

Grazing cattle began to displace the baboons and other animals. The Maasai burned areas to encourage new grasses to grow for their cattle, and overgrazing from large herds of cattle meant less food for other grazers, shifting their diets. Notably, the elephant population's new feeding habits led to additional trees being killed and prevented the woodlands from regenerating.

Over the following weeks, the Altmanns set out to assess what had happened to their beloved baboon population in the face of these changes to their habitat. It didn't take long for them to determine that the population had seen a dramatic shift since they were last there in 1964. The two scientists surveyed the area repeatedly, and the data confirmed the baboon population had dropped by more than 90 per cent.

But it wasn't just the baboon population. Vervet monkeys and several other mammals had also been affected. To Jeanne and Stuart, Amboseli appeared completely transformed—from a woodland paradise into an uninhabitable desert. In an article published in the *American Journal of Primatology* in 1985, Jeanne and Stuart Altmann, along with Glenn Hausfater, one of Stuart's graduate students, reflected that the shift they observed in Amboseli and the impact on the primate population was an important lesson in conservation. Baboons are one of the most resilient and adaptable of the primates, and for their abundant populations to be so dramatically affected meant that no primate population was safe from changing ecology.

Jeanne, Stuart and their family found themselves chasing Stuart's career from Edmonton to Atlanta and finally to Chicago. In Chicago, Jeanne found herself without a full-time job, and an idea was born.

The conversation might have happened in the car or over a glass of wine after the kids were in bed. I imagine the exchange went something like this:

"You know what we need? An instruction manual for studying animal behaviour," said Stuart.

"What do you mean?" Jeanne asked.

"Behavioural datasets are collected in so many ways. Well, I don't have to tell you that. What if there were a manual that helped researchers know how best to analyze that data?"

Jeanne nodded, and the wheels began to turn.

"You're right! There needs to be some standardization across studies so that we can confidently compare data. Even across species!" Her heart was racing.

Stuart gave Jeanne a knowing look. "You know who would be perfect to create something like that?"

Jeanne didn't need to answer the question. She could already feel it bubbling up inside of her. This kind of project would be the perfect use of her skills in mathematics and her interest in animal behaviour.

A passionate Jeanne Altmann took on a PhD-level project on methods in behavioural observation studies. She learned about techniques used in observing ants, wasps and humans. She was interdisciplinary in her approach, scouring literature from zoology, anthropology, psychology and education.

Jeanne has credited her "outsider" perspective to the success of her findings, which ultimately took shape as a seminal paper, "Observational Study of Behavior: Sampling Methods," still widely cited today. She found that few studies, especially those conducted in field settings, effectively described behaviour in enough detail to analyze the observations. She also found a lack of justification for the methods being used—it was unclear how the methods matched the questions the researchers had set out to ask.

Jeanne decided it was important to return to first principles, a technique for problem-solving that involves questioning assumptions, breaking the problem down into its basic parts and then building the solutions from scratch. Essentially, it involves leaving your assumptions at the door. The Greek philosopher Aristotle is considered a key figure in the development of this kind of thinking.

Jeanne later described the resulting publication as "a guide to thinking and planning and design."

Jeanne and Stuart Altmann had always been a team, and since Stuart had planted the seed and supported her in revisions, Jeanne offered him co-authorship on the resulting paper. Stuart declined. Years later, he told Jeanne he didn't want authorship because he felt she would only receive full recognition if she were the sole author. Jeanne didn't have her PhD at the time, and she was a woman in academia in the '70s. Stuart knew what she was up against and wanted to give her every chance of success.

The forty-page article, published in the journal *Behaviour*, described various sampling methods for direct observation of social behaviour. Jeanne detailed different kinds of behaviours: "events," which take place in an instant, and "states," which have duration. She advised researchers to think about the question they were attempting to answer before deciding whether to record behaviours as events or states. She also provided advice on how to schedule sampling sessions, how to determine the number of individuals to study in each session, and how to select those individuals.

Jeanne's paper also included several methods of behavioural sampling. Ad libitum sampling, which Jeanne defined as "typical field notes," was the method used by Jane Goodall and Dian Fossey in their field studies. Essentially, it is a journal that records everything observed. There are no formal rules with ad libitum sampling—it lives up to its Latin name, which means "in accordance with one's wishes." This kind of data is tricky to compare across researchers and studies since, well, the observer writes down whatever interests them. It is quite subjective. These observations are prone to bias, with attention often being drawn to overt, exciting behaviours.

Focal animal sampling—a term coined by Jeanne—is where the researcher observes one individual (the focal animal) for a set period, recording all behaviours and the time spent on that behaviour. This method has the advantage of capturing even subtle behaviours and is far more structured than ad libitum sampling.

Instantaneous sampling involves recording an individual's behaviour at pre-selected moments—every minute, for example. When applied to groups, Jeanne Altmann referred to it as scan sampling. This method lends itself well to analysis—researchers can calculate the percentage of time spent on activities. It is also beneficial because data can be collected quickly from many group members.

Jeanne described other sampling methods in the paper and pointed out the strengths and weaknesses of each. She urged researchers to question whether their procedures could result in biases and to consider the behavioural characteristics that are most relevant to their question. She also pointed out that no method is perfect and that researchers can use more than one in their study to get at different behaviours.

Jeanne Altmann's work outlining sampling protocols played a significant role in making an important shift in primatology. Her methods emphasized objective observations of all individuals in a group, whether male or female, and helped shift the focus from overt behaviours (such as males fighting) to more subtle behaviours of other group members.

Throughout the article, she draws on examples from rhesus macaques, baboons, chickens, gulls and even human children. As a result, her influence extends beyond primatology. After her paper was published, researchers referred to it when designing new studies and were thrilled by how the standardization of methods meant they could compare data across years, study sites and even species.

Jeanne Altmann's paper continues to be used to this day. Ask any primatologist and they will point to Jeanne Altmann as having popularized the rigorous methods that continue to be the standard for documenting primate behaviour. She herself humbly describes her paper as "the right paper at the right time," but it was more than that. Even before it was officially published, researchers were scrambling to get their hands on it. Rather than rushing to publication, though, she took a wise and measured approach: she shared drafts with experts, soliciting and carefully integrating their valuable feedback. Feminist scholar Donna Haraway points out that this approach is likely why the paper was "widely influential before its official publication." After it was published, Jeanne received letters from graduate students working in the field, asking for advice on their methods, which she generously provided.

As of today, more than nineteen thousand researchers have cited the paper, according to Google Scholar, and I have no doubt that its use by researchers is more prevalent than the citations indicate. It's no exaggeration to say that every primate behavioural researcher draws on the methods and ways of thinking that Jeanne Altmann outlined in this work. I know I did. Despite her unconventional path to academia, it's no wonder that she is widely regarded as a pioneer in the study of primate behavioural ecology.

What struck Jeanne Altmann about watching the baboons of Amboseli was just how much time they dedicated to "making a living." Each day, despite the heat, the baboons would walk several kilometres across the hot, dry short-grass savanna on all fours, searching for food. For about three-quarters of the day, Jeanne would sit quietly, diligently recording her observations as the baboons laboriously dug up bulbs and grass corms (sections of the stems) from the ground. From Jeanne's perspective, any rest they took looked to be well-earned and necessary for them to gather energy to continue their daily trek.

But Jeanne was interested in more than just the baboons' feeding behaviours. She was paying attention to the other activities associated with group living and sociality—the behaviours the baboons would display when they weren't feeding or searching for new feeding sites. These activities—mating, infant care, dominance interactions and more—were connected to the feeding behaviours, and Jeanne was interested in uncovering the links and complexities.

By 1973, Jeanne, Stuart and their family were living in Chicago. Their youngest child, Rachel, was now in full-day school, and Jeanne suddenly found herself with free time. She decided to join the University of Chicago's interdisciplinary program in human development to complete her own PhD study of the baboons. Looking to diversify, she purposefully avoided the biology program where Stuart was now a faculty member.

In June 1975, the family was again back in Amboseli, but this time Jeanne was there to conduct her own field research. Up until that point, she had always worked as part of Stuart's team—perhaps some even viewed her as rising in his shadow. Now, she was the principal investigator, while Stuart stayed back at camp with the kids.

Jeanne reflects that it was during this time that she truly found her "voice" as a field primatologist. She was beginning to gain recognition in the field as a scientist in her own right—finally, she was being invited to conferences as an independent researcher rather than an extension of Stuart—and was even elected editor of the journal *Animal Behaviour*, a position she held from 1978 to 1983. She participated in workshops, including one on women in science. In an interview with Donna Haraway, Jeanne described how the workshop unpacked how women scientists frame their questions in science based on "all those people I was and am." In a sense, Jeanne must have felt as though she was made up of many people: a mother, a scientist and a feminist, to name a few. Haraway noted that for Jeanne Altmann, being a woman meant juggling these various realities. It's also notable that, even though she had been balancing research with family since the 1950s, Jeanne is written in the history books as arriving on the "science scene" in the 1970s.

The complexities of being a woman in science during this time may have caused Jeanne to hesitate when declaring her research focus on baboon females and young infants. These topics were often considered "women's topics," which were somehow deemed "soft" or lesser. Up to this point, the focus of primatologists—particularly baboon researchers—had been on the overt, aggressive behaviours between males in a group. After all, male baboons were physically striking and muscular, with large canine teeth, and when fights broke out, it was hard not to notice. Female baboon behaviour was much more subtle, and their dominance hierarchies were more difficult to decipher. The result? Males were viewed as central to the social dynamics—including reproductive behaviour—of baboon groups.

Case closed. No further research necessary.

But Jeanne Altmann knew better. Her structured and detailed observations of baboon groups leading up to her PhD made it clear to her that we had barely scratched the surface. Ever the diligent observer, Jeanne saw immense value in understanding the reproductive challenges faced by females in the group—surely it was at least as important to understand baboon females as it was to understand the males. As a mother herself, Jeanne intimately understood the energy that went into raising her own two kids—never mind while conducting research on the savanna. Understanding the relationships of the females and infants in baboon groups was like an intricate puzzle that Jeanne was determined to solve, a challenge that fuelled her mathematically inclined brain.

Jeanne Altmann knew that baboons, like all primates, had long periods of gestation, lactation and infant carrying. There was no doubt in her mind that these behaviours played a crucial role in group dynamics and the evolutionary pressures driving primate sociality. Jeanne wanted to understand the energy and effort baboon mothers expended caring for their infants and how they managed to simultaneously maintain their social relationships with the rest of the group. She wanted to understand the ecology of motherhood.

Jeanne's study centred on a dozen baboon mothers—members of one of the five groups she and Stuart had been observing in Amboseli. Her detailed, quantitative observations finally painted a comprehensive picture of female baboon life. She published her PhD thesis in 1980 as a book titled *Baboon Mothers and Infants*.

Jeanne found that females spent most of their time and energy finding enough food to sustain themselves and their young. At the same time, she noted, they needed to maintain strong social relationships to survive within the group. Jeanne showed how baboon mothers demonstrated "knowledge of home range, of group history, of social relationships that ensured female social power." Females, it turned out, played central roles in baboon society.

Jeanne wrote, "Baboon mothers, like most primate mothers, including humans, are dual-career mothers in a complex ecological and social setting." Jeanne herself embodied the role of a "dual-career" female—a mother and a scientist—mirroring the baboon females she studied. She reflects that her own mother had taught her that "one would gain opportunities to pursue non-domestic activities by being faster and more efficient at the domestic ones, a message that I internalized early on."

She added, "That I was able to raise two truly amazing children and then also have a wonderfully satisfying career, strikes me as such marvellous luck." Jeanne also acknowledged that her success was not just due to "luck," but also to her commitment, passion and the encouragement of others.

What would turn into a decades-long research project in Amboseli began with Alto's group, one of five baboon groups living near the central waterhole in Amboseli. In July 1971, the group had thirty-five members, with Alto, an elderly baboon and the highest-ranking female, reigning over the others. The group spent most of their time near the large watering hole. In what was meant to be a one-off, short-term study, Stuart's graduate student Glenn Hausfater would study Alto's group and test Stuart's model of male priority of access to mating opportunities.

On this trip—Jeanne and Stuart's third to Amboseli—they set out to habituate Alto's group so Hausfater could collect his data. None of them had any inkling that this year would mark the beginning of a four-decade-long study—what would become the Amboseli Baboon Research Project, one of the longest-running and most detailed studies of any mammalian population.

The transition to long-term research was a gradual one. Jeanne and Stuart Altmann's work in Amboseli took place during what could arguably be considered the heyday of primate research. In the 1970s, field research was trending—if it were happening now, there most certainly would be a hashtag involved—with researchers travelling across the globe to study primate species in their natural habitats. These studies were usually brief, stand-alone projects lasting between twelve and twenty-four months. But Jeanne and Stuart knew well that a great deal of work went into setting up even the shortest field research projects. There was a multitude of logistics involved: identifying a study species and location, setting up camp and habituating the groups. Setting up a field research site—even a temporary one—could take months and would certainly cut into the valuable hours needed for primate observation.

Beyond the logistics, Jeanne's research questions and study subjects were calling out for a long-term study. For Jeanne, it felt as though the baboon population itself was literally screaming, "You need to stay here! You will not get the answers you are looking for unless you study us for years!"

Jeanne was interested in how the baboons made a living. She wanted to better understand the factors influencing baboon mothers and their infants—to deduce what influenced their survival and behaviour. One major conundrum when it comes to answering these questions, for baboons and other primate species, is their long lifespan. Unlike species like rodents or fish, to get a complete picture of a primate's life—from birth to death—takes years, not months. Baboons can live up to twenty-seven years in the wild, so to find answers to the big questions about behaviour and evolutionary fitness—which span generations—Jeanne knew they needed to study the baboons continuously and for the long term.

Stuart and Jeanne Altmann and Glenn Hausfater went on to co-direct the Amboseli Baboon Project, studying different aspects of baboon life. Stuart focused on feeding and foraging, Hausfater on male dominance and reproduction, and Jeanne on female life histories. Their projects were independent yet overlapping, each contributing to the bigger picture of understanding baboons' social lives.

Hausfater's data showed that higher-ranking males had more success with mating than lower-ranking males, supporting a model that Stuart had posited years earlier after studying rhesus macaques: the priority-of-access model. This model suggests that dominance rank predicts mating success—as if the male baboons were taking a number at a supermarket deli. Imagine the female baboons, with their hairnets fixed tightly, calling them up to the counter one by one, in order of the number they'd been assigned. The model is still used today in studies of dominance rank in multi-male social groups.

That initial year during Glenn Hausfater's project was also important because it was when the researchers formalized their data collection methods, outlining them on paper in the *Monitoring Guide for the Amboseli Baboon Research Project*. This guidebook outlines the intent of the long-term strategy in Amboseli. It urges participating team members to take their role in the project seriously and to work toward gathering the highest-quality data.

After Hausfater's study, Jeanne and Stuart split their time between Chicago and Kenya, and the project continued to expand. Stuart regularly took on PhD students or post-doctoral fellows, who would head to Amboseli to work on their individual studies. At the same time, these students collected data that contributed to the long-term project, maintaining a continuous dataset. Before long, Jeanne and Stuart found themselves with data on the baboons that could be compared across projects and over the years.

When I did my master's research in Belize, my supervisor, Mary Pavelka, followed Jeanne Altmann's model for long-term data collection. Each of us students signed on knowing we would conduct our own research while also contributing data to a long-term dataset. For my master's research, I did a population census of the Monkey River watershed, which involved travelling the region, walking trails and paddling rivers looking for monkeys. Every other day, though, I stayed near our cabin at the main research station, monitoring the four groups of howler monkeys that lived in the forest nearby. I spent hours each day walking the trail system, searching for the groups. When I found them, I would mark their location in the forest using GPS and note the time of day, the temperature, how many monkeys I saw and what they were doing. These data sets were then entered into Mary Pavelka's database, which tracked the population of monkeys at Monkey River over the long term.

Both Mary Pavelka and Jeanne Altmann would likely tell you that maintaining a long-term field research site is a challenge. For Jeanne and Stuart, one of the difficulties they faced was that they simply couldn't be there continuously. They were raising a family and for their kids' sake they needed to spend long periods of time at home. Although PhD students and post-docs helped with the data collection, there were still gaps in time that needed to be filled.

Adding to the challenge, by the early 1980s, Glenn Hausfater was ready to move on from the baboon project to pursue his own independent research. Meanwhile, Stuart was deeply involved in writing a book about infant feeding and nutrition in primates, and was too engrossed in that project to devote time and energy to fieldwork.

Jeanne, on the other hand, yearned to be back in the field collecting data. With their son Michael now in university, the Altmanns decided that if Jeanne could get funding, she would take the lead on the baboon project. She did secure the funding and was able to follow up on the findings of her mother-infant study.

Jeanne has also recalled the 1980s at Amboseli as an important time because of a shift in "primary field personnel" and the "base for the next generation of our fieldwork"—the training and participation of Kenyan researchers. Bringing locals on board to collect data was just the solution the project needed to maintain a continuous dataset.

In 1981, Jeanne hired Raphael Mututua, a member of the local Maasai community, as the first local researcher to work on the project. Mututua continued his work across decades, managing projects and collecting data. Like everyone who passed through

Amboseli, the Kenyan team was trained by the trusted monitoring guide.

Serah Sayialel, a Kenyan woman, joined the team next in 1989. She had worked previously with scientists studying vervet monkeys and had experience collecting data. Sayialel often brought her children with her into the field while assisting her husband, Philip Muruthi, who first worked in Amboseli as a master's student at the University of Nairobi. He later went on to attend Princeton University for his PhD, returning to Kenya to do conservation work. Muruthi is now the vice-president of species conservation and science at the African Wildlife Foundation.

Each person who passes through Amboseli collects their own data but always contributes to the longer-term core dataset, with the Kenyan team providing the "backbone." Jeanne Altmann has called the Kenyan team her "dream team."

Jeanne and her colleagues soon formally recognized the efforts of the Kenyan team academically by granting them co-authorship credit.

The topic of authorship of collaborators and assistants in the primate habitat countries has become a point of discussion among primatologists, particularly regarding the ethics of fieldwork. There is a growing push for primate field researchers to support co-authorship for local assistants and collaborators who contribute to field research on primates. More and more, researchers recognize the importance of building capacity in local scientists by providing support and training in technology and science, opportunities for collaboration through co-authored publications and international meetings and, perhaps most crucially, recognizing the intellectual contributions of local team members.

On these points, the Amboseli Baboon Research Project, under Jeanne Altmann's leadership, was way ahead of the curve. The project has been running continuously for nearly five decades, supporting more than twenty graduate students, including a dozen from Kenya.

Jeanne Altmann sums up her trajectory in academia as one that took place "outside of the classroom," where she balanced her relationship with Stuart, raised two young children, nurtured her love of math, and pursued her passion for teaching and interest in animal behaviour.

Jeanne's first salaried job related to primates was in the Conservation Biology department at the Brookfield Zoo in 1984—nearly twenty years after she first visited Amboseli with Stuart. There, she received financial support to continue her work in Amboseli, including training Kenyan students. Not long after, she was offered a faculty position in the Department of Ecology and Evolution at the University of Chicago.

Jeanne continued to collect data in Amboseli. Susan Alberts, who had worked in Amboseli for her master's at UCLA, entered the University of Chicago's PhD program. Alberts was interested in finding a way to determine paternity information to better understand the male behavioural data. Jeanne soon established collaborations with researchers who could contribute genetic information—notably biologist Robert Sapolsky, who facilitated studies on the hormones and behaviour of the baboons.

Meanwhile, Jeanne and Stuart's children were grown up, with their own families. Stuart transitioned to emeritus faculty status, and Jeanne accepted a faculty position at the prestigious Princeton University, where she established a steroid hormone lab. She also began creating a succession plan to continue the long-term work in Amboseli after she retired: Susan Alberts, now at Duke University, would collaborate and ultimately take ownership of the project.

Jeanne has reflected on a time when people would ask when the baboon studies would be done and has taken immense satisfaction in knowing that the Amboseli baboon project may never be "done," but will continue to grow and integrate new technologies, with generation after generation of scientists asking new questions.

Jeanne Altmann's work in Amboseli has been, and continues to be, an inspiration for many field primatologists. Even as far back as 1971, she was influencing young primatologists. One woman, about to embark on her first trip to India to study Hanuman langurs, had never been formally trained in field observation methods but had recently picked up Jeanne and Stuart's book *Baboon Ecology*. That woman, Sarah Hrdy, pored over the Altmanns' techniques for watching the baboons with grand plans to apply them to her study of infant killing among the langurs.

CHAPTER SEVEN

Lady Langur

WHEN I MET SARAH HRDY VIA ZOOM, she was seated in her home office in California, with scores of books on the shelves behind her. I squinted to try to make out the titles on the spines, but the video quality wasn't clear enough. They looked important.

I'll admit, I was a little heartbroken. We were supposed to have met in person—she had generously offered to show me around her walnut farm, Citrona Farms, in Winters, California. After the tour, we would have had dinner with our husbands. She'd even said she was going to serve lamb ("We raise lamb and often have it," she had written).

Sadly, illness got in the way, and we had to shift to an online format.

Before I clicked the call button, I prepped my workspace.

Interview questions: check.

Blank Word file open for notes: check.

Reference books arranged around me: check.

Just breathe.

I was about to meet an icon in primatology.

"So, tell me about the book you want to write," Hrdy said after we had finished with our niceties. Her voice was soft, and I picked up the slightest hint of a Texas drawl. She took notes and nodded with interest as I relayed my pitch.

I told her about Linda Fedigan's hypotheses on why women are drawn to primatology, and how these ideas and the stories of the women who emerged in the early days of the discipline would drive the narrative of my book. She jotted down her notes and then took the lead on our discussion—this woman is so clearly a force—addressing each of Fedigan's hypotheses and sharing her personal experiences.

It's hard to pick out the highlights from our conversation—there were so many gems. Hrdy told me about her meeting with Louis Leakey after a safari in Africa in 1970, and how he sent her to Tigoni Primate Research Centre in Kenya to work as a research assistant for Neil Chalmers, where she got her feet wet studying vervet monkeys. She spoke about a visit to Dian Fossey's apartment, where she admired a set of primate-themed coasters. Later, she returned home to a package from Fossey, who had sent her the coasters as a gift. Hrdy laughed a little as she referred to Jane Goodall as the "Taylor Swift of conservation." She gave me many suggestions on who else I should speak with and what literature I ought to be reading.

When I asked why she had first decided to study primates, Hrdy responded simply: "I didn't want to become a primatologist, and I didn't want a PhD. I just wanted to know why the male [monkeys] in India were behaving so badly."

She explained that she had a personal interest in primate societies and felt "galvanized" by the androcentric bias in the studies of wild primates in the 1970s. She wanted to uncover the role of female monkeys and dispel prevailing myths that placed males at the centre of primate groups.

When I think about Sarah Hrdy's story, I can find evidence for two of the hypotheses for why females are drawn to study wild primates. First, she rose in the discipline during the second wave of feminism in the 1960s and 1970s. As she put it, she'd grown up in a "patriarchal, segregated, racist part of the world" and had come out of that upbringing ready to fight the system. A true trailblazer, Hrdy was her Harvard advisor's first female graduate student, and she forged her path despite a dearth of female role models and the systemic barriers she encountered.

Second, as with Jeanne Altmann, there's evidence for the "primates themselves" hypothesis. Hrdy was acutely interested in female primates, and throughout her career, she has made a special effort to ensure that females get their due. She made it clear to me that this decision wasn't "a feminist act" but instead an effort to make sure that science paid equal attention to both sexes.

I ended my call with Hrdy with no doubt as to why I held her in such high regard. I knew it was high time for others to learn the story of the woman I've come to think of as "Lady Langur."

Primatologist Sarah Hrdy recalls spotting her first langur in 1971: a female "about the size of a springer spaniel with the slender-waisted elegance of a greyhound, an extraordinarily elegant silver-grey creature with a black face and dainty black gloves." The Hanuman langurs (also known as grey langurs) that live on Mount Abu are named after the Hindu god Hanuman who, in Hindu mythology, is the monkey commander of a monkey army. Hanuman langurs are considered sacred in India. These primates live in close association with humans and have been studied for decades. They are known for living in high population densities and typically form either all-male or one-male groups averaging around twenty-five individuals.

One day in 1972, Sarah Hrdy could sense that something significant was about to go down.

Standing nearly six feet tall, with wavy, shoulder-length blonde hair, the slim woman from Texas kept her eyes locked on the troop of Hanuman langurs feeding above her. These langurs are easily recognizable by their black faces, hands and feet. Their faces are framed with striking, white-tinged fur, giving them a look akin to a distinguished older gentleman who hasn't trimmed his beard in some time.

She watched as the lanky Old World monkeys with grey-brown fur and long, slim tails went about their activities. The leaf-eating primates moved swiftly on all fours, sometimes on the ground, sometimes in the tree canopy.

Hrdy was stationed at a study site in India, on the outskirts of the bustling northern city of Jodhpur. The site was near Abu, a town of just eight thousand people—primarily herders and wood-cutters—situated next to a lake, thirty-eight hundred feet above sea level at the top of Mount Abu. There, high atop this rocky plateau, surrounded by forest, Sarah Hrdy spent five years, on and off, observing more than two hundred individual Hanuman langurs up close. She was interested in the political dynamics of the langur troops, and the Hillside troop—one of five under study—did not disappoint.

As the sun began to set, Hrdy stood in a shaded laneway leading to Abu's school for the blind, watching as the langurs above munched on dried plums. An adult male langur arrived on the scene. It was Mug, back again. Hrdy watched carefully.

Mug was an adult male langur—about twelve years old—whom Hrdy described as a "compact, muscular specimen" and the "model of a modern langur male: aloof, swaggering, memorably loud." Hrdy recognized Mug instantly by the slit at the bottom of his left ear, his scarred tail and his crooked snout.

Back in August, Mug had been ousted from his troop—the Hillside troop—by a new, older male whom Hrdy called "Shifty Leftless." Shifty had earned his name from a bite-sized chunk missing from his left ear. Hrdy had noted Shifty's muscular frame and piercing deep-set eyes. Since Shifty's arrival, the once-peaceful troop of langurs had been thrust into disarray. One adult female and all six of the troop's infants had gone missing.

In a journal article published in *American Scientist*, Sarah Hrdy described her first encounter with the group with the missing individuals, during which she tried to convince herself that the group of langurs had not been decimated—that instead this was a different group altogether.

Then, the dark truth hit hard: Hrdy heard from locals that they had witnessed an adult male kill two of the infants in an area known to be part of the Hillside troop's range. Shifty was the prime suspect.

Shortly after the disappearances, a power struggle between Shifty and Mug ensued. When Hrdy returned to Abu in June 1972, Shifty was out, having joined a neighbouring troop, the Bazaar troop, which earned its name because it spent a great deal of time scavenging in the nearby bazaar. From what Hrdy could tell, Shifty had also wreaked havoc on that group—three of their original infants were missing, and an amateur ornithologist who lived nearby reported seeing one of them being killed by a male monkey.

But Shifty hadn't fully relinquished control of the Hillside troop back to Mug. Instead, he was behaving as though he was the male leader of two troops—perhaps the langur equivalent of running an empire. Periodically, Shifty would return to the Hillside troop, but when he was gone, Mug would swoop in and rejoin the group, whether they liked it or not. Back and forth it went.

That evening, Hrdy watched Mug carefully as he approached and lurked near the mother and infant she had named "Itch" and "Scratch." Scratch earned his name from his fur, which was black with "scratches" of white. So it was only natural that Scratch's mother be called Itch. Mug had been stalking the pair for days.

Itch and Scratch had no interest in Mug and were avoiding him. Whenever he approached the tree they were in, they would leave immediately. But Mug would follow. The females would then move back into the tree they had originally been in.

At around four in the afternoon, Mug let out a grunt and swiftly moved on all fours to a nearby rooftop. Like a soldier atop a watchtower, Mug surveyed the area, staring in one direction and then the other. Then, all at once, he lunged from the rooftop at Itch, who had Scratch clinging to her belly. Mug snatched at the infant. Itch, now cornered, turned toward Mug, baring her teeth.

What happened next gives me chills. Itch was joined by a posse of langur females. Sol and Pawless, the elder females of the Hillside troop, were among them. Pawless had earned her name because she had just one arm—perhaps this wasn't her first time in combat.

The other females positioned themselves between Itch and her attacker, Mug, fighting him off on her behalf. They lunged at Mug and chased him up a tree.

The females' response to the attacker was fascinating. When Mug attacked the mother and infant, nearby females threw themselves into battle, risking their well-being to fight Mug and protect an infant that wasn't their own.

Mug was relentless. Again and again, he descended and attacked Itch and her infant. Again and again, the females fended him off. The day's events ended when the troop was driven away by a gardener.

Really, though, it was nowhere near over. Hrdy observed Mug attacking Itch and Scratch on nine different occasions. Infants were injured, and so were adult females who fought to protect those infants.

In September, Mug finally managed to get hold of baby Scratch during one of his attacks. He carried the helpless creature in his powerful jaws and took off running, leaping up onto the rooftop of a nearby school. Again, two other older females in the group chased after Mug, trying to retrieve the infant. In the end, they were successful, but Scratch was severely wounded—Mug left him with "toothmarks inscribed on his skull" and "a deep gash across his left thigh."

Hrdy describes how, over a five-year period, she observed similar events in the Hillside and Bazaar troops—infants were dying at the hands of male attackers.

Her conclusion—one that would spark controversy in both scientific and public spheres—was that infant killing is an evolutionary reproductive strategy. When females nurse their infants, their ovulatory cycle is put on hold in a process called lactational amenorrhea. When their infant is killed, the female stops lactating and becomes sexually receptive earlier than she otherwise would. By killing the infants that weren't his, Mug would see an evolutionary benefit: he would increase his chances of mating with the females and siring his own offspring, thus passing on his genes to the next generation.

Hrdy concluded that infanticide was a result of sexual selection. The female langurs had adapted counterstrategies to combat male infanticide—older females fought off the males, risking their lives, and females mated with multiple males to confuse paternity.

These observations and Sarah Hrdy's conclusions left scientists and the public reeling.

Sarah Blaffer was born in Dallas, Texas, in 1946, and grew up in Houston with four siblings—three sisters and a brother. Her grandparents on her father's side were in the oil business. Her grandfather, Robert Lee Blaffer, had moved to Texas in 1901, the same year a massive oil geyser burst from an oil field in Spindletop, in southeastern Texas. This "gusher" reached over forty-five metres and blew for nine days, releasing roughly 100,000 barrels of oil each day. The oil industry in Texas was on the rise (quite literally), and Robert Lee "recognized that fortunes would be made." And fortunes were indeed made: he went on to found Humble Oil, which later became part of Exxon.

But young Sarah wasn't focused on money. Her childhood memories were shaped by the people around her, and largely by the strong women in her family. Hrdy later wrote that her grandmother, Kate Wilson Davis, was "a woman of tremendous determination, one of the first women from Texas to attend Wellesley College" in Massachusetts. After Wellesley, Kate ran a bookstore in Dallas and eventually married Hrdy's grandfather, a bank president and Yale graduate. Although Kate fell properly into her role as wife and mother, Hrdy recalled that she never lost her love of books. After Kate's husband passed away, she enrolled in graduate school to study English and headed to Paris to learn bookbinding. Later, as young Sarah decided to study anthropology, travel to India to observe primates in the wild and marry another anthropologist, her grandmother defended her choices against those who objected.

Sarah's mother, Camilla Davis Blaffer Trammell, also supported her decisions, even going so far as to fund her fieldwork with the langurs. Hrdy has described her mother as "a compulsive scholar and a stickler for accuracy." Camilla also graduated from Wellesley College and wanted to continue to law school, but instead, she returned home to Dallas. Now old enough to marry, Camilla's duty was to come out to the eligible bachelors and their families. In an interview, Hrdy once noted that marrying well was the only path available for her mother. Camilla pulled that off, marrying into the Blaffer oil fortune.

In her privileged position, Camilla was able to delegate her motherly duties by hiring nannies, and Hrdy remembered being raised by "a succession of governesses." If Camilla noticed the children becoming too attached to one of the nannies, she would hire a new one to maintain her maternal control.

Hrdy described her young self as shy except around friends. Beyond a fuzzy recollection of various caregivers, she wrote, she doesn't remember much about her childhood, which she chalked up to a lack of parental attachment. As the third daughter, young Sarah considered herself the "heiress to spare." To her, that was a good thing—it meant her family didn't closely monitor her every move and gave her the freedom to grow intellectually. Hrdy credited her Texas upbringing for sparking her interest in understanding female sexuality and "peoples' obsessive concerns with controlling it."

As a child, Sarah Blaffer was "bookish" yet "rambunctious," inattentive at school but a bookworm at home. She loved horses and attended horse shows around Texas and Tennessee with her beloved horse, Dusty. Recognizing her daughter's passion, Sarah's mother found a school in Maryland with a strong riding program—an all-girls school. St. Timothy's "took women's education seriously," with a "sensible and humane" headmistress. Although the school didn't offer much in the way of science classes, Sarah thrived in biology, devouring any *Scientific American* magazine she could get her hands on.

"I honestly had no idea I was becoming a scholar," Sarah Hrdy later wrote.

On April 9, 1969, a weaker-than-usual Sarah Blaffer got dressed and headed to Harvard Yard. It was a bright, sunny spring day in Cambridge, Massachusetts—the first day she could muster the strength to leave her bed after a battle with mononucleosis. As she approached the historic centre of the Harvard University campus, she noticed people milling about. Something was up.

Earlier that day, in room 4 of University Hall—a white granite building tucked away behind the statue of John Harvard—the Harvard deans had gathered for their regular meeting. Coffee was likely poured, and plates of cookies laid out and passed around the table.

Although it was their regular meeting, the topic of discussion was anything but "regular." The deans would be talking about the student rebellion that had been simmering and growing since 1966. Most would remember when, two years earlier, students had lain down in the streets between two of Harvard's dormitories, Quincy House and Leverett House, blocking the secretary of defence's motorcade in protest of the United States's involvement in the Vietnam War.

On that April day when young Sarah had emerged from her sickbed, seventy students, including factions from the Progressive Labor Party and the Worker Student Alliance, ousted the deans and staff from University Hall—some even by force. Once inside, the students chained and bolted the doors, only allowing entry to friends of the cause. At the height of the protest, 450 students occupied the building, gaining access to files and ultimately gathering in the sacred Faculty Room. Photos that later appeared in the Harvard yearbook and *Harvard Alumni Bulletin* depicted students posing with statues and seated around a large wooden table that had been a gift from the governor of the Philippines.

By the time Sarah arrived on campus, her classmates were already in the building.

As Sarah surveyed the scene, she spotted a familiar face—Professor Irven DeVore, a fellow Texan. Sarah had taken DeVore's undergraduate course on primate behaviour and was dating one of his graduate students. She made her way over to him.

"What's going on, Irv?" Sarah asked after their usual greetings, surveying the commotion around them.

With a cheeky smile, DeVore replied: "I'm not sure. But in my day, we would have called it a panty raid."

Affectionately known to his colleagues as "Irv," DeVore was a pioneer in anthropology, famous for having studied non-human primates—baboons in Kenya—and human societies, including the !Kung San (Bushmen) in Botswana. Alongside his mentor, the renowned physical anthropologist Sherwood Washburn, DeVore conducted the first detailed field studies of baboon social organization in Kenya, starting in 1959. By 1969, he had become a professor at Harvard, where he crossed paths with Sarah.

Although DeVore's field studies of the baboons took place over several short-term trips of a few months, he implemented methods that enabled him to find interesting patterns of baboon social behaviour. He identified individual animals and then observed how the individuals interacted with one another. Observing individual primates was a revolutionary approach at the time. This was 1959, before Jane Goodall had emerged on the scene, identifying the chimpanzees by name.

DeVore's observations led him to conclude that baboon societies were shaped by diverse individual relationships. Noting that females were often either pregnant or lactating and thus not sexually receptive, DeVore rejected the prevailing idea that sex was the social glue in primate societies. Instead, he argued, there were "friendships" among adult females, and the adult males in the group would form "alliances" to compete against other males. Today, we know that female "friendships" and male "alliances" are both integral components of baboon social structure, influencing individuals' reproductive success.

Beyond his research, DeVore was perhaps best known for the impact he had on his students, Hrdy among them. He was described as "larger-than-life" and "one of the greatest classroom teachers," and his lectures were referred to as "performances." In a 1997 interview with the *Boston Globe*, DeVore was quoted as saying: "I teach by humour and shock." His infamous course, Science B-29: Human Behavioral Biology, was nicknamed "Sex" by his students. Legend has it that students would sell spots in line to sign up for his always-overbooked lectures.

It was DeVore who first exposed Sarah Hrdy to the langurs—"accidentally," as she wrote in the acknowledgements of her book. She had taken his popular undergraduate course on primate behaviour in 1968, where she had read about a field study that found instances of infanticide among high-density langur populations in South India. That nugget of information stuck with her. While she was auditing a population ecology course during a brief stint studying film at Stanford University, a professor's comment about the challenges of human population growth reminded her of that interesting piece of information she had learned. She decided to transfer back to Harvard, and DeVore became her PhD supervisor. She was DeVore's first female graduate student.

Hrdy stood on the hillside, looking down at the rooftops of Abu. Just below her, a group of langurs was perched atop some large rocks. They had just finished feeding and were taking a rest, seated with their long tails dangling. She focused her attention on two female Hanuman langurs sitting near one another in the sunshine. One of the females had a tiny infant clinging to her stomach.

Hrdy held her camera to her face and brought the image of the langurs into focus, readying herself for what she knew was about to happen. As the mother sat with her infant, the other female reached out. The mother remained in a relaxed, seated posture as she relinquished the infant to the care of her fellow female group member. She willingly handed her baby over, much like a human mother who just wants a break now and then.

Chunk. Click. Click. Hrdy snapped a photograph, capturing the moment. It was evidence of how complex primate social systems are and how much there was to learn by watching the langur females. Hrdy's observations had shown that female langurs often share caregiving responsibilities for the infants in the group. They would cooperate to keep the baby safe while freeing the mother to search for food. This practice in primates is known as allomothering.

Before she got to India, Hrdy knew that allomothering was common among leaf-eating colobines like the langurs. In fact, Hanuman langur mothers would allow their newborns to be taken by other females just minutes after birth, and passed around as though the monkeys were playing a game of hot potato. On the first day of an infant's life, it wasn't uncommon for the baby langur to spend nearly half its time with individuals other than its mother.

While she was conducting her research on langurs in India in the early 1970s, Hrdy wanted to dive deeper into this practice of allomothering. She was interested in which females took the infants, how often, and how they treated them. Whenever she observed the langurs of Abu passing around an infant, she took careful notes. She learned to identify the individual monkeys to help elucidate relationships. She documented the monkeys' behaviours upon transferring an infant: What was the reaction, and did any of the parties involved resist? How was the infant ultimately returned to the mother? Was it carefully handed back or abandoned on a rock? To gather this information and ensure it was free from observer bias, Hrdy drew on the methods Jeanne Altmann had outlined in 1974.

Sarah Hrdy's results showed that infant sharing was common among langur groups. She was surprised by how the behaviour shaped group dynamics. Infants were passed from cousins to siblings, from aunts to grandmothers. Hrdy noticed that the young, inexperienced females were most enthusiastic to take their turn with the infant, her hypothesis being that taking care of infants that were not their own would help them learn the ropes of motherhood. The mothers, meanwhile, had to weigh the benefits of handing off their infant—socialization, freedom to search for food—against the possibility that the infant could be injured.

Sometimes, Hrdy observed, females would forcibly borrow infants, or kidnap them. Kidnapping can be especially risky between groups, because unrelated females have less to lose, genetically speaking, if something adverse happens to the infant. Hrdy documented a kidnapping event in 1973 when females from the Bazaar troop stole an infant from the neighbouring School troop. She watched as the poor infant was passed from female to female, flipped upside down and pushed to the ground by the females' feet. The infant tried its best to cling to each "caregiver," screaming and attempting to suckle for an hour.

In an interview with sociologist Frans Roes, Hrdy noted just how risky these kidnapping events are for the infant: "For an infant not being held by a female is paramount to death! If it is on its own, it is subject to predation. Infants are selected to cling like glue to whoever has them. So you have an allomother—a female other than the mother—pushing the baby off, the infant trying to stay on, and this is when you see langur females sitting on the baby, pushing it against a rock, this kind of abuse."

Hrdy later applied her observations of langurs to human behaviour, exploring the impact of human "helpers" on child development. She argued that there are evolutionary benefits for children who engage with helpers, making them more attuned to the thoughts and intentions of others—a precursor to language and cooperation in the human species. She highlighted how human mothers, much like the langurs, depend on others to raise their children. Grandmothers, partners, aunts—these helpers all contribute to the upbringing of human children. These insights, and others, marked a natural shift in Hrdy's focus from primates of the non-human variety to the human.

A poised Sarah Hrdy stood clutching the podium. She glanced at the crowd, a gathering of researchers with their notebooks and pencils in hand. There was a slight murmur from her peers as they waited for the presentations to begin at this session of the American Anthropological Association in Washington, DC, in 1976. Sarah shuffled her notes and took a deep breath before launching into her presentation on infant killing among the langurs of Mount Abu.

At the close of her presentation, Hrdy looked up at the audience when suddenly, as she later recounted to me: "One of the grand old men of physical anthropology who had been sitting, glowering in the front row, stood up, his back to the podium, and announced to the audience that the monkeys I had observed were abnormal since normal males did not behave that way, and, his back still toward me, stalked out of the room before I could reply."

Hrdy had gone to India initially to test the prevailing hypothesis that high population densities and overcrowding led to infant killing among the langurs. This theory suggested that infanticide was an abnormal response to an abnormal situation. Hrdy knew that at high densities, rats in Norway experience what is called a "behaviour sink," which leads to what seems to be pathological behaviours: mothers neglecting their infants, fathers killing infants, and even cannibalism.

But Sarah Hrdy soon learned that it wasn't just rats that exhibited these behaviours. She had read about a team of Japanese primatologists who observed a group of seven langur males in India oust the leader of another multi-male, multi-female group. Just a few days later, one of the males had taken over as group leader and bitten to death all six infants in the group—a gruesome act. Perhaps even more curious, in a species where mothers often carry the corpse of their dead infants for days, all the mothers whose infants had been wounded by the new male had abandoned them.

To explain this kind of behaviour, researchers at the time chalked it up to something abnormal and pathological, like with the rats. Perhaps, they argued, it was because the langurs were living at high densities in an area that was being rapidly deforested. Hrdy wondered if, like the rats, the langurs could provide a model for the behavioural effects of crowding. She decided to go to India and study infanticide in those crowded monkeys.

In June 1971, Hrdy set out for Mount Abu. She would travel there nine times between 1971 and 1980 to study the langurs. That first summer, she rented two rooms in the home of a local schoolmaster. She would rise before the sun and head out to find the langurs in the sleeping trees where she had left them the evening before. She would watch those monkeys from dawn until dusk.

The more Hrdy observed the langurs, the more her thoughts on infant killing shifted. She noticed that in one-male groups, when a new male ousted the leader, the infants of the group were often killed by the newcomer. In her second year of study, Hrdy witnessed a male stalking, attacking and wounding infants. She saw male takeovers, and infants mysteriously disappearing. Hrdy realized that infanticide was widespread among the langurs.

In an innovative approach rooted in the then-burgeoning field of sociobiology, Hrdy suggested an adaptive explanation for those instances of infanticide. Sociobiology is a discipline famously put forward by Alabama-born biologist and leading authority on ants E.O. Wilson. In 1975, the dark-haired, spectacled scientist published the seven-hundred-page book *Sociobiology: The New Synthesis*, where he introduced sociobiology as the "systematic study of the biological basis of all social behaviour." Wilson argued that social and ecological causes drove the evolution of behaviour in animals, applying natural selection to explain behaviours like altruism, fear and aggression.

Wilson's book, and indeed the entire field of sociobiology itself, were both met with controversy. Critics particularly took issue with the idea that human social behaviours could be explained by evolutionary theory—that they had a genetic component and were linked to strategies that benefited an individual's ability to survive and reproduce. Two of Wilson's fiercest critics were his Harvard colleagues, population geneticist Richard Lewontin and paleontologist Stephen Jay Gould. Lewontin and Gould argued that social environments shape behaviour and that applying natural selection to behaviours like aggression was irresponsible and dangerously close to ideas that sparked the eugenics movement in the late nineteenth century.

But Wilson's supporters argued that these critics were missing the point—it wasn't so black and white. In an interview with the *New York Times*, Wilson explained that he wasn't claiming that genes alone caused individual traits—he acknowledged that the environment plays a role in shaping behaviour. However, he maintained that some traits, even in humans, are highly heritable, pointing to evidence from cross-cultural studies, early development of the trait, and twin studies.

The field of sociobiology had become politicized. Its proponents argued that the controversy stemmed from deeply ingrained religious and political ideologies that viewed social behaviours as uniquely human. They pointed out that humans are biological organisms and, like other animals, should be studied and understood as such.

Hrdy would have been acutely aware of the growing controversy surrounding sociobiology as she stood at the podium presenting her findings, which were grounded in sociobiological concepts. After all, E.O. Wilson, or "Ed" as she knew him, was one of her mentors at Harvard. In the spring of 1972, he had co-taught a seminar with Hrdy's supervisor, Irven DeVore, where they posed the question: "Could there be a science of sociobiology?" Inspired, Hrdy got to work on her seminar paper, "The Care and Exploitation of Infants by Conspecifics Other Than the Mother," where she examined the costs and benefits of shared parental care—marking the beginning of her interest in allomothering in primates.

When she hadn't completed the paper by the semester's end, Wilson encouraged her: "This is fantastic—you must keep going." During our interview, Hrdy told me that male role models were hard to find at Harvard, but that Wilson was one of the few. She described him as "gender blind" and a supporter of women of all ages along the way.

True to his word, Wilson submitted Hrdy's completed manuscript on her behalf to a scientific journal. Penned in 1972, it was to become her first scientific publication (although a delay meant it did not appear in print until 1976). By 1972, Hrdy already considered herself a sociobiologist.

While many researchers before her chalked up infanticide to abnormal behaviour, Hrdy, as a sociobiologist, saw something different. This is when she put forward her ground-shaking argument that infanticide was a reproductive strategy built into the males—"a variant of classic Darwinian sexual selection" that increased the males' ability to sire infants of their own, and improved the chances of their own offspring to survive. Hrdy brought a unique lens to her analysis—a female lens. She paid special attention to the responses of female langurs to infanticide, and the counterstrategies they developed, like confusing paternity through sexual promiscuity and having the older females protect the infants. Sarah referred to her hypothesis as sexually selected infanticide.

Sarah's work on the langurs and her sexually selected infanticide hypothesis played a huge role in shaping the field of primatology. Before her discovery, zoologists dismissed infanticide in animals, but her research made it an important behavioural category. In her summary of the infanticide debate, "Practising Infanticide, Observing Narrative: Controversial Texts in a Field Science," published in *Social Studies of Science* in 2001, scholar Amanda Reese noted, "In this way, primatology's relation to the older and more established scientific disciplines matured." Previously, primatologists borrowed hypotheses and concepts from zoology, but with infanticide, it was the other way around.

In 1974, Sarah Hrdy published her results, making the case that in langurs "infanticide is adaptive rather than pathological male behaviour." She argued that the frequency of occurrence meant that infanticidal behaviour "must now be considered normal for this species because they are both widespread and of long duration." Her argument, rooted in evolutionary theory, was that infanticide was a by-product of male-male competition and a sexually selected adaptation. Her model is grounded in several key predictions: that males would not kill individuals they perceived as related to them, that females who lost infants would have shorter interbirth intervals, that new males would inseminate these females and that infanticidal males would gain a reproductive edge.

In 1977, Hrdy published an article about her research in *American Scientist* (a high-profile magazine with a broad audience) and released her first book, *The Langurs of Abu: Female and Male Strategies of Reproduction.* Suddenly her research was out there—in plain language—for the world to see. Biologists and anthropologists of the day questioned her work, with some even referring to the monkeys at Abu as "deranged." Her publication sparked a series of rebuttals from the primatological community, with letters to the editor questioning how the behaviours that Hrdy observed could be attributed to normal monkeys. The idea that these destructive behaviours were adaptive was unthinkable to many.

At the time that Hrdy published her findings, primatology was considered a social science with sister disciplines of social anthropology and sociology, influenced by theorists like French sociologist Émile Durkheim. Assessments of primate social groupings were rooted in theories like functionalism, where individual decisions drive a group's survival. Thus, when researchers first witnessed infanticide, it was chalked up to a dysfunctional anomaly.

In 1978, anthropologists Richard Curtin and Phyllis Dolhinow published a rebuttal to Hrdy's paper, arguing that infanticide in langurs was abnormal and possibly the result of human-induced changes to the environment in Abu. They reconstructed her observations, suggesting that the field sites were disturbed and overcrowded. They also pointed out that only some of the infanticidal acts were directly observed. When Hrdy referred to reports from locals, calling them "local informants," they were dismissed as hearsay from "casual bystanders." Curtin and Dolhinow's "social pathology" hypothesis countered Hrdy's sexual selection hypothesis, arguing that the infanticides she reported were not adaptive but instead arose from unnatural environmental conditions due to crowding.

Still, many adopted Hrdy's model—a growing number of researchers who subscribed to sociobiology. Some even went as far as to re-examine their results, using her framework to understand their observations in a new light. Her model even permeated the textbooks: the 1979 edition of John Alcock's *Animal Behavior* mentioned langur infanticide in its first chapter, elaborating on Hrdy's sexual competition hypothesis.

Despite the flurry of controversy, Sarah Hrdy did not relent. In 1979, she published a review article arguing once again that infanticide is adaptive in animals and that males benefit from it evolutionarily. While she acknowledged that evidence on infanticide came from relatively few cases and that infant deaths were often assumed rather than observed, she stressed that the observed cases of infanticide fit her sexual selection hypothesis.

For her part, Hrdy has referred to these early rebuttals as "constructive debates." She agreed that "more and better data" were needed to fully understand infanticidal behaviour in primates. She reflected deeply on her hypothesis, considering the possibility that human disturbance did play a role, even developing measures of disturbance and collaborating on an article about it. She refined her hypothesis as it applied to humans, developing nuanced explanations that could be tested when it came to the underlying evolutionary reasons for infanticidal behaviour.

But there was a second phase of the controversy that Hrdy remembers as "far less constructive." It began with the publication of *Infanticide: Comparative and Evolutionary Perspectives* in 1984, a volume co-edited by Hrdy and Glenn Hausfater (Stuart Altmann's student). The book was born out of the first international conference on infanticide in animals and humans, held at Cornell University in 1982. The volume consisted of chapters on infanticide by several prominent primatologists studying different primate species, including Jane Goodall and Dian Fossey. Hrdy made sure to include a critique of the sexual selection hypothesis by one of Phyllis Dolhinow's students. There was also a section on infanticide in other species, including carnivores, birds and even fish, as well as chapters exploring the causes of infanticide, grounded in controlled rodent experiments. Finally, there was an overview of human infanticide, including a study of maternal infanticide among the Ayoreo of Paraguay.

Sarah Hrdy believed this book would put an end to the controversy surrounding the sexually selected infanticide hypothesis. In the preface, she wrote that the current view of infanticide was as "a normal and individually adaptive activity" and that "readers ten years from now may take for granted the occurrence of infanticide in various animal species and may even be unaware of the controversies."

She was right, at least when it came to the biologists. The book was well reviewed in biology circles, and Hrdy credits its publication, along with her research on infanticide, for her election to the California Academy of Sciences in 1985 and the National Academy of Sciences in 1990. But in anthropology circles, her work was dismissed. Primatologists Thad Bartlett and Robert Sussman published rebuttals, arguing that observed infanticidal events in primates were merely by-products of other aggressive behaviours. These rebuttals led to press releases with headlines in the popular media such as "Monkey 'Murderers' May Be Falsely Accused."

Critics dismissed evidence from rodents, arguing that it could not be applied to primates, and claimed there was no genetic basis for infanticidal behaviours. They pointed out that many cases of infanticide in primates came from langurs and suggested there must be something abnormal about langurs specifically. They even argued that many of the killers were the victims' fathers, despite the data they cited showing otherwise.

When Sussman became editor for the American Anthropological Association, the organization's flagship journal suddenly began devoting more space to non-human primates and even non-primates. In 1999, Canadian zoologist Anne Innis Dagg published a work titled "Infanticide by Male Lions Hypothesis: A Fallacy Influencing Research into Human Behaviour." Hrdy noted that "the manuscript had previously been turned down by biology journals." Sussman, it turned out, had phoned Dagg and told her that if she added references to primates, the paper would be publishable in *American Anthropologist*.

In 2000, Hrdy wrote a preface for a volume on infanticide edited by primatologists Carel van Schaik and Charles Janson. The book's title, *Infanticide by Males and Its Implications*, signalled an intent to get past the controversy from anthropologists and "finally move on."

In 1979, following Sarah Hrdy's publications on primate infanticide, fellow Harvard alum and biologist Robert Trivers was asked to comment on her groundbreaking and somewhat controversial work. He said, "My own view is that Sarah ought to devote more time and study and thought to raising a healthy daughter. That way misery won't keep travelling down the generations."

This comment from a colleague—and someone who would eventually become a collaborator and friend—illustrates the ingrained perceptions about women in academia that Hrdy was up against.

"Harvard professors were like male monkeys," Hrdy told me when we spoke, "jockeying for position for access to females."

In a 2012 interview with *Scientific American*, Hrdy reflected on her academic journey. At Harvard, she noticed that studies of primate behaviour, and all of evolution for that matter, were rooted in a Victorian view of life—stuffy and prudish. Hrdy was Irven DeVore's first female graduate student, and there were no female professors at Harvard at that time. She was on the hunt for female role models but came up empty. Even her supervisor took a male-centric view of primate society.

DeVore had brought back film footage of baboons from Kenya, from which he produced several 16-mm films. He later hired a professional film crew to gather additional footage under his direction and collaborated on the editing. He would show these films to his students in class. Primatologist Thelma Rowell, in a chapter published in *Primate Encounters: Models of Science, Gender, and Society*, reflected on one of these films, made in Nairobi National Park. She noted that the film's commentary "points out very clearly the central position of the dominant adult male." However, if you turn off the sound, you might spot the peanuts being thrown at the monkeys. Rowell noted that "the centre in this case was defined by the trajectory of the peanuts, which were mostly intercepted by the adult males."

Part of the film also includes a cartoon of the baboon social organization, again showing the male at the centre, surrounded by mothers and their infants, solidifying the idea that males were at the centre of the troop—an idea that would take years to dispel. With long-term field studies, researchers (notably Jeanne and Stuart Altmann) would later show that interactions among females, although subtle, were what drove the structure of baboon social groups.

Although Sarah Hrdy found Harvard graduate school intellectually stimulating and inspiring, she couldn't shake the underlying feeling she got from faculty and students: that they were afraid that she—a woman in academia and the sciences—would be successful. Somehow, it seemed, they were rooting for her to fail. In the acknowledgements to her essay on "the myth of the coy female," she described an atmosphere "hostile to the professional aspirations of women," with professors (all male in those days) and fellow graduate students almost fearing, rather than hoping, she would succeed.

It was during this time that Hrdy began to see the world differently. While she had begun her graduate career studying infanticidal behaviour by males, a decade later she would end up focusing on female reproductive strategies—becoming a champion for bringing a female perspective to the science of primatology and uncovering the "active roles females were playing in the evolution of primate breeding systems."

In Rajasthan, India, as Hrdy bore witness to male langurs engaging in infant killing, she couldn't help but become emotionally involved. Over the course of her long-term research, Hrdy found that every twenty-seven months—a period she identified as the average tenure for a male langur to retain control of a troop—a new male would emerge, inserting himself into a group he did not belong to. He would harass and attack the females and their infants, and in many instances, infants would disappear.

As Hrdy observed and took careful notes, she became wrapped up in the female perspective. She watched as the females in the groups worked together to fight off male usurpers, and she felt a kinship with the female victims of the heinous acts that took place. Yet, despite their efforts to fight off the attacking males, the females would still end up breeding with them. Hrdy couldn't fathom this response: "Why not refuse to breed with an infanticidal male and wait until a male without any genetic propensity for infanticide showed up?"

Hrdy's interest in female langurs was linked to a growing awareness of male-female power dynamics that affected her own life. Not only was she Irven DeVore's first female graduate student, she also held the position as the only woman amid a cohort of men. Robert Trivers, one of those men, later regretted his nasty comment to reporters about Hrdy and her role as a mother, stating that he did not intend for that quote to be published and that he was sorry to have hurt his friend.

In fact, Trivers had a profound influence on Hrdy, and she has referred to him as "the most inspirational teacher" she ever had. She describes his ideas about the connections between parental investment and Darwinian sexual selection as "stunningly original." During the days that he and Hrdy overlapped at Harvard, Trivers produced many seminal papers on parental investment, reciprocal altruism and the conflict between parents and offspring. His work transformed the way that we view the evolution of social relationships and had an enormous influence on this emerging field of sociobiology.

Perhaps a sense of isolation among her peers fed Hrdy's interest in feminist scholarship. She began reading Carolyn Heilbrun, a feminist author and the first woman to receive tenure in Columbia University's English department. She also consumed the writings of Jean Baker Miller, a feminist academic, psychiatrist and social activist. She had mixed feelings about what she was reading. On the one hand, it opened her eyes to the problems that women face in society, but on the other, she was unimpressed by the lack of academic rigour behind some of these works. Still, she grew excited by the possibility of leading a feminist charge in the field of primatology.

The ceremony was held in a friend's garden in Nepal. Carleton Coon, the American consul to Nepal and son of the Harvard anthropologist of the same name, had offered the space, and Sarah and her fiancee Dan Hrdy happily accepted. Sarah wore white, though in the form of white cotton pants, and Coon's children decorated the wedding cake with plastic monkeys, even going so far as to paint estrous swellings on the female monkey's rump with red nail polish.

The day before, the couple had taken a motorcycle to the border between Nepal and China in search of langurs. On their way back to Kathmandu, they were caught in a heavy rainstorm and were forced to pull over and take shelter in a cave near the road. A shepherd, also sheltering in the cave, began speaking to them quickly, with an urgency to his tone. He gestured toward their motorcycle parked near the side of the road.

The couple realized that the man was telling them they ought to move the bike, and fast. Just minutes after Dan pulled the motorcycle to a new location, a flash flood swept through the very spot where it had been parked.

Thankfully, their only mode of transportation was spared. After waiting out the worst of the storm, Sarah and Dan hit the road again, with Dan at the helm and Sarah clinging on for dear life as the bike slid precariously down the steep, muddy road back to the capital, making it back in time to get married the next day.

Sarah and Dan Hrdy first met and fell in love as students at Harvard, both studying anthropology with Irven DeVore as their supervisor. They officially met during a course about human evolution. When Sarah left for Dharwad in South India to begin her PhD research on infanticide in langurs, Dan changed his travel fellowship plans from Peru to India to be with her. A year later, they were getting married in a garden in Kathmandu.

In her mind's eye, Sarah had pictured Dan becoming a professor of anthropology—perhaps even wearing a blazer with elbow patches—and the two of them sharing a life of research and publishing scientific articles together. Much to her surprise, when Dan met and was inspired by a medical anthropologist named Albert Damon, he opted to switch things up and go to medical school. He enrolled in the Harvard-MIT joint MD and PhD program and eventually became an infectious disease doctor. Reflecting on her relationship with Dan, Sarah Hrdy wrote, "Maintaining our partnership became one of my life's main goals, requiring compromises I did not then anticipate."

In 1977, the same year Sarah Hrdy published her book, she became a mother. She was thirty-one years old, and she and Dan had been married for a year. Although Dan had officially left anthropology to pursue medicine, he continued to join Sarah on her research trips in India whenever he could get time away from his work on rotaviruses at Harvard Medical School. They brought their daughter to India twice, which Sarah admits she probably wouldn't have done if Dan hadn't been an infectious disease specialist.

Sarah remembers feeling "overwhelmed by the child's lusciousness" when she became a mother. She was determined to be a better parent than her own mother had been to her. She recalls that in the 1950s, the prevailing notion was, "If a child cries, don't pick it up." Although she loved her mother dearly, Sarah felt that her mothering strategies were "appalling."

Balancing fieldwork and motherhood proved challenging. During the first year, Sarah brought an au pair to India to help while Dan continued his studies. Unfortunately, Sarah would soon learn the au pair was more interested in a trip abroad than in childcare. That first field season, under the care of the au pair, her daughter Katrinka experienced terrible diarrhea and diaper rash. Sarah would return from gruelling days spent watching monkeys from dawn to dusk to find a stack of dirty diapers and a hungry, fussy toddler. One memorable evening, she returned to find the toddler being harassed by a troop of monkeys who were trying to steal her cookie.

The stress proved to be too much, and Sarah Hrdy caught pneumonia. She describes being on the plane home with "a temperature of 104 degrees" and "sucking on one of Katrinka's baby bottles to stay hydrated." She decided that fieldwork and children were incompatible. She couldn't bring her babies to India anymore—it wasn't working for anyone.

But she would soon learn that not bringing Katrinka to India was also challenging. Leaving her behind with Dan and a housekeeper was hard on her, she wrote.

In 1981, Sarah followed Dan to Houston, where she secured a job as a visiting professor at Rice University so her husband could finish his medical residency at Baylor University. The following spring, now with two children in tow, the family moved to Cambridge, Massachusetts, where Dan finished his infectious diseases fellowship at the Peter Bent Brigham Hospital and his PhD in the Bernard Fields lab at Harvard Medical School. Sarah, meanwhile, held an unsalaried position at the Peabody Museum and volunteered at her children's daycare.

Balancing academic life with being a mother and a wife was not easy. Forget fieldwork—even travelling to conferences was difficult. When Sarah undertook the monumental task of co-organizing the first International Conference on Infanticide in Animals and Man in 1982, she brought along her second daughter, Sasha, who was a week old. Her co-organizer told Sarah that the conference was "no place for a baby" and that she shouldn't even bring Sasha into the building. Sarah had to ask another mother she knew to help nurse Sasha during the day while she nursed her only at night.

The more she mothered, the more Sarah Hrdy's interest in understanding maternal love, infant development and attachment theory deepened. She knew now, from personal experience, how an individual could feel a push and pull between maternal love and ambition. Her research showed that humans evolved as "cooperative breeders," and she applied that insight to her own life. She wrote that she built up "a stable network of as-if extended family, composed of daycare providers and resident allomothers."

Despite finding ways to balance work and family, Sarah Hrdy is quick to point out that she "was never paid for working full time"—she spent more on childcare than she ever made teaching. Yet, she was one of the lucky ones: she inherited enough money that she didn't need medical benefits or a pension and could devote more time to motherhood than teaching. Still, finding a "balance" took its toll. Sarah found herself torn between her academic life, being a mother and wife, and finding time for her family back home in Texas. She struggled with "classic stress symptoms," including migraines and back and neck pain.

In 1984, Dan secured a position at the University of California, Davis medical school, and Sarah landed a job as a full professor with the option to work part-time, thanks to a program targeting "outstanding women." Sarah and Dan Hrdy had managed the seemingly impossible in academia: both securing positions in the same city at the same institution.

In 1986, Sarah Hrdy received a Guggenheim fellowship to write a book about the natural history of mothering. Ironically, in that same year her son Niko was born, delaying the book. She returned to the idea in 1996, submitting it to publishers and even sparking a bidding war. *Mother Nature* was awarded the Howells Prize for outstanding contribution to biological anthropology and was cited as one of the best books of 1999 by *Publishers Weekly* and *Library Journal.* The book analyzes mothers and their relationships with their infants, integrating twenty years of Sarah's research. She posits that infanticide and the tendency of females to mate with more than one male both arose out of cooperative breeding, where females seek assistance rearing their children from various helpers, including grandmothers, fathers and even non-relatives "earning their keep."

Drawing from her experiences as a mother and her observations of langurs, Sarah believes children need security and close relationships but argues that the mother need not be the only source of attachment. She became an advocate for good, publicly funded childcare programs, arguing that they serve as the modern-day network of allomothers.

Now grown, her children speak highly of their mother. Katrinka, the eldest, has said that Sarah was a fantastic mother, and alongside Sarah's scientific approach to families and motherhood, the family maintained a sense of tradition, complete with family dinners.

Sarah Blaffer Hrdy and her husband, Dan, have three children. In 1986, they acquired land in Winters, California—known as the walnut capital of the world. The couple still lives on Citrona Farms, where they grow walnuts and much more. They've restored the habitat by planting native grasses, hedgerows, shrubs and trees, and they welcome researchers to the farm to study agricultural practices and their impact on wildlife.

Hrdy is a truly original and influential evolutionary anthropologist. She forged her path through the study of Hanuman langurs in India and used her discoveries to enhance our understanding of the human condition. Unlike many of her peers, she made a point to disseminate her work to broad audiences, bringing sociobiological hypotheses to the public.

Hrdy's findings on langur infanticide and allomothering generated debate and even controversy among scientists, yet she persevered even amid harsh personal attacks. Her work introduced a new perspective to the study of primates. She was one of the first to explore how female promiscuity could be an adaptation to infanticide and how relationships among females might be shaped by competition.

Hrdy has authored nine books. She earned a Guggenheim fellowship, was elected to the National Academy of Sciences, served as a professor-at-large at Cornell University, became an associate at the Peabody Museum of Archaeology and Ethnology at Harvard and is a professor emerita at the University of California, Davis.

In her search for female role models during her studies, Hrdy picked up a 1966 monograph on lemur behaviour. She stared at the photograph on the back of the book, captivated by the fiercely strong young woman with her long hair swept into a side ponytail who had set out into the forests of Madagascar to study ring-tailed lemurs.

When this woman later visited Harvard, Hrdy, then a graduate student, stood among the other students, mesmerized by her idol. She couldn't hold back her admiration and shocked herself when she blurted out: "But what is your *life* like?"

Not only was this woman a successful female primatologist, she also had a family—a husband and children. Hrdy was deeply curious about how one could seemingly have it all.

Through Alison Jolly, Sarah Hrdy could see clearly the path she wanted to follow.

CHAPTER EIGHT

The Mother of Lemurs

MADAME JACQUELINE IS SURPRISED TO SEE US, and she does not like surprises.

"I was not consulted about this project," Madame Jacqueline says bluntly. Her short, black hair is neat and full-bodied. She's a tiny woman—probably five feet tall or even shorter—yet she exudes strength and power. As I look into her eyes, I can see her disdain. A sinking feeling hits me like a wave. This is Madagascar, 2008.

Nearly thirty years earlier, in 1980, lemur researcher Alison Jolly published *A World Like Our Own*, which begins: "Madagascar is an island, a continent, a world." She nailed it. Madagascar is a whole strange world on an island. That island is located off the southeast coast of Africa and is roughly the size of France or Texas, depending on your frame of reference. It is the fourth-largest island in the world, after Greenland, New Guinea and Borneo—about 587,000 square kilometres. As Jolly suggests, Madagascar is filled with impressive biodiversity, much of which is found only there and nowhere else in the world: it is endemic to the country. For example, 95 per cent of Madagascar's reptiles, 89 per cent of the plants and 92 per cent of the mammals are unique to the island nation.

Alongside this incredible endemicity, the island boasts astonishing species diversity. After Madagascar separated from the African continent about 160 million years ago, the evolution of species exploded, with unique and bizarre plants and animals filling the wide variety of habitats on the island. This includes 11,000 species of plants, 400 species of reptiles, 300 species of birds and 240 species of mammals. Representing the bulk of those mammal species are the whopping 107 different species of lemurs, a type of primate found only in Madagascar and nowhere else on the planet.

I am on this strange and wonderful island nation to study a type of lemur called Coquerel's sifakas in their natural habitat for my PhD at the University of Toronto. These critically endangered lemurs are mostly white with maroon patches that remind me of distinguished professors wearing blazers and trousers. Their most distinctive feature, however, is their long, powerful hind limbs. They use these to leap from tree to tree like arboreal kangaroos, propelling themselves off a vertical tree trunk, sometimes pulling a 180-degree pivot midair, and landing softly and precisely on the next vertical substrate—a style of locomotion aptly named vertical clinging and leaping.

My research was set to take place in the northwest of the country at a site called Ankarafantsika National Park. I had travelled there by a winding, paved highway, ten hours from Madagascar's capital city of Antananarivo. Ankarafantsika is a protected area, one of the last remaining fragments of western dry forest in the country, and one of the only accessible places in Madagascar to study Coquerel's sifakas.

"Where are your permits?" Madame Jacqueline asks, breaking the silence. Her voice drips with scorn. She maintains eye contact, eyebrows raised.

I am perched on a stiff wooden chair, sitting next to my partner, Travis, and my field assistant, Lanto (pronounced Lawn-too).

Madame Jacqueline's desk is in the thatched-roofed, open-concept and open-air National Parks office in Ankarafantsika.

The man sitting next to Madame Jacqueline, another park employee in a crisp white uniform, glances at me and raises his eyebrows as if to say, "You're in for it now."

We are conversing in French, with me relying on Lanto, a slim, shy, twenty-something Malagasy university student who signed on as my research assistant for the year. He would also be working on his own research for his master's project.

No one had informed Madame Jacqueline—the head of research for the national park—that a couple of Canadians would be arriving to study the critically endangered Coquerel's sifaka. And for fourteen months? Out of the question.

"Don't worry," I assure her, producing the neatly collated papers—our permits—I've been clutching on my lap. As I release my death grip, I am startled by how white my knuckles have become. I take a breath.

It's okay, I tell myself. The evidence will speak for itself, and Madame Jacqueline will back down.

I smile a little at the thought: perhaps she'll be a bit embarrassed, but I'm ready to take the high road and forget this misunderstanding ever happened.

She frowns as she looks over the papers. I hadn't thought it possible for her brow to furrow even more.

She doubles down.

We cannot proceed without her review and sign-off on the project.

Can she tell us how long that review will take?

No, she cannot.

Is there a chance we may not get her sign-off?

Yes.

Is there anything we can do now? We had hoped to start our research in the next few days.

No, nothing to be done.

Panic sets in. I have travelled halfway across the world for the lemurs. My entire project is now in jeopardy, and I haven't made it past week one.

Madame Jacqueline makes it clear the meeting is adjourned, and Travis, Lanto and I sulk back to our research camp. The camp is shared by several research teams from all over the world. There's a team from Germany, one from Japan and us, the Canadians. The camp itself is simple, made up of several thatched-roofed, concrete-bottomed tent platforms where we researchers set up our living quarters—tents and hammocks, a clothesline, maybe a woven mat to make it feel more homey. There are also a couple of shared platforms—one for a kitchen space, the other a workspace with a few power outlets where we can charge our laptops when the national park staff, whose office building is nearby, are running the generator. Flushing toilets and cold-water showers can be found a few metres down a small hill. By fieldwork standards, the setup is slick. Certainly livable, which is important given I'm to spend fourteen months straight at this camp. All of us researchers are there with a purpose: to study the wildlife in the park. For me, that means the lemurs.

I plop down, defeated, onto the low ledge of my tent platform. I bring my head to my knees. "It's over before it even started," I say. My hot tears rise to the surface.

There is no time to secure new permissions, as Madame Jacqueline suggested. This project has been years in the making.

I've been too confident, I think, that's the problem. I've jinxed us. Is my career as a primatologist destined for failure?

Then I think about her—about Alison Jolly, nicknamed "The Mother of Lemurs," who, in 1962, conducted the first long-term field study on Madagascar's most iconic species, the ring-tailed lemur with their black-and-white-striped tails, showing that in this species of primate, females are in charge. Later, Jolly would bring community conservation to Madagascar, working to save the most endangered group of animals on the planet by considering the needs of the human population alongside the needs of the wildlife.

I hesitate to assign any hypothesis for why women are drawn to primatology to Alison Jolly. I don't believe she fits squarely within any of them. Yes, she discovered female dominance in lemurs, but she made it clear she wasn't on the lookout for that finding. She simply reported her observations. She did not benefit from the goodwill of powerful men—Jolly applied for her own grants and found her field site with the lemurs all on her own. And the "big brown eye" hypothesis? Certainly not. Jolly saw a lot during her fifty-year career, and not all of her observations demonstrated lemurs as cute or cuddly. In fact, quite the opposite: the lemurs would get into aggressive fights.

In her 2004 book *Lords and Lemurs*, Jolly described a day when she discovered her graduate student behind the bungalows, crying as an infant lemur lay dying on the ground. The infant had been injured as a result of two groups of females fighting over territory. Ring-tailed lemurs are bold, and the females frequently carry their infants even when fighting. Although Jolly's student had not observed how the infant came off its mother, it had, and none of the female lemurs had bothered to pick it up. They left, and then one of the males came over, picked it up, and began shaking and pulling at it.

"Then he just slashed it open with a canine and ran away," Jolly's student reported.

As her student relayed the story of what had happened, Jolly watched the infant quietly dying in front of her. It became too much to bear. She wrote: "I held my fingers over the soft little nose, closing the nostrils and crying mouth. It did not take long."

As Linda Fedigan argues in "Science and the Successful Female: Why There Are So Many Women Primatologists," the undeniable violence that exists in primates requires "a strong stomach to observe firsthand."

Aside from not finding the right fit, another reason I hesitate to categorize Jolly under a specific hypothesis is that she resisted seeing primatology as a female-centred field. Instead, she argued that the shift we witnessed in the discipline represented "a shift in consciousness of gender" rather than a change in "actual content." Jolly was more interested in the discoveries that had been made about the minds of animals and the "popularization of primatology," and what both of those meant for conserving our closest living relatives.

As I sit on the ledge of my tent platform with my head in my hands, my PhD research project on the brink of collapse, I take deep breaths and think about how Alison Jolly travelled to Madagascar in the 1960s. Back then, there was very little infrastructure, and she had to forge her own path. Find her own way. I thought about Jolly's work bringing conservation education to people around the world and her championing of community-led conservation to save primates on the brink of extinction.

I look up and see Madame Jacqueline in the distance, clipboard in hand, her short, swift steps propelling her toward us.

I stand up and brush the dirt off my pants. As Madame Jacqueline approaches, I notice the way she pushes her bangs away from her eyes, just like I do, and how she fumbles a little with her clipboard. At that moment, I know she is not my enemy. She is a strong woman, like me.

I am more determined than ever. I know in my heart that reason and patience will win the day. My project will happen, and Madame Jacqueline and I will become friends. I rise to my feet and start walking toward her. I nod to Travis: "I've got this."

In less than a week, she had travelled more than five hundred miles along Madagascar's dirt roads in her Land Rover. She was searching for the perfect field site to observe lemur behaviour in their natural habitat. At twenty-five years old, this six-foot-tall woman with long auburn hair and wise blue eyes was a force to be reckoned with.

It was 1962, and Alison Jolly had just graduated with a PhD in zoology from Yale University, where she had studied captive lemurs—mouse lemurs, brown lemurs and ring-tailed lemurs, to be precise. These lemurs were part of physical anthropologist John Buettner-Janusch's lab, which housed the very first collection of strepsirrhines (the primate suborder that includes lemurs). Buettner-Janusch was forging his path as a world expert on lemurs, though his later years would be marked by infamy. In the early 1980s he gained notoriety, accused of manufacturing LSD and quaaludes in his laboratory, for which he was arrested and sentenced to time in jail. After he was paroled, he was charged with attempted murder for mailing poisoned chocolates to the sentencing judge from his drug trial.

But none of this darkness had been revealed when Jolly studied lemurs in Buettner-Janusch's laboratory in the 1960s. Her research was very much on the straight and narrow, focused on object manipulation in lemurs. She compared the lemurs to other primate species, finding them less dexterous and "inferior" to all higher primates in solving manipulation problems. She argued that fine hand control likely developed slowly in primate evolution and that manipulative play was an important "pre-adaptation" for intelligence in primates. After publishing several articles on this research, she was ready to take it to the next level and study the social lives of lemurs in their natural habitat. With a grant from the National Science Foundation, she embarked on a postdoctoral study on wild lemurs in Madagascar.

Jolly had brought along a young man named Preston Boggess, a Yale undergraduate student who would assist her and help her look for a site for her study. Together, they traversed the country.

During their exploration, Jolly spoke with many people. Repeatedly, they told her: "You must visit the de Heaulme family. They have lemurs behind their houses." To Jolly, this sounded bleak. She imagined small primates tethered to trees as "miserable captives." Still, she figured, she might as well check it out.

As they arrived at the Mandrare River, Jolly and Boggess saw a sisal plantation—rows and rows of *Agave sisalana,* a two-metre-high plant that looks like a giant pineapple, with strong leaves jutting out like swords from a rounded base. Sisal is a cash crop in Madagascar; its strong fibres are used to make rope and twine.

As they neared the plantation hub, they spotted whitewashed fences and stones surrounding perfectly manicured flower beds and neat rows of white cement houses. One of the houses even had a carport with a green-and-white single-engine Cessna 172 inside.

What was this place? Why, it was the Berenty estate.

Besides the homes and plantation, Berenty boasted a gallery forest reserve, founded in 1936 by the de Heaulmes, an aristocratic French family from Réunion, an island east of Madagascar. Monsieur Henry de Heaulme had negotiated access to land with the leaders of the local Malagasy Tandroy, a nomadic group in Madagascar. He was building plantations, but there was a portion of land by the river he couldn't bring himself to cut down. "This forest is too beautiful ever to be destroyed. We must never cut it; nobody must cut it," he said.

On arrival, Jolly and Boggess were greeted by Jean de Heaulme, a man in his mid-thirties, whom Jolly described as having "smooth black hair," "round cheeks" and "merry eyes." She told him of her intention to study the lemurs in Madagascar.

Jean de Heaulme quickly welcomed Jolly into his home, telling her they were about to host a party. Jean's wife, Aline, emerged with perfectly styled curly black hair, wearing white strappy sandals. Jolly suddenly felt self-conscious about her worn-out hiking boots. She tried to protest, saying she didn't want to impose—she was there for the lemurs. But the de Heaulmes wouldn't hear of it. Soon, their friends arrived from Fort-Dauphin in two small planes, and the party commenced.

Jolly and Boggess were treated to fine wine and a four-course meal. The next day, Jean arranged for a guide to take Jolly, Boggess and Jean's nature-loving three-year-old daughter into the forest.

"The lemurs found me," Jolly writes.

She first encountered the sifakas, who leapt through the forest above her head, turning "in midair to land with both hind feet first," then folding up and clinging vertically to new trees, all the while observing her, she wrote. Next, she met the ringtails, whose "tails dangled like long fuzzy caterpillars; their pointed, raccoon-like face masks [catching] the dappled forest light."

Jolly stood there, in awe, for a full half an hour. In every other place she had visited in Madagascar, she had barely glimpsed lemurs. There was so little forest protection at the time that the lemurs feared humans—humans were hunters and predators in their eyes.

But Berenty was different. Here, the lemurs hadn't been hunted since the reserve was founded twenty-five years earlier. The lemurs were accustomed to humans, meaning Jolly wouldn't need to spend time or effort habituating them. Berenty was an ideal locale for a long-term, intensive study of lemur behaviour.

Jolly didn't waste any time after she pulled herself away from the magic of the forest. Dressed in her "crumpled khakis," she rushed to the office of Jean de Heaulme's father, Monsieur de Heaulme—a stoic and imposing man she had met at dinner the night before. The sixty-year-old had a face that "fell in straight-hewn lines, with a straight-line mouth and cleft chin." He was the man in charge.

Jolly laid out her plan and was surprised at how quickly the elder de Heaulme agreed. It was like a dream: Yes, he told her, his face unflinching. She was welcome to spend her days in Berenty forest for the next year.

Jolly once remarked to a colleague that since her mother knew everything about art and her father knew everything about literature, her only option was to become a scientist.

Alison Jolly was born Alison Bishop in 1937 in Ithaca, New York. Her mother, Alison Mason Kingsbury, was an artist, and her father, Morris G. Bishop, was a writer and scholar.

On the surface, young Alison's mother was a proper lady. According to biographer Jillian Piccirilli, who published a book about Kingsbury's art and life, she "looked, dressed, spoke and acted like a conforming Ithaca matron." However, this exterior was a façade. According to Jolly, as quoted in the *Cornell Chronicle*, her mother would advise her daughters to dress conventionally because "if you trick people into thinking you are conventional, then you can get away with doing anything you like."

Kingsbury's father was a mechanical engineer, and her mother was an amateur painter and former New York socialite. As a young woman, Kingsbury attended Wellesley, a small but serious women's college in Massachusetts, where she took a multidisciplinary approach to her education, studying art, history and physics. She spent her summers working as a draftswoman for her father's company, which she later said fuelled her determination to pursue art.

After she graduated, Kingsbury moved to New York City just as the Roaring Twenties were getting started, refining her artistic skills at the Art Students League, an independent art school. Rather than pursuing a husband like many of her contemporaries would have been doing, Kingsbury focused on her art career. In 1922, she headed to Europe to join the École des Beaux-Arts in France, studying fresco, sculpture and mural composition.

When she returned to the United States, Kingsbury worked for muralist Ezra Winter. A commission by Cornell University, the Willard Straight Hall mural, brought her to Ithaca in 1925, where she met her future husband, Morris Bishop, and settled permanently. But just because she married did not mean that Kingsbury slowed down. She became a working artist, known for her oil and watercolour paintings and murals. In addition to the mural at Willard Straight Hall, she created many beloved works of art that pepper Cornell University's campus, including impressive murals at the Gannett Health Clinic and the World War I memorial.

During the 1930s, a time when most women stayed at home, Kingsbury was producing impressive commercial work and fine art. There's no doubt that Kingsbury was a strong role model for her daughter, who grew up to be a fiercely independent woman.

Alison Jolly also inherited a literary flair unique in academia. Her words jump off the page in a 1966 publication, where she conjures the image of sifakas "soaring against the blue sky in great ballet leaps" and likens ring-tailed lemur scent-marking battles to "a kind of arboreal chess game in which opposing knights hopped to strategic branches."

Her father, a professor of literature at Cornell University, played a role in instilling this love of language. Bishop was a talented writer—a master of light prose and poetry. He frequently published his work in *The New Yorker*. He was a scholar of literary biography and history, writing biographies of famous figures like Samuel de Champlain and Blaise Pascal, as well as stories and songs about Cornell. His work was varied and creative and even included a mystery novel. Bishop was also known for spotting literary talent: in 1948, he brought Vladimir Nabokov to Cornell as a teacher, well before the publication of *Lolita* in 1955.

Jolly wrote, "Pop made sure I imprinted on Kipling early." But it wasn't just Kipling; there was also Jules Verne and others. Both her parents inspired a love for language and encouraged her vivid imagination.

In an interview, Jolly recalled a pivotal moment growing up. Her mother had purchased the first "Little Books" about science for her to practise reading. Young Alison devoured the book about dinosaurs, where she learned about the seventy-foot-long Diplodocus.

"How long is seventy feet, Ma?" she asked one day, looking up from the book.

"Well, let's find out," her mother replied and brought out the tape measure.

Mother and daughter measured the length of their living room and did the math.

"Wow," said Alison after they worked it out. "Diplodocus is two and a half times the size of the biggest dragon!"

In the interview, Jolly said, "Basically, I realized that the real world was more wonderful than anything out of the imagination."

Young Alison had looked up at her mother. "Who is it that goes out and looks at real things, Ma?"

"Well, scientists, of course!" her mother replied.

Alison paused for a moment, then nodded firmly. "Right, I am a scientist."

As Alison Jolly pursued science, she never lost her creativity. Over her fifty-year career, she made incredible breakthroughs in field science and transformed our understanding of the evolution of social behaviour in humans.

In her seminal paper on lemur social behaviour and the evolution of intelligence, Jolly detailed the results of an eleven-month study on two different lemur species—the ring-tailed lemur and, as she so eloquently put it, "the great white sifaka." Her study took place in a gallery forest by the Mandrare River in what is today called Berenty Reserve, in the far south of Madagascar. Jolly's research represented the first long-term study of wild lemurs.

She spent her days observing groups of lemurs, logging 400 hours with ring-tailed lemurs and 250 hours with sifakas. Her quest was to determine how lemur societies compared with those of other, more well-studied primates and to explore what bearing primate social behaviour had on the evolution of intelligence.

The results of Jolly's landmark study were published in the journal *Science* in 1966, one of the top-tier publications in the academic world. Articles in *Science* are rigorously reviewed, original and incredibly influential in their field of study and beyond. Alison Jolly's study certainly qualified. She showed that some lemur species have evolved complex societies and demonstrate social learning, even though they lack the capacity to manipulate objects, like monkeys or apes can. She concluded that primate societies likely developed before primate intelligence, a discovery that sent shockwaves through the scientific community. Scientists had previously believed that human tool use evolved before complex social groups—not the other way around, as Jolly had deduced from the lemurs.

But beyond the research, what stands out in her article is the way it's written. I have read my fair share of academic research, and Jolly's language and tone are not typical of a scientific article. She reported her findings, sure, but her vivid use of language is so powerful that when I read her article, I am transported to Madagascar.

Take, for example, her description of the sifakas. She begins in typical scientific fashion, detailing the group composition she observed: "*Propithecus* lived in small troops with a range of two to ten members and an average of four to five." She could have left it there, and many scientists would have, but she continues: "The members of a troop followed each other in single file, silently soaring against the blue sky in great ballet leaps, propelled by their jumping hindlegs."

Having followed the sifakas for twelve-hour days through the forests of Ankarafantsika, I can't think of a more apt description of the way they move.

Evocative language crops up throughout Jolly's paper. In another passage, she explains lemur responses to potential predators: "Lemurs gather round to mob carnivores, *Propithecus* hiccupping 'sifak, sifak,' and *Lemur catta* yapping like terriers."

Jolly's writing presents her findings and observations, but she also paints a picture, making readers feel as if they are right there with her, following groups of lemurs through the majestic forests of Madagascar.

Throughout her career, Alison Jolly continued with her delicate balance of science and creativity—a tightrope walk—making her research and conservation efforts accessible to both academics and the public. In 1980, she published *A World Like Our Own*, a first-person account of her travels with Malagasy scientists meant to bring awareness to conservation issues in Madagascar. Then, in 2004, she published *Lords and Lemurs*, which tells the history behind her field site, Berenty. Using a first-person narrative, she described the dynamics between lemurs, scientists, French expats and local Malagasy communities. She also continued her scholarly pursuits, publishing hundreds of articles in scientific journals.

Jolly was acutely aware that her work straddled the line between popular and academic writing. She reflected on this in a book chapter entitled "The Narrator's Stance: Storytelling and Science at Berenty Reserve," where she wrote that when writing *Lords and Lemurs*, "the impetus was literary," and that it was an "irresistible tale to tell." This confession reveals Jolly's unique approach to scientific writing and communication.

Leave it to a woman to discover that in ring-tailed lemurs, the females are in charge. It was a groundbreaking discovery in the 1960s, yet Jolly—an objective scientist—didn't recognize it as such.

In December 1964, Stuart Altmann organized a conference in Montreal focused on primate communication. Jolly was keen to participate and present the results of her study at Berenty, but she was living in Uganda with her husband, Richard. Not to mention, she was pregnant—too pregnant to fly to Canada. Not one to sit idle, Jolly asked her friend Thelma Rowell—the baboon researcher who had written about Irven DeVore's film—to read her paper about breeding synchrony in ring-tailed lemurs on her behalf. Rowell happily obliged.

Afterward, the two women connected.

"How did it go?" asked Jolly.

"Fine," Rowell replied with a laugh. "But now everyone thinks I study all kinds of primates. Oh, and they must think that I am obsessed with sex."

Jolly later reflected, "What is interesting is my omission of ring-tailed lemur female dominance over males from this paper, and its presentation in my 1966 book as a simple fact, not a political manifesto. It simply did not occur to me then that it was more interesting than male dominance, just different."

Before Jolly's long-term research on lemurs, primatologists assumed male primates ran the show. The idea of male dominance among primates is rooted in Darwin's theory of sexual selection, which suggests that male reproductive fitness—their ability to mate and sire offspring, thus passing on their genes—is limited by access to females. As a result, evolution favours traits that make males more appealing to females. These traits can include ornamentation (like peacock feathers) and weaponry (like antlers used by elk bulls to spar during mating season).

The poster child for sexual selection and male dominance among primates is the baboon. Baboons were of great interest to early primatologists before World War II because researchers believed that studying them could provide insight into our human ancestors. Like early humans, baboons lived in the savanna habitats of

Africa. Up to that point, studies of primates had focused primarily on the overt behaviours of the males, with females often falling into the background. Male baboon behaviours stand out and are hard to miss, with male-on-male battles helping to dictate clear dominance hierarchies. In baboon groups, males are the leaders and protectors.

In 1932, zoologist Solly Zuckerman summed it up: "Female baboons are always dominated by their males, and in many situations, the attitude of a female is of extreme passivity."

It wasn't just baboons that showed male dominance. Dian Fossey documented silverback males as the leaders of gorilla troops, and Jane Goodall observed clear male dominance hierarchies among chimpanzees.

Meanwhile, in Madagascar...

Alison Jolly observed the lemurs of Berenty—the ring-tailed lemurs and the sifakas—for nearly a year. Her study revealed that ring-tailed lemurs live in complex social groups with multiple males and females, sometimes as many as twenty-five individuals. She also discovered that females in the group "wholly dominated males," biting them, stealing fruit from them and even ousting them from their sleeping spots. In one memorable instance, Jolly watched as a lemur female pounced on a male, snatched a tamarind fruit pod right out of his hand and swatted him over the ear for good measure. Jolly referred to the swat as the "cuff," a common reaction during conflict where "one animal swats with one or sometimes alternate hands toward the other's face."

Jolly published her findings from her year with the lemurs in her 1966 book *Lemur Behavior: A Madagascar Field Study*. Near the end of the book, on page 155 of 167, she wrote: "One peculiar aspect of aggression in Lemuroidea is the relative dominance position of males and females...The troops I saw of wild *L. catta* and captive *L. macaco* are the only primates where all females can be said to be dominant over all males."

Jolly was simply reporting her observations. It was "peculiar," as she noted, but merely one of many observations she recorded during her time with the lemurs. In a later chapter of an edited volume called *Lemurs: Ecology and Adaptation*, Jolly reflected that female dominance in ring-tailed lemurs "seemed a quirk of the lemurs, not a political statement." For Jolly, her interest in the lemurs went beyond female dominance.

Yet, importantly, Jolly's study was among the first by a growing number of researchers who had bothered to look at and document what the female primates were doing. Her work also demonstrated that not all primate societies were alike, highlighting the variation within the primate order.

In *Primate Encounters*, their overview of primatology, Shirley Strum and Linda Fedigan characterized 1965 to 1975 as an era of "discovery and enigma of variability," and Jolly's findings with the lemurs were key. This was a time when field studies of new species emerged, revealing that primate behaviour varied across species and locations.

Even in 2004, however, ideas about male dominance in primates continued to influence popular media and public perception. That same year, Alison Jolly met Jeffrey Katzenberg, the CEO of DreamWorks, when he was visiting Berenty. Katzenberg, whom Jolly described as "amazingly ordinary in looks and manner," was there as part of the preparations for the animated film *Madagascar*. Not one to be shy among strangers, Jolly asked him about the movie.

Katzenberg described the plot: four animals escape from Central Park Zoo and wind up in Madagascar, where they're greeted by a singing and dancing "King of the Lemurs."

"You know," Jolly said, raising an eyebrow, "lemurs are female-dominant—so the 'King of the Lemurs' should really be a queen."

A slight pause from Katzenberg, followed by: "That boat has already left."

"Most of your friends are married by now," Morris Bishop said while he and his daughter took a drive in the family's blue Willys Jeep station wagon. A woman with a PhD might intimidate a lot of young men, he added matter-of-factly. "I think you should not be too standoffish about Richard."

"I want to marry him, but he hasn't asked me!" Alison Bishop exclaimed.

That night, in a huff and needing a distraction from her love life, Alison typed up her grant application to go to Madagascar to study lemurs. Madagascar, she reasoned, would be far enough away to forget all about Richard Jolly. She would focus on the lemurs and the majestic forests of the island.

Alison and Richard had met as graduate students at Yale. Richard, born in Sussex, England, had curly red hair and a serene temperament. His PhD thesis focused on the economics of education, and he had travelled through four African countries to collect material.

One day, possibly in his professor's office, Richard mustered the courage to make a request. "Might I have an extra hundred and fifty dollars to add a further case study?"

"Oh?" His supervisor, Lloyd Reynolds, looked at him inquisitively. "Where's that?"

"Madagascar."

The professor, who knew both Alison and Richard, as well as Alison's parents, agreed. It was settled: Richard Jolly would visit Alison in Madagascar under the pretense of research.

On the day Richard was scheduled to arrive, Alison made the three-day drive from Berenty forest to Antananarivo—or "Tana," as the city is commonly called—and then drove another two hours to Arivonimamo Airport in the central highlands. When the large Boeing airplane touched down, Alison waited expectantly.

The passengers exited the plane, crossed the tarmac and entered the building. But no Richard.

Perhaps he had taken a different flight. These were the days before cellphones and email, so Alison decided to wait a week and a half for the next Boeing to land, spending that time in the capital.

She drove the two hours to the airport again. The plane landed. This time, it was like a scene from a circus. When the doors opened, "a horde of very small Malagasy men descended the airplane steps in identical blue blazers, white trousers, and red-and-green striped ties, looking like a musical comedy of the seventy dwarves."

The plane had been commandeered for the Madagascar national soccer team, who had just returned from an international competition.

But still no Richard.

Alison waited for the next Boeing, four days later. Again, no Richard.

Enough was enough. Alison kicked herself for believing that love would carry the day. She knew she should have focused on the lemurs!

To lift her spirits after the crushing disappointment, Alison decided to go (with another Yale student, named Jeff) to the Perinet forest (today called Adasibe National Park), a few hours outside the capital, to see the indri. Indri are the largest of all the living lemurs, and their black-and-white colouration combined with their rounded, puffball ears and tail give them a look that's reminiscent of a child's drawing of a panda. They are known the world over for their song—a loud series of modulating whoops that sounds like trumpets echoing through the forests. They use these calls to maintain space between groups and to avoid competition for limited food resources.

The indri bought Richard another week, but when he still didn't show, Alison hopped back in her Land Rover and headed south to Berenty, heartbroken.

When she arrived, a stack of airmail letters awaited her. They were all from Richard, along with four "increasingly desperate" telegrams.

The first letter detailed an offer Richard had received to stay and work for a month in Addis Ababa at the Economic Commission for Africa with two of his academic heroes, Hans Singer and Dudley Seers. He planned to stop there en route to Madagascar, which meant a delay, but he hoped Alison would understand.

In the final telegram, although he hadn't heard from Alison, Richard told her he was still coming to Madagascar to do his research.

Alison panicked when she read his planned date of arrival: the day after next.

Now that she was back in Berenty, it was impossible for Alison to return to the capital in time to meet Richard. Even if she left immediately and somehow made it while he was still in Tana, there was no way to find each other in the busy capital city.

Dismayed, Alison headed into the forest, hoping for a pick-me-up, but even the ringtails were "a horrid disappointment" that day. She had been anticipating mating season for some time—there would be a lot of interesting behaviours to observe—but when she saw the lemurs, with "fresh injuries and exhausted," she knew she had missed the window. Ring-tailed lemur mating season is one of the shortest among all mammals.

As a deflated Alison trudged out of the forest, she bumped into Jean de Heaulme.

"What on earth is wrong?" he asked.

Alison relayed the whole ordeal: waiting in Tana for Richard, returning to his letters and telegrams, and missing out on mating season.

De Healme took it all in and paused a beat before saying, "Well, it just so happens that I am flying the Beechcraft to Tana tomorrow. Would you like to come along?"

The couple were reunited, and as Alison wrote, on that trip Richard found "his intellectual justification for studying Madagascar." His economist's eyes gave him a superpower: he could see the impacts of colonialism on the island nation's educational system. In 1882, the Merina kingdom of Madagascar passed a law in favour of universal primary education. Before French colonization, 160,000 children attended school; afterward, that number dropped to just 40,000. Although Richard had spent two years working as a community development officer in Kenya, it was nothing like Madagascar.

Alison felt lucky to have Richard with her in Madagascar because he revealed the full picture to her. While she might have otherwise gotten wrapped up in the lemurs and her science, Richard shone a light on the connection between human well-being and the well-being of nature. In the dedication of her 1980 book, *A World Like Our Own*, she wrote: "For Richard who said, 'Tell the whole story—ecology with people, not just your animals.'"

Alison's parents travelled to Madagascar for a visit before she and Richard flew home to marry. Richard, needing advice, went to see the head of the regional government in Amboasary. He explained they had purchased forty pointed straw hats "so all the children at the wedding can run around the Royal Pavilion in Brighton looking like little Tandroy!" But, he asked, was there a present—something that represented Madagascar—that he could give her parents as an engagement present?

The official grinned and told him there was just one gift that would be appropriate: a zebu, of course.

Zebu are Malagasy cattle that look something like a cross between a cow and a camel, with a large fatty hump on their back. Zebu hold immense cultural significance in Madagascar. They are a sign of wealth and social status. People use them for transport, meat, milk and even to help tread down rice fields. Zebu play significant roles in many ceremonies, including, as Richard was learning, weddings.

"The wedding would hardly be legal without a gift of zebu," the official explained.

Richard loved this idea. "That means Pop Bishop can actually have milk in his morning coffee!"

Three days later, Richard purchased a small black cow and her nursing calf.

When Richard proudly told the local official what he had done—he had gone ahead and bought a zebu for his in-laws!—the official was less than impressed.

"Just one?" he scoffed. "You do realize that you have a very cheap wife!"

Despite the scant zebu, Alison and Richard married in 1963 in the Royal Pavilion in Brighton, England.

"I would so love to do that!" Alison exclaimed to Richard, waving the letter that had just arrived in the mail. "But four children—who else can I recommend as author?"

The letter was from renowned conservation biologist Thomas Lovejoy, whom Alison knew from Yale. Lovejoy was asking if she would like to write a popular book about conservation in Madagascar. He had secured funding through the World Wildlife Foundation for an author and a photographer to travel throughout the island, writing about its unique environment for public audiences.

Richard wouldn't let Alison pass up such an opportunity. After all, it was 1975, he pointed out—International Women's Year! It was Alison's time to shine.

Alison later wrote about Richard's response in *Lords and Lemurs*: "You take the book; I'll stay home to look after the kids," he said. "Or perhaps I can find a temporary job in Madagascar? Then we'll go as a family!"

After writing to the International Labour Organization in Geneva, Richard—a superstar in his field of economics—was offered a post in Madagascar's planning office. They had been looking for an economist who was interested in social issues, and Richard's experience and expertise were a perfect fit.

In 1975, the adventurous family of six—all four children under the age of eleven—made their way to the other side of the world. Alison Jolly would team up with Russ Kinne, a freelance wildlife photographer, and together they would travel the country for five months. Their mission was to create a book that conveyed the "scientific excitement of Madagascar."

The Jolly family set up their home base in Antananarivo, at the Tsimbazaza Zoo and Botanical Gardens, next to the home of ornithologist George Randrianasolo. The Jolly's eldest daughter, Margaretta, recalled that she and her siblings were "thrilled that we would live in the country's zoo, in a whitewashed house." The children were enrolled in an American Lutheran missionary school for the few months they were in Madagascar, freeing Alison to travel and research her book while Richard worked at the planning office.

That year, Madagascar was in political turmoil. Just a few years earlier, in 1972, there had been a government coup. Crowds, led mostly by students and farmers, took to the streets, demanding that Philibert Tsiranana, the president of Madagascar, resign. Tsiranana, a former teacher, was a Christian and a socialist and had ruled Madagascar since its independence from France in 1960. However, by the 1970s, there was growing unrest. Farmers were frustrated by tax collection during a time when disease had struck their cattle herds. Students were upset by French domination of their school systems; they were pushing to replace the educational programs designed for schools in France and taught by French teachers with programs focused on Malagasy culture, taught by Malagasy teachers. They also emphasized the need to increase access to education for the underprivileged.

As antigovernment protests grew, the French government distanced itself from the situation. Ultimately, on May 18, 1972, the military, led by politically conservative General Gabriel Ramanantsoa, took power. Three years later, following allegations of corruption, Ramanantsoa's government was nearly overthrown, forcing him to resign. Amid the upheaval, in June 1975, Didier Ratsiraka, a military commander nicknamed the "Red Admiral" for his socialist policies, took over as the head of state, marking the beginning of a two-decade dictatorship.

When Alison Jolly arrived in Madagascar in 1975, she quickly learned that the new military government had a disdain for Western nations, especially France and the US. The government had expelled the US ambassador, closed a NASA tracking station and nationalized the operations of two US oil companies. Research visas were not being granted to Western scientists, and French researchers had been ousted altogether.

As a scientist and lemur researcher, Jolly worried her book would be a no-go. Luckily, she and Kinne were able to enter Madagascar on tourist visas, emphasizing that their book was a popularization, not a scientific study.

Jolly and Kinne travelled across the country, from Berenty in the far south—Jolly's home away from home—to an island called Nosy Be on the northwest coast, seeking to document Madagascar's diversity and share it with the world. Along the way, they were helped by their Malagasy colleagues, and were treated with kindness and hospitality in the villages they visited. The two absorbed all they could about the wildlife, the environment and the human condition. It was during this trip that, according to her daughter, Margaretta, Jolly began to fully appreciate the plight of Madagascar and truly understand how humans interact with nature—the politics of conservation. She began to ask, "Who pays for conservation—and who benefits?"

The result of their work was *A World Like Our Own*, published by Yale University Press in 1980. The publication, a hardcover coffee-table book, featured nearly 190 of Russ Kinne's photographs, including a few select colour images. Jolly penned the stories that captured the essence of Madagascar, complete with its incredible biodiversity, geologic history and intertwined economic and educational challenges. The book's title summed up Jolly's perspective on the country: what was happening there was not unique. Jolly believed that Madagascar is a "microcosm" for the whole world, providing a snapshot of how human actions influence nature around the globe.

A riveting section of the book documents Jolly's experiences on the island of Nosy Mangabe, a five-kilometre hilltop reserve created by the International Union for Conservation of Nature. No humans live on the island; it is just for the wildlife. Alison had hoped to glimpse an aye-aye, those bizarre bat-eared lemurs that fill a niche more typical of woodpeckers elsewhere, eating grubs out of trees. Back in 1966, French primatologist Jean-Jacques Petter released nine aye-ayes on the beach of Nosy Mangabe to save the species, which was persecuted and killed by humans due to folklore, from extinction.

"Where are they now?" Jolly lamented in her book, having travelled the island and failing to see an aye-aye or any evidence of the endangered lemur.

One of their Malagasy colleagues, a professor of forestry at the University of Madagascar, told Jolly and Kinne that the aye-ayes might be dead. However, others had reported spotting their leaf nests.

"For my part," Jolly wrote, "I can only say you could hide a dozen aye-ayes in my field of vision on Nosy Mangabe, and in that density of forest, I might not see them."

The lack of scientific research on the island due to government visa restrictions left many questions unanswered, including whether the aye-ayes were still roaming Nosy Mangabe.

In the mid-1980s, there was good news: scientists were able to successfully make their case for the importance of allowing Western researchers into Madagascar to study its unique biodiversity. In 1985 and 1987, Eleanor Sterling, a Yale University graduate student, surveyed Madagascar for the endangered aye-ayes. In the 1990s, Sterling answered the question Jolly had posed years earlier: the aye-ayes were still living on Nosy Mangabe. She estimated that the small island reserve was home to as many as forty-five aye-ayes, and she tracked them and studied their behaviour and ecology—the first long-term study of this elusive lemur.

Of course, Jolly had to pay a visit to Berenty to show her colleagues the site where it all began for her. She was struck by how the lemur populations had hardly changed, even after twelve years. The forest, too, still under protection, was intact—could Berenty serve as a model for large-scale habitat protection?

In the dry deciduous forests of the west, Jolly met up with Rachel Rabesandratana, a botany teacher from the University of Toliara. As they observed the flowers and lemurs of the region, Jolly noted the human impact on the forests through overgrazing cattle and uncontrolled fire. Fires are an annual problem in this area, encroaching on and burning the forest—"suicide by fire," as Rabesandratana called it. Jolly noted that it was a "fragile equilibrium," with people setting fires to encourage the growth of new grasses for grazing their cattle. The people rely on cattle for their livelihoods, and shifting agriculture is an important source of income through cash crops like cotton or peanuts.

"Is there hope?" Jolly asked in the conclusion of *A World Like Our Own*. "It depends," she continued, "on whether we have the wisdom to conserve our future."

Jolly's experience travelling through Madagascar awoke a passion for conservation and highlighted the complexities surrounding the plights of lemurs and people in Madagascar. She recognized that the fates of humans and animals were intricately linked.

In her diary from 1983, Alison Jolly jotted down several New Year's resolutions. Chief among them was, "To say I like New York, when asked."

The Jolly family had moved the year before from their home at the zoo in Madagascar to fast-paced New York City—"the city that never sleeps," home to Times Square and Broadway. Richard had followed Alison to Madagascar, first visiting her during her post-doctoral research in Berenty and later while she wrote her first popular book. But now it was Alison's turn to support Richard in his new post as deputy executive director with the United Nations. The family found an apartment on Roosevelt Island with views of the iconic Chrysler Building and the Empire State Building.

Nature-loving Alison was out of her comfort zone in the big city. While Richard worked to launch programs for oral rehydration for diarrhea and vaccination for childhood diseases in countries that needed them most, Alison wrote that she and the children "learned to live at the top of the world's heap."

Alison wondered if she had done right by her children in moving to New York, particularly when it came to being a role model. She reflected in her diary: "I brought up the kids as I wanted to be—with freedom and excitement and little nagging about the rules and appearance. Clearly, this was wrong. But how wrong? Should I not have done what I did about [my] career?"

Alison also struggled with her role as a hostess and wondered whether she should have "tried to make NYC more of a home" for her kids. When Margaretta, as Alison's literary executor, read these words after her mother passed away, she suddenly saw Alison as a woman in her own right—a forty-year-old, successful in her career, "trying to please her own mother."

Despite her disdain for the big city, Alison understood that living in New York was for the greater good. Richard's new post at UNICEF involved overseeing 130 countries and developing support strategies to reduce child mortality. Madagascar was one of those countries.

The Jollys exemplified the give-and-take required for a lasting relationship. It's rare for schedules, desires and dreams to align perfectly, and sacrifices are often necessary. The Jollys took these challenges in stride.

Although their home life centred on Richard's career, Alison made it a point to return to Madagascar many times over the years. She advised on films, attended international conferences, held various academic positions, and researched and published many popular and scientific books and articles.

In 2000, after his retirement from the United Nations, Richard visited Alison in Madagascar for, as she put it, "an actual holiday." A highlight of their trip, which she described in her book *Lords and Lemurs*, was attending a Malagasy funeral. Alison had heard about Malagasy funerals and had been dying to attend one—pun intended—as part of the research for her book. Of course, she did not wish for anyone's death, but was eager to understand the cultural significance of the ceremony. It would demonstrate how Tandroy traditions remain strong, even in the modern world.

With the help of a friend, it was arranged. It was a morning affair and started with just the intimate family. As Alison and Richard sat near the deceased man's house where the coffin lay, they were startled by gunfire. A herd of fifty zebu stampeded straight toward them, followed by young Malagasy men firing blank cartridges into the air. Hundreds of villagers cheered as the cattle flew past them. By the time the "dance of the cattle" was done, there were nearly seven hundred cattle in the village.

The day continued with a festive lunch, music and dancing. Even Richard got up for a dance, much to the villagers' delight. Each branch of the family then offered a zebu to the host. Finally, they paid their respects to the deceased by covering the zebu with a cotton cloth called a lamba.

Two weeks later came the public funeral, which culminated in the sacrifice of twenty-three zebu. The cattle were stripped, and the meat was divided among the funeral attendees. But the family did not consume the meat, as the sacrificed cattle now belonged to the deceased man, and he would bring them with him to the land of the ancestors.

Against the backdrop of this intricate Malagasy funeral, Richard and Alison stood in the early morning, watching the villagers setting up a series of mortars. I can picture them there: the sky pink, the cool morning fog beginning to dissipate, the sun just peeking over the horizon. In *Lords and Lemurs*, Alison Jolly remembered the morning fondly. Richard turned to her and said, "Remember our life in New York?" He then launched into a playful impression of their daily routine in the Big Apple: "Eat up your breakfast, you'll be late for school, Dad is going to be late for the office, you shouldn't have stayed up watching TV if you are going to be late, don't forget your homework, GOODBYE."

They shared a laugh and soaked in the calmness of the village morning where nobody hurried.

Soon after, the couple moved to Lewes, England, where they had lived in the early days of their marriage in 1969. Alison became a visiting senior research fellow at the University of Sussex.

Alison and Richard Jolly embodied #couplegoals. Although it must have been challenging to raise four kids while balancing their respective careers, they made it appear seamless by following their passions and finding areas of overlap.

Their dedication paid off. Alison continued to spread the word about Madagascar and the plight of the lemurs, while Richard's contributions to international development were recognized with a knighthood in 2001. The couple would become Sir and Lady Jolly.

"Don't you know why I first came with you? I was a spy!" the young woman told Alison Jolly. "I had to write a report to the authorities to say what you were really up to in the woods with all those Americans!"

Hanta Rasamimanana and Alison Jolly met in 1983, when Earthwatch, an American environmental charity that connects people and scientists worldwide, came to Berenty. Jolly could hardly fathom that amateurs would pay to volunteer, fly across the world and spend two weeks getting up at 5 a.m. to study the lemurs for fun. Even better, they would help her collect standardized data. She was thrilled—finally, she could gather data on all six groups of lemurs simultaneously.

The Malagasy government required Jolly to include Malagasy interns among the Earthwatch volunteers. One of these interns was a petite, pretty woman named Hanta. Although Rasamimanana, as she confessed later to Jolly, had been sent to check on things for the government, she couldn't help but become inspired by the lemurs.

Jolly quickly recognized Rasamimanana's work ethic. On one memorable occasion, a huge storm was brewing over Berenty. Jolly ran through the woods to extricate the volunteers but couldn't locate Rasamimanana. She hooted and hollered for her and finally found the quiet young woman still observing a group of lemurs. The two hightailed it back to camp. When Jolly asked why she hadn't headed back when she saw the storm, Rasamimanana replied, "You said never to lose our lemur troops, even if it rains."

Rasamimanana was born and raised in Antananarivo, and won scholarships to study abroad. At eighteen, she travelled all the way to Moscow to study biology, where she was inspired to study animal husbandry and attended Moscow's agricultural university as the only foreigner among a class of Russians.

After seven years, Rasamimanana returned home to Madagascar and took a job at the zoo as a nutritionist. She was then assigned to Jolly's Earthwatch contingent, where she was inspired to write a doctoral thesis on ring-tailed lemur nutrition, and she and Jolly became friends for life. Over the years, Rasamimanana studied the lemurs and published on their feeding behaviour, energy expenditure and unique dominance structure. She supervised students at Berenty and contributed to developing a new master's degree in primate conservation, which was offered in Mahajanga and the Comoros.

Both conservationists and mothers, Jolly and Rasamimanana were inspired in 2006 to create the Ako Project to bring education about Madagascar's unique wildlife to children around the globe. *Ako* is Malagasy for aye-aye. Along with New York artist Deborah Ross, Jolly and Rasamimanana produced a series of six illustrated children's books about lemurs, written in Malagasy and English. The first book focused on Ako the Aye-Aye, followed by books about the mouse lemurs, the ring-tailed lemur, the red ruffed lemur, the sifaka and the indri. For each book, Jolly penned the English text, Rasamimanana took on the Malagasy and Ross painted dreamy watercolours to go along with the inspiring words. The books were accompanied by posters and teaching materials, all focused on Madagascar's lemurs and their habitats.

The goal was to provide a creative way for Malagasy children to learn about the precious wildlife in their own backyards—to bring biodiversity and conservation into the primary school curriculum. Since publication, UNICEF has distributed tens of thousands of copies, written in Malagasy and English, to schools in Madagascar, and the Lemur Conservation Foundation has printed English versions for sale in North America.

The Mother of Lemurs.

Alison Jolly earned this nickname for her tireless efforts studying the lemurs in Madagascar for more than fifty years. During her work, Jolly witnessed a conservation crisis unfolding in the country—wildlife on the brink of extinction, people starving and struggling to live day-to-day, all against the backdrop of political instability and economic uncertainty.

Jolly questioned how it is possible to conserve wildlife without also helping and working with the people. On the surface, it might seem easy to blame Madagascar's conservation issues on its human population. After all, the two biggest threats to lemur survival are habitat loss, due to slash-and-burn agricultural practices, and hunting. But Jolly understood that the problem was nuanced and complex. People in Madagascar take part in these activities out of necessity, simply to feed their families. Recognizing these complexities early on, Jolly was one of the first to advocate for addressing the issues facing both wildlife and humans in Madagascar simultaneously. She began working with the Malagasy government, the World Bank and high-level conservation officials to bring about change for the country.

Jolly also connected with Malagasy community members, taking the time to understand their perspectives. She uncovered the complexities of why a Malagasy man named Jean took a job as a "rainforest executioner," cutting down rosewood trees for profit despite conservation issues. Like a third of Madagascar's people, Jolly pointed out, the man was undernourished and barely surviving. Jolly also learned about Bedo, a young Malagasy naturalist who died tragically because of jealousy over the money he earned as a tour guide. She was convinced that saving Madagascar's wildlife required working directly with its people—a concept now known as community conservation. In a 2001 article published in *Science*, she wrote, "Awareness and the will to conserve cannot be imposed from the outside but must be built on people's pride and delight in their own country's wildlife."

In her final book, *Thank You, Madagascar*, published posthumously, Jolly reflected on the ongoing destruction of Madagascar's environment and what it might mean for the lemurs and other wildlife. She warned: "If its forest destruction continues, we could be left with only lemurs confined to zoos and the rarest palms and baobabs in botanic gardens and seed banks."

Alison Jolly's approach inspired my partner, Travis, to create a charity called Planet Madagascar. I sit on the board, helping to write grants to fund our various projects. Our aim is to work closely with the Malagasy people—implementing community conservation approaches inspired by Jolly—to help save lemurs and improve people's lives in remote communities. To date, we have created fire management and forest restoration programs and have run numerous education initiatives for adults and children. We have learned firsthand that it is impossible to save Madagascar's biodiversity from extinction without considering the needs of the people. Alison Jolly was right.

Alison Jolly died of breast cancer on February 6, 2014, at the age of seventy-six. During her lifetime, she held positions with the New York Zoological Society, Rockefeller University, Princeton and the University of Sussex. She wrote half a dozen books and hundreds of articles, all while teaching courses and raising a family. In 2010, four years before her passing, Alison Jolly received the International Primatological Society's Lifetime Achievement Award.

Epilogue

AS I HAD DONE FOR THE PAST SEVEN MONTHS and would continue to do for the next seven, I packed my black-and-yellow daypack with the essentials. I gathered everything I needed for data collection on the lemurs: notebooks, data sheets, pens and pencils, binoculars, a GPS, a range finder, measuring tape and a handheld weather meter. Then, there was the equipment required to navigate my way through the northern dry forest of Madagascar throughout the long day ahead: handheld garden pruners to cut through the tangled lianas—check. A raincoat for sudden downpours—check. Bug spray and a mosquito net hat for when the mosquitoes got unbearable—check. Water bottle—got it. I also had food, since I would be spending more than twelve hours in the forest. And, of course, I had my lightweight chair for when the lemurs were resting. Into the pack it all went. I shook my head and laughed. Sometimes it was hard to believe I was halfway through my fourteen-month PhD research project on Coquerel's sifakas—those fuzzy white-and-maroon lemurs found only in Madagascar. It was funny to think that my job as a graduate student was to hike through Madagascar's forests in search of lemurs, and then, like a crazed stalker, follow groups of these cute and cuddly primates all day, writing down everything they did.

My days began before the sun rose. My guide, Zama—a boisterous Malagasy man with salt-and-pepper hair, who spoke loudly in broken French and limped with a bowlegged gait—and I would trek into the forest in the early morning hours. We would split up, each carrying blue, weatherproof Motorola hand-held walkie-talkies. We walked the trail system quietly, eyes locked on the forest canopy above, holding our breath in anticipation of a flash of white fur, an irregular shaking of a branch or the pitter-patter of fruits raining down from the canopy as the lemurs ate their breakfast. Some days, finding the groups was a snap. My radio would crackle, and Zama's voice would come through: "Keriann, *ils sont ici*."

On other days, we walked in circles for hours before we found them. Sometimes, we didn't find them at all. On those days, I thought about Jane Goodall and her initial struggles to find the chimpanzee groups. Like Jane, I would not quit.

That memorable day was a happy one. We had found the group without incident and spent the morning following them through the forest. These lemurs live an arboreal lifestyle—moving through the trees in search of food. They will spring off of a tree trunk, propelled by their powerful hind limbs, and after completing a 180-degree spin in midair, they will reach out and grab on to the next tree trunk. Again and again, they leap from tree to tree, sometimes covering a ten-metre gap in a single bound.

Every hour, I collected three ten-minute behavioural samples using methods developed by Jeanne Altmann to get a sense of their activities throughout the day. When the group moved, I took the lead. My job was to keep my eyes on the individuals in front, craning my neck to watch the canopy above and noting the lemurs' behaviour as I followed. Zama stayed back, sticking close to the individuals bringing up the rear. That way, we always had eyes on the group members, and there was less chance we would lose sight of them if they decided to split off in different directions.

Usually, the lemurs spent the first hours of the morning feeding, moving through the forest canopy and grooming. After a few hours of that, they typically stayed put in a tall, shady tree for a nap.

That day, the lemurs settled at around 10 a.m. An hour passed, and I turned to Zama. "You might as well head back," I said.

I stood watching the lemurs a while longer and took a behavioural sample.

Inactive, I wrote. *END*.

I closed my data book and wiped the sweat off my brow. I used the waterproof yellow notebook to fan myself a little. I was starting to feel weak. I found a patch of shade near a large tree trunk a few feet away from where the lemurs were resting in the canopy. I strategically set up my chair so I could take a break while keeping the lemurs in my sightline.

I took a swig of water.

I would kill for some ice, I thought.

I sighed and unzipped my backpack, pulling out my snacks. First, the plastic sleeve of dry, sliced toast—Madagascar's answer to Melba toast. I had to handle these crispy pieces of dried bread carefully, as they easily crumbled into pieces. Next, I pulled out my Ziploc bag containing La Vache qui rit cheese. The image of the laughing cow on the little triangle packets of soft cheese mocked me.

Not what I would eat back home, I thought as I unwrapped the foil. But with no refrigeration, dried bread and processed cheese was as good as it could get. I took out my pocketknife and began carefully spreading the soft cheese on the dry toast.

I was about to take a bite when I heard rustling. The lemurs had started to slowly lower themselves down the tree trunk, inching their way to the forest floor.

I gently set my toast on top of a Ziploc bag on the sandy soil. *Were the lemurs getting ready to move*? If so, I had to be ready to follow, which meant forgoing lunch.

But wait.

One by one, all five lemurs descended until they were seated directly on the ground, arms and legs still hugging the tree trunk. I couldn't believe my eyes. One of their predators, the fossa, a relative of the mongoose, was a ground-dwelling species. There was no doubt the lemurs were safer up in the canopy. But there they were, just a few feet away from me, seeking refuge in the shade, just like I was. After a few moments, the lemurs closed their eyes.

As quietly as I could, I picked up my toast. Then I couldn't help but let out a guffaw.

Here I was, in the forests of Madagascar, quite literally having a picnic with some of the most endangered primates in the world.

I had the women to thank. One of those women was, surprisingly, Madame Jacqueline. After she'd signed off on our permits, she and I became friends. She would tell me about her kids and how she loved watching them grow. When I went to town for supplies, I would bring her chocolates because I knew they were her favourite treat. One day, she even came into the forest with Zama and me to see my research in action. We all shared a laugh as she struggled through the sandy soil in her high-heeled shoes.

Then there were the other women. The women whose stories had stuck with me: Linda, Jane, Dian, Biruté, Jeanne, Sarah, Alison, and many, many more whom I would have included in this book if space was unlimited.

There's no doubt I was drawn to primatology because of these women. I wanted to be like them—explorers, travelling to all ends of the world in search of answers to questions about evolution and the human condition. To contribute to conservation.

Digging deeper into the personal stories of these women has been an adventure in itself. They come from different walks of life, yet it's easy to see how each was driven to the primates.

A critically thinking Linda Fedigan saw the world with her military father, learning many languages, being exposed to different cultures and challenging the status quo. Jane Goodall, a role model to young women everywhere, was raised by a mother who supported her in everything she did and encouraged her passions, even when they went against accepted social norms for a girl. Dian Fossey saw the gorillas as family because her own family was cold and distant. Biruté Galdikas's immigrant family valued education and work ethic above all, which she brought with her in rehabilitating orangutans and trekking through the harsh forests of Indonesia. Jeanne Altmann was a city kid who yearned to travel and wound up camping in Kenya amid the baboons, applying her mathematical skills to improve primate observation methods. Sarah Hrdy was raised by strong-willed women who supported her dreams of being a scholar and travelling to India. Alison Jolly, the daughter of artists, landed in the sciences but never lost her creative spark.

No two stories are alike, yet all of these women ended up in a discipline where they studied our closest living relatives. My conclusion from their stories and my own experience is that there is no single answer to why women have been drawn to primatology. Perhaps unsurprisingly, the reasons are varied and nuanced. Writing this book has made me realize that the question of why women are drawn to primatology is perhaps less important than the question of how these women have shaped the discipline as we know it today.

Each of the founding women primatologists made new discoveries about primates in their natural habitat—tool use in chimpanzees, infanticide in langurs, female dominance in lemurs and more. Collectively, they changed the way we understand primate societies and, ultimately, ourselves. Many of these women contributed to a shift in focus from males as the central players in a group, highlighting that females play crucial roles. Others emphasized conservation, working to save endangered species.

I feel a thrill when I think about how these women emerged at a time when society expected them to stay at home, to be good wives and mothers. They each defied all expectations, travelled across continents, coped with the harsh conditions of primate habitats, many having children and families, all while completely transforming the discipline of primatology. They persisted and persevered, and by doing so, they gifted me the strength to do the same. I have carried these women, their stories and their discoveries with me as I have navigated my path to the primates.

Acknowledgements

"JANE GOODALL'S MOM!" my mother cries. "Look here!" She taps her finger on the program for tonight's lecture. "She went with Jane to Tanzania! Served as her chaperone!"

I see where this is going: "Yes?"

"You never told me this! You kept it secret!"

We are sitting near the back of the Jack Singer Concert Hall in Calgary, Alberta—then my hometown. We don't have the best seats in the house. In fact, the event hasn't even started and we've already swapped seats. My mother is five foot two, and a large man had plunked down in front of her. "Why do the tall ones always sit in front of me?" she had moaned—a little too loudly—to no one in particular.

I had laughed and stood and shuffled sideways to trade seats. I'm five foot seven, and knew that a mildly obstructed view of the stage wouldn't bother me at this point. I'm excited just to be here. I mean, it's *her*. She is here in the same building as me right now. And, in just a few minutes, we will be in the same *room*. I can hardly believe that I will be so close to my idol, Dr. Jane Goodall.

"What do you mean, I kept it a secret?"

"Jane's mom," she says, excitedly. "Her mom travelled with her to Tanzania as her chaperone. The government wouldn't let her go alone, so she brought her mother, who had been to Africa before. While Jane was studying the chimps, her mom was cooking and helping out around camp."

She pauses, waiting for me to fill in the blanks. When I just smile back at her she fills them in for me.

"When you go to the field to study the primates," she says, "I could come too. Help out around camp. Like Jane's mom!"

I start to laugh but catch myself when I see my mother raise her eyebrows. My mother teaches elementary school. Slim and demure, she exudes warmth. The kids in her classroom love and respect her. She is lovely, but an adventurer? She certainly does not look the part. Yet...what is it...something about books and covers? In her younger years, she and my father had shared more than a few adventures. They had worked as fire lookouts in the Canadian Rockies—just the two of them on a mountain in a small cabin, scanning the valley below for signs of fire. And, more relevant to her current excitement, for a time, she and my father had lived in Africa.

On August 4, 2024, my mother, Sheena Fraser McGoogan—my constant inspiration—passed away. First and foremost, I wish to acknowledge her. My mother instilled in me kindness, dedication and curiosity, and without her this book would never have materialized.

Truthfully, this book has been germinating inside of me for years. The seed was planted while I was completing my undergraduate degree at the University of Calgary and I learned of the countless women who shaped the science of primatology. I'd like to thank these women for forging a path that I could follow. This includes the women in this book, of course—Linda Fedigan, Jane Goodall, Dian Fossey, Biruté Galdikas, Jeanne Altmann, Sarah

Hrdy and Alison Jolly. I would like to especially thank Linda Fedigan and Sarah Hrdy for allowing me to interview them. Thanks, too, to Samara Greenwood, a scholar examining how the women's liberation movement affected primate field studies, for speaking with me about our shared interests. I would also like to acknowledge that there are many, many other female primatologists who inspired me and others—too many to name here or include in this book.

I would like to thank the various scientists who directly helped me along my path to the primates, including Brian Keating, Mary Pavelka and Shawn Lehman. Without them, I would never have completed a degree in primatology nor travelled to Belize and Madagascar in pursuit of primates.

I am grateful to the Writers' Trust Rising Stars program and to award-winning author Deborah Campbell, who selected me for the program and provided mentorship invaluable to refining the structure for this book. Through that program, I also had the honour of receiving mentorship from author Lawrence Hill and Sue Goyette during a writing retreat at the Banff Centre for Arts and Creativity. At that retreat, I met the other Rising Stars in the program, who provided boundless inspiration, each of them going on to do great things. Thanks to the Canada Council for the Arts for providing grant funding for this work. Funds from the Access Copyright Foundation allowed me to attend the Orion Environmental Writers' Workshop, where I learned from other nature-loving writers and from my workshop instructor, author Alison Hawthorne Deming.

A huge thanks goes out to my early readers: my father, author Ken McGoogan, who taught me everything I know about writing; my husband, Travis Steffens; and my good friend Brooke Crowley.

I am grateful to Douglas & McIntyre for bringing me aboard as an author, amongst an impressive list of Canadian writers. Thank you to publisher Anna Comfort O'Keeffe, for sharing my vision, and to managing editor Ariel Brewster for guiding me through the publishing process with a steady hand. Editor Jen Lauriault was crucial in shaping this book through her substantive edit—thanks, Jen for lending me your sense of structure and style and for making this book the best it could be. Thanks to copy editor Melissa Edwards for her eagle eye for detail and proofreader Melanie Little for a meticulous editing job.

Most of all, I want to thank my family: Ken and Sheena; Carlin and Sylwia; James and Veronica; Cecile and Bob; and the Steffens family. Fellow primatologist Travis Steffens is my husband, travel companion and all-around partner in crime. Thank you, Travis, for sharing your passion, your love for adventure and your overall positive vibes with me every day.

Selected Sources

Addessi, Elsa, Marta Borgi, and Elisabetta Palagi. "Is Primatology an Equal-Opportunity Discipline?" *PLoS One* 7, no. 1 (2012): e30458.

Alberts, Susan, and Jeanne Altmann. "The Amboseli Baboon Research Project: 40 Years of Continuity and Change." In *Long-Term Field Studies of Primates*. Edited by Peter Kappeler and David Watts. Springer, 2012.

Alberts, Susan, and Joan Silk. "The Contributions of Jeanne Altmann." *Evolutionary Anthropology: Issues, News, and Reviews* 22, no. 5 (2013): 198–199.

Alberts, Susan, Jeanne Altmann, E. A. Archie, Jenny Tung, Stuart Altmann, and Susan Alberts. *Monitoring Guide for the Amboseli Baboon Research Project*, 2018.

Allan, John. "A Voice in the Wilderness." *On Wisconsin*, 2010. https://onwisconsin.uwalumni.com/features/a-voice-in-the-wilderness.

Altmann, Jeanne, Glenn Hausfater, and Stuart Altmann. "Demography of Amboseli Baboons, 1963–1983." *American Journal of Primatology* 8, no. 2 (1985): 113–125.

Altmann, Jeanne. "Motherhood, Methods, and Monkeys: An Intertwined Professional and Personal Life." *Leaders in Animal Behavior* (2009): 39–58.

Altmann, Jeanne. "Observational Study of Behavior: Sampling Methods." *Behaviour* 49, no. 3–4 (1974): 227–266.

Altmann, Jeanne. *Baboon Mothers and Infants*. University of Chicago Press, 2001.

Altmann, Stuart, and Jeanne Altmann. "The Transformation of Behaviour Field Studies." *Animal Behaviour* 65, no. 3 (2003): 413–423.

Altmann, Stuart, and Jeanne Altmann. *Baboon Ecology*. University of Chicago Press, 1970.

Altmann, Stuart. *Foraging for Survival: Yearling Baboons in Africa*. University of Chicago Press, 1998.

Alvey, Mark. "The Cinema as Taxidermy: Carl Akeley and the Preservative Obsession." *Framework: The Journal of Cinema and Media* 48, no. 1 (2007): 23–45.

Arbour, Jessica, and Sharlene Santana. "A Major Shift in Diversification Rate Helps Explain Macroevolutionary Patterns in Primate Species Diversity." *Evolution* 71, no. 6 (2017): 1600–1613.

Asquith, Pamela. "A Woman of Science: Sorting Fact and Illusion in Gender and Primatology." In *Primate Life Histories, Sex Roles, and Adaptability:*

Essays in Honour of Linda M. Fedigan. Edited by Urs Kalbitzer and Katharine Jack. Springer, 2018.

Barnet, Andrea. *Visionary Women: How Rachel Carson, Jane Jacobs, Jane Goodall, and Alice Waters Changed Our World*. HarperCollins, 2018.

Bartlett, Thad, Robert Sussman, and James Cheverud. "Infant Killing in Primates: A Review of Observed Cases with Specific Reference to the Sexual Selection Hypothesis." *American Anthropologist* 95, no. 4 (1993): 958–990.

Bass, Carole. "Alison Jolly '62PhD Dies at 76; Was World Expert on Lemurs." *Yale Alumni Magazine*, February 19, 2014. https://yalealumnimagazine.org/blog_posts/1713-alison-jolly-62phd-dies-at-76-was-world-expert-on-lemurs.

Battiata, Mary. "Dian Fossey: The Crusade, the Conflict, the Night of Horror." *Washington Post*, January 25, 1986. https://www.washingtonpost.com/archive/lifestyle/1986/01/25/dian-fossey-the-crusade-the-conflict-the-night-of-horror/7dab897d-3933-4ebf-9a17-263610b1758a.

Baumgartner, Aly, and Daniel Peppe. "Paleoenvironmental Changes in the Hiwegi Formation (Lower Miocene) of Rusinga Island, Lake Victoria, Kenya." *Palaeogeography, Palaeoclimatology, Palaeoecology* 574 (2021): 110458.

Bell, Loren. "What Is Peat Swamp, and Why Should I Care?" *Mongabay*, July 20, 2014. https://news.mongabay.com/2014/07/what-is-peat-swamp-and-why-should-i-care.

Boswell, Percy. "Human Remains from Kanam and Kanjera, Kenya Colony." *Nature* 135, no. 3410 (1935): 371.

Britannica. "Amboseli National Park." Retrieved August 18, 2024. https://www.britannica.com/place/amboseli-national-park.

Brittanica. "Obsidian: Volcanic Glass." Accessed August 12, 2024. https://www.britannica.com/science/obsidian.

Burt, Jonathan. "Solly Zuckerman: The Making of a Primatological Career in Britain, 1925–1945." *Studies in History and Philosophy of Science Part C: Studies in History and Philosophy of Biological and Biomedical Sciences*, 37, no. 2 (2006): 295310.

Campbell, Colin. "Anatomy of a Fierce Academic Feud." *New York Times*, November 9, 1986. https://www.nytimes.com/1986/11/09/education/anatomy-of-a-fierce-academic-feud.html.

Cepelewicz, Jordana. "Why Primates Kill Their Offspring." *Nautilus*, October 31, 2016. https://nautil.us/human-infanticide-signals-a-lack-of-social-support-5389.

Chambers, David Wade. "Stereotypic Images of the Scientist: The Draw-a-Scientist Test." *Science Education* 67, no. 2 (1983): 255–265.

Christopher, Ben. "The Massacre at Monkey Hill." *Priceonomics*, October 6, 2016. https://priceonomics.com/the-massacre-at-monkey-hill.

Cleveland Clinic. "Polio." Accessed September 6, 2024. https://my.clevelandclinic.org/health/diseases/15655-polio.

Cole, Sonia Mary. *Leakey's Luck: The Life of Louis Seymour Bazett Leakey, 1903–1972*. Collins, 1975.

Curtin, Richard, and Phyllis Dolhinow. "Primate Social Behavior in a Changing World." *American Scientist* 66, no. 4 (1978): 468–75.

Dagg, Anne Innis. "Infanticide by Male Lions Hypothesis: A Fallacy Influencing Research into Human Behavior." *American Anthropologist* 100, no. 4 (1998): 940–950.

Denworth, Lydia. "Curriculum Vitae: Jeanne Altmann's 'Twisty' Path to Baboon Research." *Princeton Alumni Weekly*, March 29, 2021. https://paw.princeton.edu/article/curriculum-vitae-jeanne-altmanns-twisty-path-baboon-research.

Dowling, Claudia Glenn. "Maternal Instincts: From Infidelity to Infanticide." *Discover Magazine*, February 28, 2003. https://www.discovermagazine.com/health/maternal-instincts-from-infidelity-to-infanticide.

Dunbar, Robin Ian MacDonald. *Primate Social Systems*. Springer Science & Business Media, 2013.

Encyclopedia.com. "Fossey, Dian (1932–1985)." Accessed September 6, 2024. https://www.encyclopedia.com/women/encyclopedias-almanacs-transcripts-and-maps/fossey-dian-1932-1985.

Fedigan, Linda, and Laurence Fedigan. "Gender and the Study of Primates." *Critical Reviews of Gender and Anthropology* (1989): 41–64.

Fedigan, Linda. "A View on the Science: Physical Anthropology at the Millennium." *American Journal of Physical Anthropology* 113, no. 4 (2000): 451–454.

Fedigan, Linda. "My Path to Primatology: Some Stories from the Field." *Primates* 63, no. 4 (2022): 313–325.

Fedigan, Linda. "Reflections of an Imperfect Anthropologist." *Annual Review of Anthropology* 49 (2020): 1–12.

Fedigan, Linda. "Science and the Successful Female: Why There Are So Many Women Primatologists." *American Anthropologist* (1994): 529–540.

Fedigan, Linda. *Primate Paradigms: Sex Roles and Social Bonds*. University of Chicago Press, 1992.

Fossey, Dian. *Gorillas in the Mist*. Houghton Mifflin Harcourt, 1983.

Fuentes, Agustín. "Being Human and Doing Primatology: National, Socioeconomic, and Ethnic Influences on Primatological Practice." *American Journal of Primatology* 73, no. 3 (2011): 233–237.

Galdikas, Biruté. *Reflections of Eden: My Years with the Orangutans of Borneo.* 1st edition. Little, Brown, 1995.

Gaur, Rajan. "Louis Leakey and Mary Leakey: The First Family of Palaeoanthropology." *Resonance* 20 (2015): 667–679.

Gaveau, David, Sean Sloan, Elis Molidena, Husna Yaen, Doug Sheil, Nicola Abram, Marc Ancrenaz, et al. "Four Decades of Forest Persistence, Clearance, and Logging on Borneo." *PloS One* 9, no. 7 (2014): e101654.

Glazer, Gwen. "You've Seen Her Murals Around Campus—Now She's Rediscovered in New Book." *Cornell Chronicle*, May 5, 2011. https://news.cornell.edu/stories/2011/05/little-known-artists-work-abounds-campus.

Goodall Jane. "Learning from the Chimpanzees: A Message Humans Can Understand." *Science* 282 (1998): 2184–2185.

Goodall, Jane, and Phillip Berman. *Reason for Hope: A Spiritual Journey.* Grand Central Publishing, 1999.

Goodall, Jane. *In the Shadow of Man.* Houghton Mifflin Harcourt, 2000.

Goodall, Jane. *My Life with the Chimpanzees.* Simon and Schuster, 1996.

Goodall, Jane. *The Chimpanzees of Gombe: Patterns of Behaviour.* The Belknap Press of Harvard University Press, 1986.

Gruen, Lori, Amy Fultz, and Jill Pruetz. "Ethical Issues in African Great Ape Field Studies." *Ilar Journal* 54, no. 1 (2013): 24–32.

Haraway, Donna. *Primate Visions: Gender, Race, and Nature in the World of Modern Science.* Routledge, 2013.

Hausfater, Glenn, and Sarah Blaffer Hrdy. *Infanticide: Comparative and Evolutionary Perspectives.* Routledge, 2017.

Hayes, Harold. *The Dark Romance of Dian Fossey.* Simon and Schuster, 1990.

Henning, Justine. "Jeanne Altmann." *Math4Science.* Accessed September 6, 2024. https://math4science.org/jeanne-altmann.

Herzfeld, Chris. *The Great Apes: A Short History.* Yale University Press, 2017.

Hooton, Earnest. "The Importance of Primate Studies in Anthropology." *Human Biology* 26, no. 3 (1954): 179–188.

Hrdy, Sarah Blaffer, and Ruth Bleier. "Empathy, Polyandry, and the Myth of the Coy Female." *Conceptual Issues in Evolutionary Biology* 131 (1986): 119–146.

Hrdy, Sarah Blaffer. "Infanticide as a Primate Reproductive Strategy." *American Scientist* 65, no. 1 (1977): 40–49.

Hrdy, Sarah Blaffer. "Male-Male Competition and Infanticide Among the Langurs (Presbytis entellus) of Abu, Rajasthan." *Folia Primatologica* 22, no. 1 (1974): 19–58.

Hrdy, Sarah Blaffer. "Myths, Monkeys, and Motherhood: A Compromising Life." In *Leaders in Animal Behavior: The Second Generation*. Edited by Lee Drickamer and Donald Dewsbury. Cambridge University Press, 2009.

Hrdy, Sarah Blaffer. *Mother Nature*. Chatto & Windus, 1999.

Hrdy, Sarah Blaffer. *The Woman That Never Evolved.* Revised Edition. Harvard University Press, 2009.

Huffman, Michael, Linda Fedigan, Paul Vasey, and Jean-Baptiste Leca. "A Brief Historical Time-line of Research on the Arashiyama Macaques." In *The Monkeys of Stormy Mountain*. Edited by Jean-Baptiste Leca, Michael Huffman, and Paul Vasey. Cambridge University Press, 2012.

Huffman, Michael. "History of the Arashiyama Japanese Macaques in Kyoto, Japan." In *The Monkeys of Arashiyama: Thirty-five Years of Research in Japan and the West*. Edited by Linda Fedigan and Pamela Asquith. Suny Press, 1991.

Humle, T., F. Maisels, J.F. Oates, A. Plumptre, and E.A. Williamson. *Pan Troglodytes.* Errata version. *The IUCN Red List of Threatened Species* 2018. Accessed September 6, 2024. https://dx.doi.org/10.2305/IUCN.UK.2016-2.RLTS.T15933A17964454.en.

International Union for Conservation of Nature. "The IUCN Red List of Threatened Species." Version 2024-1. https://www.iucnredlist.org.

Isbell, Lynne, Truman Young, and Alexander Harcourt. "Stag Parties Linger: Continued Gender Bias in a Female-Rich Scientific Discipline." *PloS One* 7, no. 11 (2012): e49682.

Jahme, Carole. *Beauty and the Beasts: Woman, Ape and Evolution*. Soho Press, 2003.

Johnson, Eric Michael. "Raising Darwin's Consciousness: An Interview with Sarah Blaffer Hrdy on Mother Nature." *Scientific American*, March 16, 2012. https://blogs.scientificamerican.com/primate-diaries/raising-darwins-consciousness-an-interview-with-sarah-blaffer-hrdy-on-mother-nature.

Johnson, Eric Michael. "Women and Children First." *Times Higher Education*, 2012. https://www.timeshighereducation.com/features/women-and-children-first/419301.

Jolly, Alison, and Margaretta Jolly. "A View from the Other End of the Telescope: Review of 'Primate Visions' by Donna Haraway."

New Scientist, April 21, 1990. https://www.newscientist.com/article/mg12617133-900-a-view-from-the-other-end-of-the-telescope.

Jolly, Alison. "Lemur Social Behavior and Primate Intelligence: The Step from Prosimian to Monkey Intelligence Probably Took Place in a Social Context." *Science* 153, no. 3735 (1966): 501–506.

Jolly, Alison. "Monkeys in the Back Garden." *Science* 291, no. 5509 (2001): 1705–1706.

Jolly, Alison. "Story-telling and Science at Berenty Reserve." In *Centralizing Fieldwork: Critical Perspectives from Primatology, Biological and Social Anthropology*. Edited by Jeremy MacClancy and Agustín Fuentes. Berghahn Books, 2010.

Jolly, Alison. "The Bad Old Days of Primatology?" In *Primate Encounters: Models of Science, Gender, and Society*. Edited by Shirley Strum and Linda Fedigan. University of Chicago Press, 2000.

Jolly, Alison. *A World Like Our Own: Man and Nature in Madagascar*. Yale University Press, 1980.

Jolly, Alison. *Lemur Behavior: A Madagascar Field Study*. University of Chicago Press, 1966.

Jolly, Alison. *Lords and Lemurs: Mad Scientists, Kings with Spears, and the Survival of Diversity in Madagascar*. Houghton Mifflin Harcourt, 2004.

Jolly, Alison. *Thank You, Madagascar: The Conservation Diaries of Alison Jolly*. Bloomsbury, 2015.

Jolly, Margaretta. "Travelling Through Time / Voyage dans le Temps." *Madagascar Conservation & Development* 5, no. 2 (2010): 125–126.

Jones, Jeannette Eileen. "Gorilla Trails in Paradise: Carl Akeley, Mary Bradley, and the American Search for the Missing Link." DigitalCommons@University of Nebraska – Lincoln, September 1, 2006.

Kalbitzer, Urs, and Katharine M. Jack, editors. *Primate Life Histories, Sex Roles, and Adaptability: Essays in Honour of Linda M. Fedigan*. Springer, 2018.

Lambert, Tim. "A History of Reading, Berkshire." *Local Histories*. Accessed September 6, 2024. https://localhistories.org/a-history-of-reading.

Leakey, Louis. "A New Fossil Skull from Olduvai." *Nature* 184, no. 4685 (1959): 491–493.

Leakey, Richard. *The Making of Mankind*. Michael Joseph, 1981.

Lee, Richard Borshay. "Irven DeVore 1934–2014." *Hunter-Gatherer Research* 1, no. 1 (2015): 135–137.

Leighty, Katherine, Annie Valuska, Alison Grand, Tamara Bettinger, Jill Mellen, Stephen Ross, Paul Boyle, and Jacqueline Ogden.

"Impact of Visual Context on Public Perceptions of Non-human Primate Performers." *PloS One* 10, no. 2 (2015): e0118487.

Lewin, Roger. "The Old Man of Olduvai Gorge." *Smithsonian* 33, no. 7 (2002): 82–89.

Lewis, Amanda. "Africanizing Science in Post-colonial Kenya: Long-term Field Research in the Amboseli Ecosystem, 1963–1989." *Journal of the History of Biology* 51, no. 3 (2018): 535–562.

Luft, Joan, and Jeanne Altmann. "Mother Baboon." In *The Natural History Reader in Animal Behavior*. Edited by Howard Topoff. Columbia University Press, 1987.

MacKinnon, Katherine, and Erin Riley. "Ethical Issues in Field Primatology." *Ethics in the Field: Contemporary Challenges* 86 (2013): 98–107.

Marchese, David. "Why Jane Goodall Still Has Hope for Us Humans." *New York Times*, July 12, 2021.

Maréchal, Laëtitia, Stuart Semple, Bonaventura Majolo, and Ann MacLarnon. "Assessing the Effects of Tourist Provisioning on the Health of Wild Barbary Macaques in Morocco." *PloS One* 11, no. 5 (2016): e0155920.

Maugh, Thomas II. "Orangutans in the Mist: Woman's 20-Year Study of Elusive Rain Forest Apes Finds They're Not Antisocial After All." *Los Angeles Times*, January 13, 1992. https://www.latimes.com/archives/la-xpm-1992-01-13-me-231-story.html.

McNulty, Kieran, David Begun, Jay Kelley, Fredrick Manthi, and Emma Mbua. "A Systematic Revision of Proconsul with the Description of a New Genus of Early Miocene Hominoid." *Journal of Human Evolution* 84 (2015): 42–61.

Mestel, Rosie. "Monkey 'Murderers' May be Falsely Accused." *NewScientist*, July 15, 1995. https://www.newscientist.com/article/mg14719862-300-monkey-murderers-may-be-falsely-accused.

Mikkelsen, T., W. Ladeana, E. Eichler, M. Zody, D. Jaffe, and S. Yang. "Initial Sequence of the Chimpanzee Genome and Comparison with the Human Genome." *Nature* 437 (2005): 69–87.

Milam, Erika Lorraine. "Landscapes of Time: Building Long-Term Perspectives in Animal Behavior." *Berichte zur Wissenschaftsgeschichte* 45, no. 1–2 (2022): 164–188.

Miller, David, Kyle Nolla, Alice Eagly, and David Uttal. "The Development of Children's Gender-Science Stereotypes: A Meta-Analysis of 5 Decades of US Draw-a-Scientist Studies." *Child Development* 89, no. 6 (2018): 1943–1955.

Montgomery, Sy. *Walking with the Great Apes: Jane Goodall, Dian Fossey, Biruté Galdikas*. Chelsea Green Publishing, 2009.

Morell, Virginia. *Ancestral Passions: The Leakey Family and the Quest for Humankind's Beginnings*. Simon and Schuster, 2011.

Morgans, Courtney, Truly Santika, Erik Meijaard, Marc Ancrenaz, and Kerrie Wilson. "Cost-Benefit Based Prioritisation of Orangutan Conservation Actions in Indonesian Borneo." *Biological Conservation* 238 (2019): 108236.

Mowat, Farley. *Woman in the Mists : The Story of Dian Fossey and the Mountain Gorillas of Africa*. Warner Books, 1987.

Mukanjari, Samson, Birgit Bednar-Friedl, Edwin Muchapondwa, and Precious Zikhali. "Evaluating the Prospects of Benefit Sharing Schemes in Protecting Mountain Gorillas in Central Africa." *Natural Resource Modeling* 26, no. 4 (2013): 455–479.

Nelson, Lynn Hankinson. *Biology and Feminism: A Philosophical Introduction*. Cambridge University Press, 2017.

New World Encyclopedia. "Great Rift Valley." Accessed September 6, 2024. https://www.newworldencyclopedia.org/entry/great_rift_valley.

Nienaber, Georgianne. "International Court Acquits Suspected Murderer of Dian Fossey." *Huffpost*, November 17, 2009. https://www.huffpost.com/entry/international-court-acqui_b_360379.

Nienaber, Georgianne. *Gorilla Dreams: The Legacy of Dian Fossey*. iUniverse, 2006.

Nijman, Vincent. "Orangutan Trade, Confiscations, and Lack of Prosecutions in Indonesia." *American Journal of Primatology* 79, no. 11 (2017): 22652.

Nissen, Henry Wieghorst. *A Field Study of the Chimpanzee: Observations of Chimpanzee Behavior and Environment in Western French Guinea*. Johns Hopkins Press, 1931.

Onyango, Patrick Ogola. "Altmann, Jeanne." In *The International Encyclopedia of Primatology*. Edited by Agustín Fuentes. John Wiley & Sons, 2017.

Packer, Craig. "Infanticide Is No Fallacy." *American Anthropologist* 102, no. 4 (2000): 829–831.

Pandong, Joshua, Melvin Gumal, Zolkipli Mohamad Aton, Mohd Shahbudin Sabki, and Lian Pin Koh. "Threats and Lessons Learned from Past Orangutan Conservation Strategies in Sarawak, Malaysia." *Biological Conservation* 234 (2019): 56–63.

Peaker, Malcolm. "London Zoo's Monkey Hill (1925–1955) Revisited." *Zoology Jottings*, May 3, 2016. https://zoologyweblog.blogspot.com/2016/05/london-zoos-monkey-hill-1925-1955.html.

Perelman, Polina, Warren Johnson, Christian Roos, Hector Seuánez, Julie Horvath, Miguel Moreira, Bailey Kessing, et al. "A Molecular Phylogeny of Living Primates." *PLoS Genetics* 7, no. 3 (2011): e1001342.

Peterson, Dale. *Jane Goodall: The Woman Who Redefined Man*. Houghton Mifflin Harcourt, 2008.

Razafindramanana, Josia. "In Memory of Dr. Alison Jolly." Duke Lemur Center, 2014. https://lemur.duke.edu/in-memory-of-dr-alison-jolly.

Rees, Amanda. "Practising Infanticide, Observing Narrative: Controversial Texts in a Field Science." *Social Studies of Science* 31, no. 4 (2001): 507–31.

Rees, Amanda. *The Infanticide Controversy: Primatology and the Art of Field Science*. University of Chicago Press, 2009.

Rimmer, Brandy. "Dian Fossey's Controversial 'Active Conservation' Proves Useful in Increasing Mountain Gorilla Awareness." *Earth Common Journal* 3, no. 1 (2013).

Robbins, Martha, Markye Gray, Katie Fawcett, Felicia Nutter, Prosper Uwingeli, Innocent Mburanumwe, Edwin Kagoda, et al. "Extreme Conservation Leads to Recovery of the Virunga Mountain Gorillas." *PloS One* 6, no. 6 (2011): e19788.

Sabuhoro, Edwin, Brett Wright, Ian Munanura, Ingrid Nyonza Nyakabwa, and Carmen Nibigira. "The Potential of Ecotourism Opportunities to Generate Support for Mountain Gorilla Conservation Among Local Communities Neighboring Volcanoes National Park in Rwanda." *Journal of Ecotourism* 20, no. 1 (2021): 1–17.

Schülke, Oliver, and Julia Ostner. "Ecological and Social Influences on Sociality." In *The Evolution of Primate Societies*. Edited by John Mitani, Josep Call, Peter Kappeler, Ryne Palombit, and Joan Silk. University of Chicago Press, 2012.

Setchell, Joanna, and Adam Gordon. "Editorial Practice at the International Journal of Primatology: The Roles of Gender and Country of Affiliation in Participation in Scientific Publication." *International Journal of Primatology* 39 (2018): 969–986.

Shaffer, Marguerite. "A Transnational Wildlife Drama: Dian Fossey, Popular Environmentalism, and the Origins of Gorilla Tourism." *American Quarterly* 67, no. 2 (2015): 317–352.

Shoumatoff, Alex. "The Fatal Obsession of Dian Fossey." *Vanity Fair*, January 1, 1995.

Shutt, Kathryn, Michael Heistermann, Adetayo Kasim, Angelique Todd, Barbora Kalousova, Ilona Profosouva, Klara Petrzelkova, et al. "Effects of Habituation, Research, and Ecotourism on Faecal Glucocorticoid

Metabolites in Wild Western Lowland Gorillas: Implications for Conservation Management." *Biological Conservation* 172 (2014): 72–79.

Sineo, L., and C. Veracini. "Primatology in the Italian Universities: From the Colonial Experience to the End of the xx Century." In *History of Primatology: Yesterday and Today. The Mediterranean Tradition*. Edited by Francesco Scalfari, Cecilia Veracini, and Catarina Casanova. Aracne Editrice, 2019.

Spalding, Linda. "The Jungle Took Her." *Outside*, May 1998. https://www.outsideonline.com/outdoor-adventure/jungle-took-her.

Spelman, Lucy, Kirsten Gilardi, Magdalena Lukasik-Braum, Jean-Felix Kinani, Elisabeth Nyirakaragire, Linda Lowenstine, and Michael R. Cranfield. "Respiratory Disease in Mountain Gorillas (Gorilla beringei beringei) in Rwanda, 1990–2010: Outbreaks, Clinical Course, and Medical Management." *Journal of Zoo and Wildlife Medicine* 44, no. 4 (2013): 1027–1035.

Stanford, Craig. *The New Chimpanzee: A Twenty-First-Century Portrait of Our Closest Kin*. Harvard University Press, 2018.

Stiles, Daniel, Ian Redmond, Doug Cress, Christian Nellemann, and Rannveig Knutsdatter Formo. "Stolen Apes." In *The Environment in Anthropology*. 2nd edition. New York University Press, 2016.

Strum, Shirley, and Linda Fedigan, editors. *Primate Encounters: Models of Science, Gender, and Society*. University of Chicago Press, 2000.

Strum, Shirley, and Linda Marie Fedigan. *Primate Encounters: Models of Science, Gender, and Society*. University of Chicago Press, 2000.

Trivers, Robert. "Parental Investment and Sexual Selection." In *Sexual Selection and the Descent of Man 1871–1971*. Edited by B. Campbell. Routledge, 1972.

Turner, Trudy. "Changes in Biological Anthropology: Results of the 1998 American Association of Physical Anthropology Membership Survey." *American Journal of Physical Anthropology* 118, no. 2 (2002): 111–116.

UBC Okanagan News. "Primatologist Tells of the Heart, Soul, and Struggle of the Orangutan." 2014. https://news.ok.ubc.ca/2014/04/10/primatologist-tells-of-the-heart-soul-and-struggle-of-the-orangutan.

Van Schaik, Carel, and Charles Janson, editors. *Infanticide by Males and Its Implications*. Cambridge University Press, 2000.

Van Schaik, Carel, and Joan Silk. "Contributions of Sarah Blaffer Hrdy." *Evolutionary Anthropology: Issues, News, and Reviews* 22, no. 5 (2013): 200–201.

Walker, Alan, Dean Falk, Richard Smith, and Martin Pickford. "The Skull of Proconsul Africanus: Reconstruction and Cranial Capacity." *Nature* 305, no. 5934 (1983): 525–527.

Walker, Alan. "Louis Leakey, John Napier, and the History of Proconsul." *Journal of Human Evolution* 22, no. 4–5 (1992): 245–254.

Whitlock, Gillian. "Remediating Gorilla Girl: Rape Warfare and the Limits of Humanitarian Storytelling." *Biography* 33, no. 3 (2010): 471–497.

Wich, Serge, David Gaveau, Nicola Abram, Marc Ancrenaz, Alessandro Baccini, Stephen Brend, Lisa Curran, et al. "Understanding the Impacts of Land-Use Policies on a Threatened Species: Is There a Future for the Bornean Orang-utan?" *PloS One* 7, no. 11 (2012): e49142.

Wildlife Conservation Society. "Census Finds Mountain Gorillas Increasing." *ScienceDaily*. Accessed September 5, 2024. www.sciencedaily.com/eleases/2004/01/040119082707.htm.

Wilson, Edward. *Sociobiology: The New Synthesis*. Harvard University Press, 2000.

Wilson, Michael, Elizabeth Lonsdorf, Deus Mjungu, Shadrack Kamenya, Elihuruma Wilson Kimaro, D. Anthony Collins, Thomas Gillespie, et al. "Research and Conservation in the Greater Gombe Ecosystem: Challenges and Opportunities." *Biological Conservation* 252 (2020): 108853.

Wrangham, Richard, Michael Wilson, and Marc Hauser. "Does Participation in Intergroup Conflict Depend on Numerical Assessment, Range Location, or Rank for Wild Chimpanzees?" *Animal Behaviour* 61, no. 6 (2001): 120316.

Zuckerman, Solly. *The Social Life of Monkeys and Apes*. K. Paul, Trench, Trubner & Co., 1932.

Index

Page numbers in bold indicate a photo.

Abu (India), 200
ad libitum sampling, 183–84
Aep, Mr., 138–39
Akmad (orangutan), 143–45
Ako Project, 259
Alberts, Susan, 194
Alexander, John, 94–95, 96, 97
allomothering, 208–10, 213, 225, 226
Altmann, Jeanne
  changes to Maasai-Amboseli, 180–81
  data tabulation and analysis, 171
  female baboons study, 168–69, 177, 187–89, 190, 192
  guide to primate observation, 173
  legacy, 195
  long-term study of wild baboons, **XI**, 169–70, 171–73, 177–79, 180, 186–87, 189–91, 192–93, 194–95
  mathematics study, 174, 176–77
  methods used by other researchers, 167–68, 209, 264
  as mother, 169, 170, 171, 172–73, 176–77, 178–79, 182, 186, 188–89, 194
  observational sampling of behaviour, 168, 173, 182–85
  PhD and thesis, 186–87, 188
  as primatologist, xxi, 168–69, 173, 186–87, 194
  publications, 168, 178, 181, 182–85, 188
  romance and marriage, 175–77
  youth and background, 173–77
Altmann, Stuart
  background, 170, 175
  conference on primate communication, 243
  as faculty, 194
  and Jeanne's paper, 182, 183
  long-term study of wild baboons, 168, 169–70, 171–73, 177–79, 180, 189–91
  romance and marriage, 175–77
Alto (baboon), 189
Amboseli Baboon Research Project, 189–95
Amboseli National Park. *See* Maasai-Amboseli Game Reserve
American Anthropological Association, presentation of Hrdy, 211
American Anthropologist journal, 218
Animal Protection Institute, 15–16
Ankarafantsika National Park (Madagascar), **XVI**, 230–32
anthropology, and North American primatology, xviii
"Arashiyama West" group of macaques, **I**, **II**, 10–11, 12–14, 15–16
Avern, Frida (Henrietta Wilfrida), 41

See also Leakey, Frida
aye-ayes, 253–54, 259

baboons
 description as group, xv
 displacement and population decreases, 181
 hamadryas baboons at Monkey Hill, 6–9
 human influences and feeding, 169–70
 life history, 186, 190
 males as dominant, 219, 243–44
 social behaviour, 207
 studies of, 169–70, 187, 207, 219, 244
baboons, yellow
 data collection and observation methods, 178, 191
 description and as study animal, **XI**, 172
 females study, 168–69, 177, 187–89, 190, 192
 infant relationships, 188–89
 long-term study by Altmann, 169–70, 171–73, 177–79, 180, 186–87, 189–91, 192–93, 194–95
 in Maasai-Amboseli Game Reserve, 172–73, 177–79
Bartlett, Thad, 217–18
Baumgartel, Walter, 97, 99, 106, 108, 109
Belize, author's research in, xvii
Berenty estate (Madagascar), 236–38
Berenty Reserve (Madagascar), **XV**, 241, 254, 258, 259
Beth and Bert (orangutans), 150–51
Binti, Mr., 158–59, 162
Binti (son of B. Galdikas), 162–63, 164
Bishop, Alison, 238–40
See also Jolly, Alison
Bishop, Morris G., 238, 239–40, 246
Blaffer, Robert Lee, 203–4
Blaffer, Sarah, 203–5
See also Hrdy, Sarah
Blaffer Trammell, Camilla Davis, 204, 205
Boggess, Preston, 236
Borneo
 Camp Leakey, 143, 147, 155–56
 deforestation and logging, 136–37, 155–56, 157–58
 forests description and as challenge, 147–49
 orangutans, 136–37
 research of Galdikas on orangutans, 136, 145, 146–55, 159–60, 165, 166
 slash-and-burn agriculture, 156
 See also Tanjung Puting
Boswell, Percy George Hamnall, 45
Bramblett, Claud, 13, 15
Brindamour, Rod
 and logging in Tanjung Puting, 155, 157, 158
 orangutans and pet trade, 138–39, 143, 165
 orangutans research with Galdikas, 146–53, 155, 159–60
 as photographer, 135–36, 146, 160
 as primatologist, xxi

romance and marriage to Galdikas, 145–46, 159–65
Buettner-Janusch, John, 235
Buffon, Georges-Louis Leclerc, comte de, xvi
Burkhart, Michael, 124–25

Campbell, Robert/Bob, 121–23, 125–27
capuchins, **III**, 19–20, 21–23
Carr, Rosamond, 112, 126
Catarrhines (Old World monkeys), description and features as group, xiv–xv
Ceram, C.W., 2
Chambers, David, ix–x
Chimpanzee Project
  early days and start, 70–72, 73–74
  funding, 68–70, 80–81
  observations, 75–77, 82–83, 84
chimpanzees
  activism by Goodall, 86–88
  conference of 1986 in Chicago, 86
  conservation efforts, 87–88
  description and closeness to humans, xiv
  and early human ancestors, 49–50, 51–52, 77
  early research, 74–75
  meat-eating, 76–77, 80
  "not-so-cute" behaviour, 24
  polio epidemic, 84–86
  population decreases and endangered status, 86–87
  termites and tools, 62
  See also Goodall, Jane – and chimpanzees
classification of primates
  overview, xiii–xiv, xvi
  lemurs and lorises, xv
  monkeys, apes and tarsiers, xiii–xv
Coco (gorilla), 117, 119, 123
Cole, Sonia, 56
Colin (son of Leakey and Frida), 46, 47, 56
collaborative approach to research, 14
Cologne Zoo, 115, 118–19
Committee for Conservation and Care of Chimpanzees (the cccc), 87
community conservation, 131, 233, 260–61
Coquerel's sifakas
  critically endangered status, 230
  description, xvii, 230
  research of author, xvii, 167–68, 230, 234–35, 263–66
Costa Rica, as study site for Fedigan, 16, 18
Curtin, Richard, 216

Dagg, Anne Innis, 218
Darwin, Charles, xvi, 214, 243
David Greybeard (chimpanzee), 61–62, 76
Davis, Kate Wilson, 204
DeVore, Irven, 52, 169, 206–8, 219
Digit Fund, 121
Digit (gorilla), **VIII**, 111, 113, 120–21
Dilley (Texas), 15–16
Dolhinow, Phyllis, 216
Dryden, Edward, Jr., 13–14, 15

Emlen, John, 10–11, 13

Fedigan, Larry, 4, 10
Fedigan, Linda
  capuchins research, 19–20, 21–23
  collaborative approach to research, 14
  description and traits, 1, 9, 15
  education, 3–5
  female primates study, 9, 15, 16, 19, 22
  on history of primatology, xvi–xvii, xviii–xix, 245
  Japanese macaques research, **I**, **II**, 9–10, 14, 15
  long-term field station and research, **II**, 16–20, 23
  as mentor, 14–15, 23
  as primatologist, xix, 5–6, 9
  in primatology, 5, 25
  publications, xii, xvi, 9, 14, 15, 23, 26
  and women as primatologists, xii, xix, 1–2, 23–29
  work in Alberta, 14–15
  youth and background, 2–4
female primates
  dominance by males, 7–8, 190–91, 243–45
  "friendships" and reproduction, 207
  as perspective of studies, 220–21
  reproduction and food resources, 7
  reproduction research, 15, 22
  role in social groups, 9
  study by Altmann, 168–69, 177, 187–89, 190, 192
  study by Fedigan, 9, 15, 16, 19, 22
  study by Hrdy, 198, 199, 201–2, 208–9, 214, 220–21
  study by Jolly, 243–47
feminism, 25–27, 221
fissioning of monkeys/primates, 10–11
focal animal sampling, 184
Fossey, Dian
  and R. Campbell, 121–23, 125–27
  description and traits, 90–91, 123–24
  first visit and safari to Africa, 39–40, 93, 94–98
  gravesite, **VIII**
  and Leakey, 39–40, 95, 99, 108, 110–11
  legacy, 131–33
  murder of, **VIII**, 90–92, 128–31, 133
  observation techniques, 103–4
  photos of, 121–22, 123
  as primatologist, xx–xxi, 89–90
  problems with Burkhart, 124–25
  publications, 39–40, 89, 95
  rebellion in Kivu (Zaire) and escape to Uganda, 99, 105–10
  return to Africa, 98–99
  romance, 123, 125–27
  as romantic interest of Leakey, 55–56
  visa renewal issues, 127–28
  youth and background, 92–94
Fossey, Dian – and gorillas
  capture of infants, 114–19
  conservation efforts, 114, 119, 121, 131, 132–33

first visit and encounter, 95–98
long-term study at camp Karisoke, **VII**, **VIII**, 90, 111–12, 133
long-term study at Kabara, 40, 99–105, 110–11
personal attachment to gorillas, **VIII**, **IX**, 90, 111, 113–14, 121–22
poachers at Karisoke, **VIII**, 111–12, 114–15, 119–21, 128, 129, 131
See also Karisoke Research Center
Fossey, George, 92, 122
Fossey, Kitty (mother of Fossey), 92–93

Galdikas, Biruté
forests in Tanjung Puting, 148–49, 155–56, 166
habitat protection and logging, 156–59, 166
and Leakey, 31–32, 33, 42–44, 136, 145–46
legacy, 165–66
as mother, 162–63
PhD and presentation, 142, 164
photos and article, **IX**, 135–36
pregnancy and birth of child, 162–63
as primatologist, xxi, 136, 151, 166
publications, 31, 33, 138, 160, 166
romance and marriage, 145–46
trips to North America, 160–61, 164
wait for Borneo project, 146
youth and background, 140–42
See also Borneo
Galdikas, Biruté – and orangutans
infant captured, 143
orangutans family of, 139–40, 144–45, 152–54, 165–66
pet trade, **X**, 138–39, 143
research, 136, 145, 146–55, 159–60, 165, 166
Galdikas, Filomena and Antanas, 140–41
gender
imbalance in STEM, ix–x, xii
and scientific study, 25–27
Glander, Ken, 16, 21
Gombe Stream National Park (Tanzania)
chimp population and health today, 87
Chimpanzee Project, **VI**, 70–72, 76–77, 82–83, 84
description, 60–61, 71
polio epidemic, 84–86
Goodall, Jane
event in Kitchener, ON, **XVI**
Jane Goodall Institute, **XVI**, 85
and Leakey, 34–35, 36, 48, 50–51, 54–55, 66–67
on Leakey, 33
lecture in Toronto, 59–60, 88
legacy, **XVI**, 60, 87–88
malaria, 72, 73
on murder of Fossey, 129
National Geographic article about, 83
at Olduvai, 51
on orangutans, 149
PhD and presentation, 77–80
photos and article, 80–81, 82, 83

practices and observations, 75–76
as primatologist, xx, 88
publications, 24, 33, 64, 68, 83
romance and marriage, 83–84, 160
trip to Africa, 65–66
youth and background, 63–65
Goodall, Jane – and chimpanzees
activism, 86–88
and "not-so-cute" behaviour, 24
research at Lake Tanganyika, **VI**, 51–52, 61–63, 68–69, 76–77, 82–83, 84–86
stuffed chimpanzee as child, 63–64
and termites, 60, 62–63
tool use discovery, 62–63
See also Chimpanzee Project
Goodall, Mortimer, 63–64, 65
Goodall, Vanne (Margaret Myfanwe Joseph Goodall), 55, 56, 63, 65, 70, 72, 82
gorillas
conservation efforts, 131–33
description and social structure, 103
ecotourism, 131–32
health concerns, 132
capture of infants and killing of family, 114–15
long-term study by Fossey, 40, 99–105, 110–12, 133
at Mount Mikeno, 97–98
poaching as threat, 113, 114, 119, 128
population decreases and endangered status, 112, 113
research by Schaller, 96
for zoos and pet trade, 114–16, 118–19
See also Fossey, Dian – and gorillas
Gorillas in the Mist (movie), **IX**, 89, 95
Gould, Stephen Jay, 213
gray langurs. *See* Hanuman langurs
great apes, 1–2, 137, 166
sifaka, 241–42, 244
Griffin, Louise, 15
Gundul (orangutan), 153–55

hamadryas baboons at Monkey Hill, 6–9
Hamzah, Mr., 143–44
Hanuman langurs (or gray langurs)
allomothering, 208–9, 210
attacks on infants and mothers, 202–3
description, 199–200
infant killing (*See* infant killing [or infanticide])
kidnapping of infants, 210
male tenure of troop, 220
research by Hrdy, **XII**, **XIII**, **XIV**, 199–203, 208–10, 212, 226–27
Haraway, Donna, 25, 119, 185, 187
Harrisson, Tom, 44
Hausfater, Glenn, 181, 189, 190–91, 192, 217
Hayes, Harold, 95, 123, 124–25
Heaulme, Jean and Aline de, 236–37, 248–49
Heaulme, Monsieur de, 237–38
Henry, Mary White, 93

Hillside troop of Hanuman langurs, 200–202
Hinde, Robert, 77–78
Homo genus, classification, xvi
Homo habilis "the toolmaker," 47
howler monkeys, xiv, xvii, 150, 191–92
Hrdy, Dan, 222–23, 224, 225, 226
Hrdy, Sarah
  allomothering and kidnapping of infant langurs, **XIV**, 208–10, 213
  allomothering in humans, 225, 226
  criticisms of, 216–19
  and I. DeVore, 206, 208
  education and academic journey, 205, 206, 208, 213–14, 219–20, 221
  female langurs study, 198, 199, 201–2, 208–9, 214, 220–21
  feminist scholarship, 221
  on human behaviour, 210
  infant killing (infanticide) study and theories (*See* infant killing)
  langurs research, **XII**, **XIII**, **XIV**, 199–203, 208–10, 212, 226–27
  legacy, 226–27
  marriage and motherhood, 222–26
  meeting online with author, 197–98
  as mother, 223–25, 226, 227
  PhD, 208, 222
  presentation of research, 210–11, 213–14
  as primatologist, xxi–xxii
  publications, 201, 213–14, 215, 216, 217, 218, 220, 225, 227
  student rebellion at Harvard, 205–6
  on women as primatologists, 198, 220, 221
  youth and background, 203–5
human-primate interface, 11–12, 17, 169–70
humans
  allomothering, 225, 226
  closeness to chimpanzees, xiv
  evolution and ancestors, and non-human primates, 43, 49–50, 51–52, 68–69, 77, 99
  "helpers" with children, 210, 225
  origins in Africa, 35–36, 41–43, 44–45, 47–48
  population in Africa, 87, 112–13
hyoid bone, xiv

indris, description and features, xv, 247
infant killing (or infanticide) in Hanuman langurs
  as evolutionary reproductive strategy, 203, 214
  occurrences and as behaviour in Abu, 201, 203, 208, 212
  presentation of results and reaction to, 210–11, 213–14, 216–18
  prevailing hypotheses, 211–12, 214, 215
  process in troops, 220
  research by Hrdy, 199–203, 208–10, 212, 226–27
  results and theories of Hrdy, 203, 211, 212, 214–18

sexually selected infanticide, as hypothesis, 214–15, 217
instantaneous sampling (scan sampling), 184
International Primatological Society, women in, xii, 27, 28
Itch (langur), 201–2

Jacqueline, Madame, 229, 230–32, 234, 266
Jane Goodall Institute, **XVI**, 85
Janzen, Daniel, 18–19
Japanese macaques
  at Arashiyama, 10–14
  at La Moca Ranch (Texas) and Dilley, **I**, **II**, 9–10, 14, 15–16
  on Yakushima island, **I**
Jolly, Alison
  book on conservation in Madagascar, 250–51, 252–53
  conservation as concern, 252–53, 254–55, 260
  and Earthwatch volunteers, 258–59
  female lemurs study, 243–47
  legacy, 260–61
  long-term field study of lemurs, **XV**, 232–33, 235–36, 238, 240–41, 258
  in Madagascar for research, **XV**, 234, 235–38
  marriage and romance, 246–51, 257–58
  as mother, 250, 251, 255–56, 261
  New York City life, 255–56, 257
  PhD and research in lab, 235, 240–41
  at "The Primates" symposium (1962), 79
  as primatologist, xxii
  publications, 79, 229, 233, 235, 240–41, 242, 244–45, 250, 253, 256, 259, 260–61
  travels to Madagascar, 256–57
  on women as primatologists, 25, 234
  writing style and creativity, 239, 240–41, 242
  youth and background, 238–40
Jolly, Margaretta, 25, 251, 252–53, 255–56
Jolly, Richard
  holiday in Madagascar, 256–57
  research and work, 249, 251, 255, 256
  romance and marriage, 246–51, 257–58

Kabara, long-term study of gorillas, 40, 99–105, 110–11
Kanam fossil site, 44–45
Karisoke Research Center
  cattle herders, 111, 112, 128
  description, 111
  murder of Fossey, 90–92, 128–31, 133
  poachers at, 111–12, 114–15, 119–21, 128, 129, 131
  problems at camp, 124–25
Katzenberg, Jeffrey, 245–46
Kawamura, Syunzo, 10–11, 13
Kayu Mas company, 157–58
Keating, Brian, xi
Kikuyu people and society, 37–38
Kingsbury, Alison Mason, 238–39, 240

Kinne, Russ, 251, 252, 253
Kumai (Indonesia), orangutans as pets, 138–39

La Moca Ranch (Texas), **I**, 9–10, 14, 15
langurs. *See* Hanuman langurs
Lawick, Hugo van, 81, 82–86, 160
Leakey, Frida (wife of Louis), 41, 42, 46, 47, 52
Leakey, Harry, 36–37
Leaky, Jonathan (son of Leakey and Mary), 53–54
Leakey, Louis
- as archaeologist, xix–xx, 40–42
- expeditions to Kenya and Tanzania, 41–42, 44, 46, 48–49, 66–67
- headstone and grave, 53–54
- Kanam jaw controversy, 45
- marriages, 41, 45, 47
- and National Geographic, 70, 81, 82
- non-human primates and human evolution/ancestors, 43, 49–50, 51–52, 68–69, 77, 99
- Olduvai Gorge work, **IV**, **V**, 36, 42–43, 44, 46–47, 51, 66–68, 70
- and origin of humans in Africa, **IV**, 35–36, 41–43, 44–45, 47–48
- publications, 38, 41, 42, 47, 49
- on tool use by chimps, 62–63
- youth and background, 36–39, 40–41

Leakey, Louis – and women
- and Fossey, 39–40, 55–56, 95, 99, 108, 110–11
- and Galdikas, 31–32, 33, 42–44, 136, 145–46
- and Goodall, 34–35, 36, 48, 50–51, 54–55, 66–67
- influence on and as champion to women as primatologists, xix–xx, 29, 33, 34
- interest in women, 34, 46, 50, 52–56
- marriages, 41, 45, 47
- on women as better scientists, 32–33

Leakey, Mary "May" (mother of Louis), 36, 37
Leakey, Mary (wife of Louis)
- cremation, 54
- and Fossey, 95
- meeting and marrying Leakey, **IV**, 46, 47
- own work and discoveries, 47–48
- work with Leakey, **IV**, **V**, 35, 36, 46–47, 49, 51, 66–67

Leakey, Richard (son of Leakey and Mary), 53–54, 56, 82, 121
lemurs
- conservation, 260, 261
- description as group, xv
- dominance of females over males, **XV**, 243, 244–45
- endangered status, xvii
- long-term field study by Jolly, **XV**, 232–33, 235–36, 238, 240–41, 258
- research of author, xvii, 167–68
- studies on, 235, 241, 259

See also Coquerel's sifakas; ring-tailed lemur
Lewontin, Richard, 213
Linnaeus, Carl, xv–xvi
London Zoological Society, and hamadryas baboons at Monkey Hill, 6–9
long-term study or research on primates
in natural settings, 80
transition to and importance, 190–91, 194–95
Louisville Courier Journal, 95
Lovejoy, Thomas, 250
Loveridge, Arthur, 38, 39

Maasai-Amboseli Game Reserve (now Amboseli National Park)
changes to, 180–81
description, **XII**, 171–72
local researchers, 192–93
long-term project in, 189–94
yellow baboons study, **XI**, 172–73, 177–79
Maasai pastoralists, 180–81
macaques, range and conflict with humans, 11–12
See also Japanese macaques
McClellan, Anita, 110
McGoogan, Keriann
behavioural sampling methods, as example, 167–68, 264–65
charity for Madagascar, 261
Coquerel's sifakas research, xvii, **XVI,** 167–68, 230, 234–35, 263–66
data collection methods, 191–92
experience for field research, 170–71
and hardships of the forest, 147–48
howler monkeys research, xiv, xvii, 150, 191–92
in human-primate interface example, 11–12
in Madagascar for research, xvii, **XVI,** 230–32, 234–35, 246
malaria, 72
path to primatology, ix–xi, 94
studies and research in primatology, xvii–xviii, 14–15
techniques in forest, 150
McGuire, Wayne, 91–92, 130
MacKinnon, John, 147
Madagascar
as animated film, *Madagascar,* **XV**, 245-46
biodiversity and human impacts, 229–30, 254–55, 259
books about lemurs, 259
charity for, 261
community conservation, 233, 260–61
conservation and Jolly, 250–51, 252–53, 254–55, 260
education and social aspects, 249, 251–52, 253, 260
funerals in, 256–57
as home of lemurs, xv, **XV**
political turmoil in 1970s, 251–52
research and travels of Jolly, **XV**, 234, 235–38, 256–57

research of author, xvii, **XVI**, 230–32, 234–35, 246
zebu, 249–50, 256, 257
malaria, 72–73
male primates, 7–8, 190–91, 243–45
Mano, Tetsuzo, 14
men
"goodwill of powerful men" as hypothesis, xix, 34, 89
Michael (son of Altmanns), 170, 171, 172–73, 178–79
Miller, David, x
Monkey Hill (London Zoological Society), and hamadryas baboons, 6–9
monkeys
anatomy *vs.* humans, xv
classification as primates, xiv–xv
darting and marking for research, 21
See also individual species
Morell, Virginia, on Leakey family, 34, 37
wives and women, 34, 41, 45–47, 50, 52, 53, 56
work of, 50
motherhood, and Hrdy's research, 223–26
Mount Abu (India), **XII**, **XIII**, **XIV**, 199, 200
Mount Mikeno gorillas, 97–98
Mowat, Farley, 55, 89, 107–8, 109
Mr. McGregor (chimpanzee), 84–86
Mug (langur), 200, 201–3
Muruthi, Philip, 193
Mututua, Raphael, 192
Nairobi National Park, study of baboons in, 169–70
Napier, John, 79
National Geographic Society and *National Geographic* magazine
and Fossey, 121–22, 123
and Galdikas, **IX**, 135–36, 160
and Goodall, 80–81, 82, 83
and Leakey, 70, 81, 82
Nemeye (tracker), 120
New World monkeys (Platyrrhines), description and features as group, xiv
Newsam, Bernard, 41
Nicol, Mary, 45–47
See also Leakey, Mary
Nienaber, Georgianne, 110
Nissen, Henry, 74–75
non-human primates. *See* primates
North American primatology, xvi–xviii
Nosy Mangabe (Madagascar), 253–54

"Observational Study of Behavior: Sampling Methods" (J. Altmann), 168, 173, 182–85
use by author, 167–68, 264–65
Old World monkeys (Catarrhines), description and features as group, xiv–xv
Olduvai Gorge (Tanzania)
description of site, **IV**, **V**, 36
Fossey at, 40, 95
Goodall at, 51, 66–68
Leakeys' work, 36, 42–43, 44, 46–47, 51, 66–68, 70

Orangutan Foundation International, 166
orangutans
 critically endangered status, 136–37
 description and species, 136
 elusiveness, 149–50
 forced copulation, 151–52, 154–55
 hunting and in pet trade, x, 137–39, 143–44, 165
 capture of infants and killing of family, 143
 mange disease, 159
 mating system and sexual behaviours, 152–53, 154
 and palm oil production, 137
 rehabilitation and return to the wild, x, 145, 165–66
 research of Galdikas, 136, 145, 146–55, 159–60, 165, 166
 studies in the wild, 147
 See also Galdikas, Biruté – and orangutans
Osborn, Rosalie, 50, 52–53, 54, 79

Paranthropus boisei, 70
Pavelka, Mary, 15, 191–92
Pawless (langur), 202
Peanuts (gorilla), 122
Peterson, Dale, 54, 64, 77–78, 79, 110
Piccirilli, Jillian, 238
Planet Madagascar charity, 261
Platyrrhines (new-world monkeys), description and features as group, xiv
poaching
 at Karisoke, 111–12, 114–15, 119–21, 128, 129, 131
 orangutans, 137
 as reality for local people, 112
 as threat to gorillas, 113, 114, 119, 128
Pongo pygmaeus and *P. abelii,* 136–37
Price, Richard (stepfather of Fossey), 92–93
Pricilla (daughter of Leakey and Frida), 47
Primate Paradigms: Sex Roles and Social Bonds (Linda Fedigan), 9
"primate pattern," xiii
primates (non-human)
 allomothering, 208–9, 210, 213
 characteristics and traits as group, xiii
 classification, xiii–xvi
 closeness to humans, xviii
 conservation efforts, 87–88, 131–32
 distribution, xiii–xiv
 diversity and variability, xiii, xviii
 dominance and mating, 7–8, 190–91, 243–45
 endangered or critically endangered status, xvii, 87, 113, 136–37, 230
 in entertainment industry, 19–21
 evolutionary pressures and group dynamics, 7–8
 guide to observation, 173
 and human evolution/ancestors, 43, 49–50, 51–52, 68–69, 77, 99
 humans as, xvi

hunting by, 77
interface with humans, 11–12, 17, 169–70
kidnapping of infants, 210
longer-term research in natural settings, 80
names for, by observers, 75–76, 104, 139–40
study – early, xv, xvi
study – modern, xvii–xix
violence in, 24, 234
See also female primates; individual species
"The Primates" symposium (1962), 79
primatologists
data collection and analysis, 151, 191
experience for field research, 170–71
hardships of the forest, 147–48, 149
looking good in the field, 123–24
women as (*See* women as primatologists)
primatology
and anthropology, xviii
authorship of collaborators and assistants (co-authorship), 193
beginning and history, xv, xvi–xvii
expectations towards students, 93–94
feminist charge led by Hrdy, 221
field research as focus, xvii–xviii
growth in 1960–70s, xvi–xvii, xvii, 24–25
at Harvard, 208, 219–20
as inclusive science, 27
local teams and researchers/scientists, 192–94
in North America, xvi–xviii
"sociobiological era," xviii–xix
starting point, xv
Proconsul ape-like species, 35–36, 48, 49
provisioning of monkeys/primates, impact of, 10, 11
psychology, as path to primatology, 136
Pucker (gorilla), 118, 119, 123

Rabesandratana, Rachel, 254
Ranthambore National Park, **XIII**
Rasamimanana, Hanta, 258–59
Redmond, Ian, 120
Reese, Amanda, 214
ring-tailed lemur
death of infant, 233
female lemurs study, 243–47
long-term field study by Jolly, **XV**, 232–33, 240–41
work of Rasamimanana, 259
Root, Joan and Alan, 97–100
Ross, Deborah, 259
Rowell, Thelma, 219, 243
Rusinga Island (Kenya), 48–49
Rwelekana, Emmanuel, 130

St. Kitts, as study site for Fedigan, 16–17
sampling, methods used, 183–84
See also "Observational Study of Behavior: Sampling

Methods" and paper of Altmann
Santa Rosa National Park (Guanacaste, Costa Rica), **II**, **III**, 18–19, 21–23
Sanwekwe (guide and tracker), 102, 103, 104, 105
Sapolsky, Robert, 194
Sayialel, Serah, 193
scan sampling (instantaneous sampling), 184
Schaller, George, 96, 104, 112
Schiebinger, Londa, 26
"Science and the Successful Female: Why There Are So Many Women Primatologists" (L. Fedigan), xii, 23–24, 26, 234
Scratch (langur), 201–3
sexual selection, 214, 243–44
Shifty Leftless (langur), 200–201
sifakas. *See* Coquerel's sifakas
Sinaga, Walman, 158
snow monkeys of Japan, xiv–xv
sociobiology, as field, 212–13
Sol (langur), 202
Solomon, John, 42
spider monkeys of Guatemala, 17
Steffens, Travis, 11–12, 59–60, 170–71, 231, 232, 261
STEM disciplines (science, technology, engineering and mathematics), women in, ix–x, xii
stereotypes, women as scientists, ix–x
Sterling, Eleanor, 254
Stewart, Kelly, 129
Strum, Shirley, on history of primatology, xvi–xvii, xviii–xix, 245
Sugito (orangutan), 139, 152–53
Sumatra, orangutans, 136
Sussman, Robert, 217–18

Tanganyika, Lake
- chimpanzees research, 49–50, 51–52, 61–63, 76–77, 82–83, 84–86
- description, 60–61, 70–71

Tanjung Puting
- forests and logging, 148–49, 155–56, 157, 166
- as nature reserve, **X**, 157, 158, 166

taxonomy, xv–xvi
tool use, by chimps or apes, 62–63
Trace, Gillian, 51, 67
Trevor, Jack, 49
"the Trimates"
- championing by Leakey, 33–34
- description, xix–xx
- as influence on women as primatologists, 1–2, 28–29, 136
- as nickname, 33, 34
- *See also* Fossey, Dian; Galdikas, Birutė; Goodall, Jane

Trivers, Robert, 218, 221
Tyson, Edward, xv

United States, education of scientists, 3

van Lawick, Hugo 81, 82–86, 160
Verschuren, Jacques, 95–96
vervets, study by Fedigan, 5, 16–17

Virunga Mountains
conservation efforts, 131–33
gorilla research, **VII**, **VIII**, 90, 96–97, 100–105, 111
population of gorillas, 112
See also Karisoke Research Center

Washburn, Sherwood, xvii–xviii
Whitlock, Gillian, 110
Wilkie, Leighton, 69–70
Wilson, E.O., 212–14
women
as better scientists (according to L. Leakey), 32–33
in conference and symposia, 27
dismissed as scientists, 69, 218–19
at Harvard and in academia, 208, 219, 220, 221, 225
in mathematics, 174
as scientists and in STEM, ix–x, xii, 28, 187
workshop about women in science, 187
See also Leakey, Louis – and women
women as primatologists
overview of women in this book, xix–xxii
appeal of primates ("primates themselves") hypothesis, 27–28, 169, 199
article by Fedigan, xii, 23–24, 26, 234
"big brown eyes hypothesis," 23–24, 90
growth since 1970s, xii–xiii
impact and contribution to primatology, xiii, 266–68
influence of Leakey, xix–xx, 29, 33, 34
Jolly's views on, 25, 234
media coverage of, 28–29, 83, 89–90
as mothers and wives, 268
"National Geographic effect," 1–2, 28–29, 136
reasons and hypotheses for, 23–29, 89–90, 136, 169, 198–99, 267–68
role models, 28–29, 90, 136, 227, 266, 268
as trend, xi–xiii
"the Trimates" as influence, 1–2, 28–29, 136
women's movement and feminism, 24–27, 199, 221
women's movement, 24–27, 199, 221
Wood, Linda, 2–4
See also Fedigan, Linda
A World Like Our Own (A. Jolly), 229, 242, 253, 254
Wylie, Laurence, 4

yellow baboons. *See* baboons, yellow
Yuni (nanny), 163–65

zebu, 249–50, 256, 257
Zigiranyirazo, Protais ("Monsieur Z"), 130–31
"Zinj" or *Zinjanthropus boisei*, **V**, 43, 47
Zuckerman, Solly, 6, 8–9, 79–80, 244